W9-AXW-179

The Anchor

The Anchor

Finding Safety in God's Harbor

by Stephen & Tony Fortosis

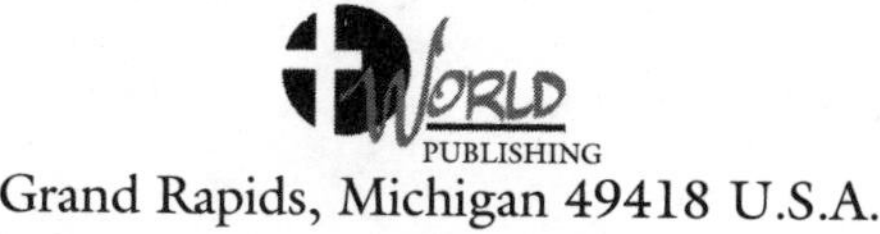

World Publishing
Grand Rapids, Michigan 49418 U.S.A.

The Anchor: Finding Safety in God's Harbor

Published by World Publishing, Inc.
Grand Rapids, MI 49418

Many of the meditations in this book appeared originally in Anchor devotional booklets distributed by Haven of Rest Ministries, Hollywood, Calif. Permission to reprint these meditations is gratefully acknowledged.

Book Design by Scott Pinzon.
Edited by Heather Stroobosscher.

ISBN 0-529-10861-5

Library of Congress Catalog Card Number 97-62292

Printed in the United States of America

Contents

Dedication

From Stephen Fortosis:
This book is dedicated to individuals such as Joyce Gibson, Bee Justamante, Fred Wilson, Lawrence Boadt, my brother, Dave, and other friends and family who taught me, encouraged me as a writer, or gave me my first significant opportunities to be published.

From Tony Fortosis:
I dedicate this book to my beloved grandchildren. May they grow in courage, compassion, and in deep, intimate commitment to their first love, Christ himself.

Introduction

Writing devotionals brings with it some distinctive challenges. One involves the idealistic style and superlative aspirations of many devotional thoughts. The reader may be tempted to give up, assuming that most other Christians have reached lofty spiritual peaks he or she views as hopelessly unscalable. Yet if the challenges in Scriptural meditations were all easily attained, how truly valuable would they be and how much would readers mature through them?

My father and I are sensitive to how far short we fall in some areas we write about with such bravado. We have attempted to intersperse our own vulnerabilities and failings in the collection in an effort to assure readers that we are only fallible pilgrims, stumbling our way along the same narrow road upon which they travel. We have also inserted many insights voiced by great giants of the faith who dwarf us in their holy knowledge of God.

A second challenge is the tension between interpreting Scripture and applying it to life. Our goal was to reach a fair balance between the two. In other words, you will find some of the meditations devoted almost entirely to the meaning and exposition of the focus Scripture. Others will describe true life examples, thus translating the biblical text into the grind of daily experience. Though we tried, it is difficult to both interpret the text and apply it adequately to life in each brief devotional. Therefore, some may say the book doesn't expound the Scriptural text enough; the cry of others may be that there aren't enough real life applications.

The writing of 366 Bible meditations is, in a sense, a draining experience. In other words, it drains to the dregs what the author has inside himself to pass on. The experience pressed us, rebuked us, and challenged us, showing how far we've come; but more profoundly, showing how infinitely far we are from full maturity in Christ.

God uses life as a teacher—triumphs, obstacles, tragedies, but mostly encounters with people: Learning encounters . . . encounters of comfort, friction, encouragement, reproof, inspiration, and on it goes. In his book, *Telling Secrets,* Frederick Buechner describes this process well: "The events were so small that I was surprised to remember them, yet they turned out to have been road markers on a journey I didn't even know I was taking. The people involved in them were often people I had never thought of as having played particularly significant roles in my life yet looking back at them I saw that, for me, they had been life-givers, saints."

We would like to thank all those life-givers in our own lives: some are written of in this book; others live on forever in our minds. We will always be grateful to these friends, family members, writers, Christian leaders—each of whom had a part in making the truths of this book real. Most of all, we thank God for calling us, forgiving us, putting up with our ongoing messes and failures, befriending us in the deepest, most giving, most eternal sense.

Publisher's Note: Entries written by Tony Fortosis are noted.
All other entries are by Stephen Fortosis.

JANUARY

In the Beginning, God . . .

⚓ JAN. 1 ⚓

ACTS 17:22–29

THE ONE TRUE CREATION ACCOUNT

In the beginning God created heaven and earth (Genesis 1:1).

I was confused as a college student to learn that Christians are not the only people with a creation story. There are Mesopotamian and Babylonian accounts of a universe created by other gods. Thus, some people may think the writer of Genesis just piggybacked his story on the other accounts. While it's possible that the writer was aware of certain creation myths, the Bible account uniquely contrasts with others.

Other accounts include many gods; the biblical account presents one majestic God over all. In Babylonian stories, the divine spirit and cosmic matter exist side by side through eternity; in the Christian story, the eternal God is distinct from all he creates and creation depends upon him for existence and sustenance. In Near Eastern legends, the heavenly bodies and sea monsters are actually powerful gods; Genesis reports they are only creations of matter. In the myths, mankind seems to have only a walk-on part; in the Bible mankind's creation in God's image is a high point in the narrative.

The Bible doesn't tell us how God did any of it. It just says he created the heavens and the earth and declared it good. Using only seventy-six word-forms in a poetic pattern, God gives us in Genesis 1 everything that humans of all ages, maturity levels, and backgrounds need to know about creation. Read the narrative again and marvel at its bold simplicity.

LIFE FOCUS: Thank God that in the confused conglomeration of creation accounts and evolution theories, you can be quietly confident that your brief, simple account is the truth.

⚓ JAN. 2 ⚓

PSALM 134:10–31
ONLY FOR GOD'S GLORY

Then God said, "Let the earth produce every type of living creature: every type of domestic animal, crawling animal, and wild animal." . . . God saw that they were good (Genesis 1:24–25).

God is amazingly inventive. Out of his mind sprang the thousands of multi-hued plants, and his animals overwhelm the imagination with their variety and sheer splendor. Animals can be amusing, too. It seems impossible to picture a harsh, humorless God creating them.

For years I've watched nature documentaries on television. I'm always taken aback when animals I've never seen before flash onto the screen. And surprisingly some plants and animals don't seem to have any special purpose. They don't serve humanity, they can't be used for food, products, or medicine, and they may be rarely seen. Why do they exist?

I recently heard of a genet—a spotted, cat-like animal with oversized ears and turquoise eyes. It lives in the deep darkness of African jungles and is rarely observed by humans. Here is an animal that apparently exists for no other purpose than simply to give glory to God. We often tend to be very utilitarian. If something or someone doesn't prove useful to us, we ignore or discount it.

Daily and nightly, creation speaks unendingly of God. Worship him for creatures and creations who speak silently of an astounding Creator.

LIFE FOCUS: Listen for God's voice whispering through the pines and roaring in thunder's crash. Look for him in the intricacy and orderly grandeur of his craftsmanship.

⚓ JAN. 3 ⚓

1 John 1:5–7, 8–11
The Light of Life

Then God said, "Let there be light!" So there was light. God saw that the light was good (Genesis 1:3).

God's first act in the creation process was to create light. The light divided itself from the darkness. And all through the rest of Scripture God used light and darkness in powerfully figurative ways.

Prophecy described the coming Messiah as a great luminary to the Gentiles. Jesus came to earth claiming to be the light of the world. John affirmed He was the true light which lights all who come into the world.

God's words are like a light to guide us through life, while the godless are blind to these spiritual realities. Many are also said to love darkness rather than light because they want to conceal evil actions. Someday the Lord will bring to light their hidden deeds of darkness and expose even the thoughts and motives of the heart. In contrast, our good works are to shine as lights, and the daytime is represented as the time to fulfill God's work—the night comes when no one can work.

Why is light used so often as a symbol? It is pure, it is bright, it is focusing, and it reveals what is shameful or hidden. We are reflectors, not the light source. Whenever we want to hide a word or deed from the light, there's a good chance its source is evil. God's light can guide us safely through life. Someday, as children of light, we will come face to face with light so luminous and pure that our only response will be to fall prostrate before him who dwells in light unapproachable.

Life Focus: When you are filled with the pure light of God's Word, you see the path he has marked out for you, and you draw others to the light.

⚓ JAN. 4 ⚓

HEBREWS 3:12–19

DON'T SUGARCOAT SIN

"You certainly won't die!" the snake told the woman. "God knows that when you eat it your eyes will be opened. You'll be like God, knowing good and evil" (Genesis 3:4–5).

Our Sunday school lesson today was about hard times. Before the lesson even started, Angela blurted out, "Steve's back on alcohol again," and she began to cry. "This time," she quavered, "he says he's given up. He says God just can't help him quit for good."

Steve had been coming alone to our class off and on for months. At times he seemed happy in Christ and on top of his addictions. But sin has a way of slowly, almost imperceptibly, luring us back into habits we thought we'd licked.

When Adam and Eve sinned, God said that woman would bear children in great pain and the earth would fight man's cultivation of it at every turn. God chose not to mention at that time the gravest results of sin—bitter tears, sadness, evil addictions, shattered relationships, alienation, and death.

We try to sugarcoat sin so it doesn't sound so bad. Adultery becomes an affair or having a fling. Business cheating becomes playing with the figures. Divorce becomes following your dreams. People even have a way around coveting—maxing out their credit cards gives them what they covet. But there is absolutely nothing good about sin.

LIFE FOCUS: Ask God to help you not to rationalize away your sin but to face it, repent, and hate it the way he does.

⚓ JAN. 5 ⚓

Psalm 90:1–6
Envisioning Eternity

"I am the A and the Z," says the Lord God, the one who is, the one who was, and the one who is coming, the Almighty (Revelation 1:8).

As kids, we'd try to blow the minds of our friends by challenging them to try to picture time without end. Try it yourself sometime. It's impossible for such terribly time-bound creatures to envision eternity.

Genesis 1:1 states, "In the beginning God created heaven and earth." No one created God. He was already there because he has no beginning. That may really disturb you if you think hard about it. We have this incorrigible need for things to have a beginning and an ending. If an important matter doesn't have closure, it can drive us to distraction.

Yet God doesn't even try to describe eternity in a way we can understand it. He simply affirms that it exists. We have no way of experiencing this spiritual realm of reality with our limited senses. While still on earth, humans have been allowed glimpses into that world, but the snapshots have been rare indeed.

God promises that his children will live eternally, but he tells us little about what will comprise that existence. We are left with the assurance that God is the Alpha and the Omega, knowing the end from the beginning, and whatever he plans for us is surely a thousand times better than our imaginations can conjure. So how do we deal with eternity? By preparing now for what it will hold.

Life Focus: You don't need to grasp eternity or understand what it will hold. You can simply prepare for it by fulfilling God's pleasure day by day.

⚓ JAN. 6 ⚓

Genesis 3:1–6
The Anatomy of Temptation

Everyone is tempted by his own desires as they lure him away and trap him. Then desire becomes pregnant and gives birth to sin. When sin grows up, it gives birth to death (James 1:14–15).

The Apostle John wrote, "Don't love the world and what it offers. . . . Not everything the world offers—physical gratification, greed, and extravagant lifestyles—comes from the Father" (1 John 2:15). Over and over again, those three avenues draw us like evil magnets into temptation.

When Eve turned her attention to the forbidden fruit, the three magnets kicked in immediately. She saw it seemed good for food, it was a delight to the eyes, and it would make one wise. So she finally rationalized that God must be denying her something that was actually quite harmless and enjoyable.

Satan even appealed to Jesus on the basis of these three avenues. He challenged the famished Christ to turn stones into bread and to worship him in exchange for all the lavish world kingdoms. Then Satan said angels would save Jesus from an ostentatious leap off a pinnacle of the temple to win the admiration of the multitudes below (Matt. 4:1–11).

Beware of what your eyes covet, what your body yearns for, and what your ego dreams of. Check the Scriptures, judge your true motives. Don't talk yourself into something that, deep in your heart, you know is just plain wrong.

Life Focus: Ask God to let a red light from his Spirit flash on in your heart when you begin entertaining evil possibilities. Trust him for power to turn away.

⚓ JAN. 7 ⚓

Jeremiah 17:9–10
Ways to Belittle Sin

God is faithful and reliable. If we confess our sins, he forgives them and cleanses us from everything we've done wrong (1 John 1:9).

When Adam and Eve sinned, surely they weren't ready to face the true evil of their rebellion and its results. If we admitted how bad sin is, we would have to admit how bad we can be. So we try incessantly to minimize it. One way we do this is by forcing it out of our minds. We figure if we stay busy enough working, watching TV, listening to the radio, etc., we can ignore our sin long enough so it'll go away.

C.S. Lewis reminds us that another ploy we use is comparing ourselves with those around us. After all, if I am only envying what others own, I'm not nearly as bad as Sam, who is stealing the company blind. Or we pontificate about the corporate sin of our nation or our neighborhood instead of facing our personal sin.

We also tend to act as if time cancels sin. We may laughingly describe sins of childhood or adolescence as "sowing our wild oats," but did we ever make things right with those we hurt or used? Our selective memories often forget all the pain our past sins caused others.

At times, we assume there is safety in numbers. In other words, if people we know are engaging in a particular behavior, then it must be OK. It's true that some Christians feel the biblical freedom to do certain things others may not have the liberty to do, but we must base our freedom on honest, well-thought-out convictions, not on the perceived actions of the majority.

Life Focus: God will bless us if we face our sin head-on, confess it, and turn from it. No excuse is ever quite adequate.

2 PETER 1:16–21

MAGIC FRUIT AND TALKING SERPENTS?

We apostles . . . didn't base our message on clever myths we made up. . . . No prophecy ever originated from humans. Instead, it was given by the Holy Spirit as humans spoke under God's direction (2 Peter 1:16, 21).

Some have labeled the Bible's creation story an ancient fable or legend about the origin of the universe. They say it seems preposterous for the Bible to claim that an infinite, omnipotent God took one week to create the universe and had to rest the seventh day. They scorn the idea of a fruit that dispensed knowledge of good and evil and another that dispensed eternal life. And they snicker about an evil, talking serpent that tempted Eve.

The story may seem a bit fanciful until we take a closer look. First, we don't know if God meant literal twenty-four-hour days when he described the creation process, though it seems as if he did. He may have created in an instant and then spent some time surveying his new creations. It could also be that the six days of work followed by a Sabbath rest was primarily enacted for our benefit, so we would later understand God's decree that one day each week should be set aside for rest and worship.

And surely there was nothing inherent in the fruits that could give a knowledge of good and evil or dispense eternal life. The fruit prohibition was simply a test of human obedience. The penalty for rebellion was spiritual and eventual physical death.

Eve was not tempted by an ugly, slithering snake but most likely an attractive creature that stood upright. Satan apparently used this creature, and after the Fall it was cursed to become a dangerous serpent, sliding covertly along the ground.

LIFE FOCUS: Speaking about the Bible, C.S. Lewis, a master of literature, writes, "I have been reading poems, romances, vision-literature, legends, myths all my life. I know what they are like. I know that not one of them is like this." The Bible is not myth; it is truth of the purest sort.

DEUTERONOMY 8:11–18
PRIDE: THE ULTIMATE EVIL

You morning star, son of the dawn! . . . You thought, "I'll go up to heaven and set up my throne above God's stars . . . I'll be like the Most High" (Isaiah 14:12–14).

The Bible says little about Satan's origin. However we gather he was originally a chief angel. At some point, he apparently led an angelic rebellion against God and he and his cohorts were banned from heaven. At the root of Satan's sin was pride—he desired equal authority with God.

When Satan attempted to lead Eve and Adam into disobedience against God, he used the same approach. First, he cast doubt into Eve's mind: "Did God really say 'You shall not eat of every tree of the garden'?" "No," answered Eve. "God said we could eat of any tree except the one tree. If we eat it, we will die." Satan wanted Eve to begin thinking of God as unreasonable.

Satan answered, "You certainly won't die. God knows that when you eat it, your eyes will be opened and you will be like God, knowing good and evil." If that's true, thought Eve, God not only lied to us, but He's depriving us of the knowledge and status we deserve. The more Eve thought about Satan's lie, the more truthful and attractive it appeared. Why shouldn't we be like God? she thought. Maybe he's selfishly holding us back from our highest potential. So Eve took the fruit and gave some to Adam.

LIFE FOCUS: Pride can be subtle. Anytime we sin, we are sowing an ounce of rebellion, saying, in effect, "God, you don't really care about my best interests. If I'm my own authority, I can do a better job than you can." But pride precedes destruction, and a conceited attitude brings a fall.

⚓ JAN. 10 ⚓

HEBREWS 9:22–28
A COVERING FOR SIN

The LORD God made clothes from animal skins for the man and his wife and dressed them (Genesis 3:21).

Somehow I ended up with the unlikely opportunity of teaching a group of non-Christians a college survey Bible course. As they began reading the Bible for the first time, some of them found surprises. I remember how one woman was appalled at the blood and violence that she found. Apparently she expected every page to exude the gentle compassion of God.

But, the entrance of sin into the world brought all sorts of ugly and patently unpleasant byproducts. Violence, brutality, and death are only a few. Even our faith involves blood and death. The first physical death was not Cain's murder of his brother. It was the killing of animals, which God himself performed so Adam and Eve could cover their nakedness with skins.

With sin, mankind suddenly had something to hide. Even the innocence of nakedness seemed suddenly shameful. Death was unknown before sin came. Animals had not been created to be murdered, but it was their skins that God chose to cover Adam and Eve's nakedness.

On the surface, bloody animal sacrifice seems savage. But God proclaimed that the very life of the flesh is in the blood and blood must be shed in sacrifice for sin. It was never possible for the blood of lambs and goats to take away sin—they were only stand-ins for the one perfect Lamb of God.

LIFE FOCUS: Praise God that all our numberless sins are permanently covered through the blood that ran down that coarse crossbeam at Calvary.

⚓ JAN. 11 ⚓

PSALM 8
GOD OF INFINITY

When I look at your heavens, the creation of your fingers, the moon and the stars that you have set in place—what is a mortal that you remember him? (Psalm 8:3–4).

Only a few centuries ago, astronomers taught that the earth was the significant focal point of a relatively small solar system. Now we know better. Earth is an infinitesimal speck dwarfed in a galaxy of billions of stars. Our closest galactic neighbor is Andromeda, and its distance from us means that we view it as it existed two million years ago. Scientists claim there are about one hundred billion additional galaxies out there.

The author of Genesis says God created the sun, the moon, and the stars. What an amazingly understated way to announce the creation of a staggeringly enormous universe. Only one phrase is devoted to the stars, yet multiple words in the account announce the creation and purpose of humans.

What is the purpose of the endless galaxies? The only reason that appears clear is to show forth God's majestic and infinite power. Isaiah raved, "Look at the sky and see: Who created these things? Who brings out the stars one by one? He calls them all by name. . . ." We know the invisible God partly through his handiwork. Thus, he places the endless fabric of heaven and earth before us that he may invite us to a knowledge of himself.

LIFE FOCUS: The next time there is a cloudless night, turn your head upward, gaze at the starlit heavens, and worship.

⚓ JAN. 12 ⚓

1 Samuel 15:16–23

Blame Shifting

"To follow instructions is better than to sacrifice. To obey is better than sacrificing the fat of rams" (1 Samuel 15:22).

Comedian Flip Wilson wasn't the first to say, "The devil made me do it." When God asked Eve if she'd eaten of the forbidden tree, she answered, "The snake deceived me, and I ate." When God confronted Adam, he said, "That woman, the one you gave me, gave me fruit from the tree, and I ate it."

Adam blamed Eve and Eve blamed the serpent. We have great tendency to shift blame. A boy once asked, "Mother, why is it that whenever I do anything bad it's because I am a bad boy, but whenever you do anything wrong, it's because you are nervous?"

As a child when I displeased my father, he responded to my explanations with a curt, "Don't defend yourself." This angered me because, at times, there were extenuating circumstances. Most likely, though, he didn't want me to grow up spouting excuses whenever I messed up.

Blame shifting—Adam was essentially saying, "God, you're partly to blame here! If you hadn't given me this wayward woman, I wouldn't have fallen into sin." Eve was saying, "God, if you hadn't allowed Satan to enter that snake, I wouldn't have been fooled. It was just too tricky."

When King Josiah rediscovered in the rubble-strewn temple the words of the Law, he ripped his robe in deep remorse over sin. No excuses there, no sidestepping—just a deep sorrow for sin and a determined desire to change.

Life Focus: The next time you open your mouth to blame your sin on circumstances or on someone else, ask God to remind you that you are the one to blame.

⚓ JAN. 13 ⚓

GENESIS 1:26–28
RESPONSIBLE CARETAKERS

God blessed them and said, "Be fertile, increase in number, fill the earth, and be its master. Rule . . . all the animals that crawl on the earth" (Genesis 1:28).

When God created humans he said to, "Be fertile . . . [and] fill the earth." Next God said to subdue the earth and rule over the animals. This job was kicked off with the task of naming all the animals. Evidently, thousands of animals were named by Adam.

Martin Luther believed that before the Fall, Adam and Eve were superior to the animals in every way. "I am fully convinced," he said, "that before Adam's sin his eyes were so sharp and clear that they surpassed those of the lynx and the eagle. He was stronger than the lions and bears . . . and he handled them the way we handle puppies."

Still, even after the Fall, human intellectual superiority has usually enabled people to subjugate animals. The trouble is our fallen humanity tends either to violate creation, subjecting it to our own selfish ends, or to bow down and worship creation in place of the Creator.

We do not have to be overzealous environmentalists or animal rights activists to believe in our responsibility as stewards over the earth. Dangerous chemical dumping or the wholesale slaughter of animals simply for a valuable appendage or organ are just two small examples of exploitative domination of an environment entrusted to us by God.

LIFE FOCUS: We are to be servant preservers and sustainers of the earth—its creatures and resources. That is what God said.

⚓ JAN. 14 ⚓

JOHN 14:1–4
A SECOND PLACE PREPARED

"If I go to prepare a place for you, I will come again. Then I will bring you into my presence so that you will be where I am" (John 14:3).

The biblical account says that God spent six days creating our home planet and the universe. Of course, God has no limits —if he wished, he could have spoken it into existence in a microsecond.

Centuries later, Jesus placed another creative, divine act within the scope of time. He told his disciples that he was leaving earth to prepare a place for all believers. Of course, in heaven Christ is outside the realm of earth-time, so it may not be proper to say, for example, "Jesus has been spending the past two thousand years preparing a place for us."

It is obvious, though, that God expressed both the universe creation and heaven's preparation within the context of time. Thus, it may be legitimate to say that if God placed the universe creation within the context of six days, what he is now preparing for those who love him must be infinitely beyond our wildest imagination.

The countless and vastly complex aspects of earth alone reflect a God who is endlessly inventive and who knows what humans need and what fascinates us pleasingly. I encourage you to prepare for a hereafter that will make earth's fascinations pale to nothingness.

LIFE FOCUS: You can only dream of what Christ has planned for you in eternity. Thank him for loving you that much.

⚓ JAN. 15 ⚓

Psalm 102:25–28
The Law of Entropy

To God we are the aroma of Christ among those who are saved and among those who are dying. To some people we are a deadly fragrance, while to others we are a life-giving fragrance (2 Corinthians 2:15–16).

In simple terms, the scientific law of entropy states that the universe is constantly, inexorably wearing out and going downhill. This law actually says more to support biblical creation than the theory of evolution, which hold that the universe is becoming more complex, advanced, and efficient. The evidence supports that truth that the universe is gradually decaying.

In describing the Fall, Vinet writes, "We believe in the wreck of humanity; we believe that its unfortunate ship has perished; the remains of that great catastrophe float upon the waves." And ever since that moment, the universe has groaned in pain for deliverance. Paul added that we, as Christians, also "groan inwardly. We groan as we wait eagerly for our adoption, the freeing of our bodies from sin" (Rom. 8:23). While it is true that much of the universe appears beautiful, it is apparently a sad, broken-down planet compared to its original pristine glory.

If you're observant, you can see reminders of the curse. The thorny weeds in your garden, your ever-decaying belongings, that chronic pain or health problem, the ravages of age, let alone the moral ravages of our sin and the sin of others. All these things, at times, make us long for deliverance from this life. Yet God must have good reasons for keeping us on earth. Perhaps we can be the fragrant aroma of Jesus rising from a small corner of a decaying earth.

Life Focus: In a world that is dying, you can spread the hope Christ brings. Your testimony to the truth can spread the fragrance of vibrant life to the living dead.

⚓ JAN. 16 ⚓

MATTHEW 11:28–30

GOD IS NO CRUEL TASKMASTER

On the seventh day [God] stopped the work he had been doing. Then God blessed the seventh day and set it apart as holy (Genesis 2:2–3).

Modern forecasters such as Alvin Toffler have claimed that as technology exploded Americans would work less and less and have much more leisure time—so much time they wouldn't know what to do with it. But this prediction hasn't materialized for many people. In fact, most seem to be working harder than ever. Maybe the lure of the almighty buck will never let people ease up.

During the 1600s what some people call the Protestant work ethic saturated the Christian community in America and continued through succeeding generations. "Work for the night is coming" became a frenetic slogan of missionaries and ministers who "burned their lives out for God." On the negative side, many pastors and Christian workers fail in ministry, fallen to nerves or depression, or have problem kids because they spend so much time "doing ministry" that staying healthy themselves and building family relationships simply doesn't happen.

God rested from the work of creation on the seventh day. He blessed this day and set it apart. Later he instructed us to spend one day each week in rest. And that's not all. Many feast days and weeks were to be periods of complete rest. One year in seven the Israelites were to leave the ground untilled and unplanted. Not only that, but new grooms were not to work during the first year of marriage, but were to spend it in restfulness with their brides. It's true that the Bible condemns laziness, but God is obviously not a cruel, driven taskmaster. He wants us to take time for rest and refreshment.

LIFE FOCUS: Rest and be refreshed. The infinite, omnipotent God is fully able to accomplish his almighty purposes even if you take a break.

⚓ JAN. 17 ⚓

HEBREWS 10:24–25
HUMAN COMPANIONSHIP

Then the LORD God said, "It is not good for the man to be alone" (Genesis 2:18).

Among all the animals, none was found suitable as a life partner and helper for Adam. And God said, "It is not good for the man to be alone." Some have used this verse as a proof that God wants everyone to marry, but here God was speaking specifically to Adam. The first man had no human companionship at this point and no helper. Besides, how was he to be fruitful and replenish the earth if he had no female partner?

Today we can enjoy many different types of companionship—family, friends, assistants, roommates, teammates. It is important that we not isolate ourselves and become alienated and reclusive. I board with a pastor's widow and retired school teacher. I suppose it's still possible I may marry, but I am learning to seek contentment with whatever God has for me.

The Apostle Paul writes, "I would like everyone to be like me. However, each person has a special gift from God, and these gifts vary from person to person. I say to those who are not married, especially to widows: It is good for you to stay single like me." Marriage and singleness each has its blessings and positive aspects.

LIFE FOCUS: God can help you find spiritual contentment and maximum fullness of life whether you are single or married.

⚓ JAN. 18 ⚓

JEREMIAH 6:13–15
"YOU SHOULD BE ASHAMED"

The LORD God called to the man and asked him, "Where are you?" He answered, "I heard you in the garden. I was afraid because I was naked, so I hid" (Genesis 3:9–10).

Picture the scene. God moves through the Garden of Eden as the evening breeze brushes the trees. But Adam and Eve are nowhere in sight.

"Where are you?" God calls. Then he sees them hiding in a cluster of trees, covered by crude outfits of fig leaves. Embarrassed and ashamed, Adam says, "I heard you in the garden. I was afraid because I was naked, so I hid."

Sin brings a sense of guilt. Some psychologists today claim that no one should experience guilt and shame—these are caused by childhood dysfunction or puritanical, oppressive religious teachings. It's true that in rare cases people become obsessed with such self-perpetuating guilt and shame that it becomes sick and twisted. These psychologists, however, appear blind to the fact that if there were no shame and guilt about sin and crime, the crime rate would skyrocket out of control overnight.

The most terrifying citizens are those who have sinned so constantly and horrifically that their consciences no longer sense any guilt. This is occurring today even in some adolescents.

We need to allow ourselves and others to sense guilt. This can motivate us to confess sin and turn from it.

LIFE FOCUS: Though it's far from enjoyable, you should be thankful for the shame and guilt you sense when you sin. Without it, you'd run hopelessly to evil without qualms.

⚓ JAN. 19 ⚓

EPHESIANS 5:28–31
WOMAN: FLESH OF MAN'S FLESH

A man will leave his father and mother and will be united with his wife, and they will become one flesh (Genesis 2:24).

What does it mean for a man and woman to become one in marriage? God's plan is for marriage to be a union of body and body, soul and soul, spirit and spirit. If one of these points of union is missing from a marriage, trouble is likely to arise.

If the relationship is based primarily on sexual attraction, when the glamour wears off, the relationship is often considered finished. Total indifference sets in, and adultery or divorce court are not far away.

Many non-Christian marriages survive simply because there's been a union of soul with soul. That is, the emotional and intellectual sides of a couple meld into a mutual closeness. These couples communicate and experience life together, sharing intimate times, the same friends, a similar livelihood, or similar interests and hobbies.

But the most important union is spirit to spirit, where both husband and wife must have a close relationship with God. It is paramount that Christians marry Christians and live in mutual acceptance and mercy.

Four great attacks on marriage in our day are: (1) the idea that the chief goal in life is our pleasure, (2) the widespread acceptance of adultery, (3) ease of divorce, and (4) decline of character traits such as integrity and perseverance. Christians need to be on guard so as not to fall prey to these weaknesses.

LIFE FOCUS: God is honored when we do whatever it takes to show the world his perspective of marriage—both in what we say and in how we live.

⚓ JAN. 20 ⚓

1 Corinthians 15:21–23, 45
First Adam, Last Adam

As everyone dies because of Adam, so also everyone will be made alive because of Christ (1 Corinthians 15:22).

In First Corinthians, the Apostle Paul distinguishes between the first Adam (Adam) and the last Adam (Christ). How did the experience of Adam and Christ contrast?

First, when Adam was placed in the Garden of Eden, he faced nothing but good. It was the optimum environment, perfect in every way. When Christ came to earth, he faced certain death—physical death in a long, excruciating crucifixion and spiritual death from which even he shrank in horror.

Second, while Adam and Eve lackadaisically conversed with Satan in the garden, Christ conversed with his Father in Gethsemane's agony. Minds were obviously tuned in opposite directions in those pivotal moments.

Third, Adam and his wife fell into sin and seemed to do so without great struggle. Christ wrestled mightily with God that the awful cup would pass from him, but in the end Christ did not turn from it but willingly carried out the will of his Father.

Fourth, the first Adam's spiritual death plunged all humanity into the curse of sin. The last Adam's death—physically and spiritually—redeemed all the millions the Father had given him. The last Adam's resurrection crippled Satan for all time and set the stage for Satan's final crushing on the Last Day.

Life Focus: The last Adam repaired all the awful damage caused by the first Adam. It cost him more dearly than can be imagined. Have you thanked him lately?

Romans 1:21–26

In God's Likeness, Not His Equal

God created humans in his image. In the image of God he created them. He created them male and female (Genesis 1:27).

Jim Jones, leader of the People's Temple cult, charmed masses of followers into a dysfunctional dependence on him. Then he began revealing his true colors. He raved, "I'm going to cause you to know that you are what Jesus was. It is written that 'ye are gods.' I'm a god and you're a god. I'm going to stay god until you recognize that you're a god. When you recognize that you're a god, I will go back into principle and will not appear as a personality."

Jones failed to differentiate between being created in God's image and arrogantly claiming oneness with God. When God created Adam and Eve in his image, he created beings who had an immortal soul and spirit. They possessed mind, will, and emotions which made it possible for them to feel, choose, and reason intelligently. They could also relate to and fellowship with him in a reciprocative, loving way.

Being in the image of God did in no way elevate humans to God's level. We are not infinite and possess none of God's unique divine traits. However, after sin came, we began seeing ourselves and others as if through one of those funhouse mirrors found at county fairs. The gross distortions have often resulted in two equally wrong responses. We may either deny the image and degrade ourselves to animal status, or we elevate the image and behave as if we are equal to or above God himself.

Life Focus: Through the Scriptures and accountability with mature Christians, we can maintain an authentic concept of ourselves and others as servants of God, created for his honor in his image.

⚓ JAN. 22 ⚓

HEBREWS 11:13–16
QUEST FOR UTOPIA

If they had been thinking about the country they had left, they could have found a way to go back. Instead these men were longing for a better country—a heavenly country (Hebrews 11:15–16).

Ever since Adam and Eve were banished from their Eden, humanity has yearned for utopia. That first couple left their perfect habitat unwillingly—a flaming sword and angels on guard lest they return.

As long as humans have a sinful nature, utopia will never be a reality. Yet Thoreau had Walden Pond, Jones had Guyana, the hippies had communes, and even Communists envisioned a utopia where no one would suffer poverty. There is this tenaciously persistent lie that says if leadership is capable enough, if the cause is noble enough, if the people are committed enough, a perfect environment can be a reality.

But every one of us is self-centered. In the end, issues arise on which we stubbornly refuse to compromise. One person begins hoarding instead of sharing. Another develops a grudge that festers into a bitter feud. What began as a big happy family eventually degenerates to small splintered factions.

As Christians, we can live in unity and love if we constantly keep in mind our own imperfection. This ushers in concepts like confession, apology, forgiveness, patience, and compromise. Our fellowship in this life, however, will always fall short of our dreams. Only in heaven will humanity's longings for utopia be fully realized.

LIFE FOCUS: It's sad that many whose utopian efforts devoured their brief lifetimes failed to give a moment's attention to preparing for the only possible utopia—an eternal one in Heaven. Are you preparing for that one?

Isaiah 40:13–22

A Lesson in Humility

God is enthroned above the earth, and those who live on it are like grasshoppers. He stretches out the sky like a canopy, and spreads it out like a tent to live in (Isaiah 40:22).

Robert Ruark wrote a captivating book about childhood days with his grandfather. In the book he tells about a period when he began skipping Sunday school and was waxing cocky and crude.

One day his grandfather announced that it was time for the boy to learn a little humility. He took his grandson fishing. Ruark writes, "That day, out on the Cape Fear River, I was the lonesomest boy in the world. In the utter hush a million noises intruded. A bittern roared. A kingfisher rattled. A deer snorted and barked. A bird screeched. A crow cawed. There was a rising miasma of mist as the air cooled and I was lost in the million slivers of vibrant life."

On the way home that evening the boy whispered to his grandfather, "Feel like I been to church. I feel like I got—that word you said."

"Humility?" the old man asked gently.

"Yessir, I feel awful little and unimportant somehow, and a little bit scared."

"You're beginning to learn, boy," he answered. "You're beginning to learn."

If you ever sense you are starting to act as if you're the master of your own universe it may be time to go off alone into God's backyard and contemplate again the vastness and majesty of his natural wonders. You will come back home a quieter, humbler person.

Life Focus: It may be time to acknowledge again that you're not the master, God is. You are just a lone creature whispering worship in a boundless universe.

⚓ JAN. 24 ⚓

EPHESIANS 5:21–25

EQUAL VALUE, DIFFERING ROLES

"You will long for your husband and he will rule you" (Genesis 3:16).

Nowhere in the Bible is man represented as being superior to woman or possessing greater innate worth in any sense. However, both before and after the Fall, the roles of man and woman are distinct from one another. Eve was created to be a helper fit for Adam. And after the Fall, God said that one aspect of the curse was that the husband would rule the wife.

Some women today may bristle at a statement like that. They envision a self-centered, domineering dictator stifling them and controlling them. These wives want equal authority in the relationship, yet when husbands and wives lock angry horns over and over, steadfastly refusing to bend, bitter divorces often result. Spiraling gender wars are multiplying divorces even among Christians.

Though biblically, man is to be a leader in marriage, how he enacts that leadership appears a key to success. Paul challenged husbands to cherish their wives as they love themselves. One facet of love is caring what another thinks and trying to meet the needs of another. If a husband caringly discusses with his wife the decisions he makes, the decisions can usually be mutual negotiations of what is best for both partners. If your marriage is a battleground, can you make a mutual agreement to begin submitting to one another in love? It begins with one unselfish act.

LIFE FOCUS: In a country where marriages are self-destructing in droves, ask the Lord to help you be an example of marital submission and mutual love.

⚓ JAN. 25 ⚓

ISAIAH 29:15–16

THE HIDDEN PARTS

We have refused to use secret and shameful ways. We don't use tricks, and we don't distort God's word (2 Corinthians 4:2).

Following their trespass, the eyes of Adam and Eve were opened and they realized they were naked. In one of his books, R.C. Sproul draws a broad parallel between the shame of their nakedness and our paradoxical desire to be noticed, mixed with fear of personal exposure. In other words, if a person ignores us, we become offended because we believe we're worthy of being noticed. However, if that same person stares hard at us, suddenly we become uneasy.

Because we're created in God's image, we do not want to be alienated from others; we have a need to relate to those around us. But our sinful nature leaves us with much to hide. Thus, if we believe people are prying into our inner selves, sometimes we try to hide. Or we wear masks, pretending to be what we think others will respect or admire.

Have you spent any time with the mentally challenged? There is a certain innocence in much that they say and do—a simplicity and transparency in their nature. They are missing much of the subterfuge and phoniness we "normal" folks practice.

Though it's painful, we must tear away the layered facades from our faces. We must admit to God who we really are. We must not be afraid or ashamed to show ourselves to others. Maybe multi-masked people will begin removing their masks if they see you doing it first.

LIFE FOCUS: Ask the Lord to make you more transparent, unashamed to show your true self to him and to others.

⚓ JAN. 26 ⚓

GENESIS 6:5–13
KEEP US FROM EVIL

Turn me away from a life of lies. Graciously provide me with your teachings. I have chosen a life of faithfulness. I have set your regulations in front of me (Psalm 119:29–30).

The Bible says that during the time of Noah, God saw how evil humans had become. All day long their deepest thoughts were nothing but evil. As we know, God wiped out all of humanity except one family.

Down the many centuries, human life on earth has never again reached the point of such total wickedness. Is that because, beginning with Noah's generation, we received a different, more spiritual nature? No, we have the same fallen nature inherited from Adam. Is it because people simply became more wise and conscientious? No, we still breed our share of fools.

What's the answer then? The Bible doesn't spell this out, but it seems as if God initially began focusing on single families or clans. He revealed himself to Noah and his family, to Abraham, Isaac, and Jacob. God nurtured a holy relationship with these patriarchs. Then, through Moses, he gave his selected people the Book of the Law—his guidelines for successful godly living. They learned a system of worship and sacrifice for sin. Then more Scriptures were written for their benefit. Jesus came with fuller teachings about God and his ways and then died and rose to conquer sin. The church was founded, God's Spirit came to empower disciples from the inside out, and more Scriptures gave greater guidance. Thus, throughout history, a strong human remnant have remained faithful to Yahweh.

LIFE FOCUS: The nurturing presence of God and Word of God preserve us from complete apostasy and abandonment to evil. We must always stay close to him.

⚓ JAN. 27 ⚓

PSALM 103:13–17
WE ARE BUT DUST

He certainly knows what we are made of. He bears in mind that we are dust (Psalm 103:14).

We are not created from gold dust, diamond dust, or powder of pearl. God forged man from the common dust of the earth and breathed into his nostrils the breath of life. This is not very flattering to us, but our bodies are composed of water and the compounds that make up ordinary brown mud.

Dust is not the stuff dreams are made of. Throughout the Bible, dust and ashes were a sign of utter humiliation or repentance. People mourned by sitting on a heap of dust and ashes, sprinkling dust on their heads. The tempting creature was condemned to eat dust down throughout history as a slithering serpent. God judged humans by declaring we would labor in the dust by the sweat of the brow, we would age, and eventually return to the dust from whence we came.

We use the expression "I know what she's made of." It means that we know the most glaring weaknesses or solid strengths of an individual. God also knows and understands each of us in a total sense from the time our tissues were forming in a womb.
He knows what he can genuinely expect from us, and he comprehends our finite limitations. He, better than anyone, knows we are but dust.

LIFE FOCUS: Be glad today that though God knows you're but dust, his mercy toward you never changes or ebbs.

⚓ JAN. 28 ⚓

PSALM 16
A LIFE TO BE SAVORED

Complete joy is in your presence. Pleasures are by your side forever (Psalm 16:11).

God could easily have created people as exceedingly boring creatures who consumed bland fodder, mated purely by instinct, viewed nature as purely utilitarian, plodded grimly through life, and even related to God mechanistically. Instead, God allowed our mouths to water for grilled steak. Humans tirelessly romance the opposite sex. Splashes of brilliant autumn leaves take our breath away. We split our sides laughing about silly escapades. And God is someone we can trust implicitly and worship deeply.

God made life something rich beyond words, something to be cherished and enjoyed. It is these special added touches that make us believe God is not a harsh, thundering tyrant, but is gentle, approachable, and joyful. Undoubtedly, God's capacity to enjoy is infinitely greater than ours, for his is uncluttered by selfishness, decline, or sin's grief.

When you relish that lasagna today, or look into your friend's dancing eyes, gaze across a shadowed lake or laugh at your child's antics, remember that God made it all possible.

LIFE FOCUS: Take time today to thank God for the thousand enjoyments that help make your life so worth living.

⚓ JAN. 29 ⚓

Job 38:1–18
A God Beyond Criticism

Job answered the Lord, "I'm so insignificant. How can I answer you? I will put my hand over my mouth" (Job 40:3–4).

Job fell fast and landed hard in the pit of despair. Looking up, he couldn't glimpse even a sliver of light at the mouth of the pit. Though the core of his being still clung to God, there were times when his cries to God were laced with acid. He couldn't understand why God had allowed such catastrophe to occur to a man who had lived so righteously and compassionately.

When God finally confronted Job face to face, he didn't mollycoddle him. He didn't explain his purposes in detail, and he didn't defend himself in any sense. Surprisingly, God simply laid out before Job the vast panoply of his universe: "Who is this that belittles my advice with words that do not show any knowledge about it? . . . Where were you when I laid the foundations of the earth? . . . Who determined its dimensions? Certainly, you know! Who stretched a measuring line over it?" (Job 38:2, 4–5). On and on God roared, laying out before Job his vast creations and challenging him to explain it all.

When God was finished, Job lay bruised and humbled in the dust: "'I have stated things I didn't understand,'" [he whispered,] "'things too mysterious for me to know. . . . I had heard about you with my own ears, but now I have seen you with my own eyes. That is why I take back what I said, and I sit in dust and ashes'" (Job 42:3, 5–6).

Life Focus: When you are in the dark throes of pain or disappointment, review God's immensely majestic universe, place your hand over your mouth, and bow low at his feet.

⚓ JAN. 30 ⚓

ACTS 17:22–28
THE SELF-SUFFICIENT GOD

"The God who made the universe . . . doesn't live in shrines made by humans, and he isn't served by humans as if he needed anything. He gives everyone life, breath, and everything they have" (Acts 17:24–25).

Something in us humans needs to be needed. We crave to know that someone cannot do without us. It makes us feel useful and important, and, in itself, there's nothing wrong with that.

However, some try to erroneously attribute to God this need to be needed. We imagine we have value because of what we can do for God. We forget that God is not helplessly dependent. He needs no one at all to maintain either his existence or sustenance. A.W. Pink writes, "God was under no constraint, no obligation, no necessity to create. That he chose to was purely a sovereign act on his part . . . determined by nothing but his own good pleasure." God is in no need for creatures to glorify him. He is perfect glory as the triune God.

And God doesn't grovel for helpers or defenders. It's true he commissioned us to fill the earth, subdue it, and, later, go and make disciples of all nations. But there are many other ways God could have fulfilled these tasks. We may rightfully defend his character, but God will be God regardless of evil charges.

LIFE FOCUS: Relax in the palm of the self-existent, self-sufficient God. He will work powerfully in and through your life simply because he wants to.

⚓ JAN. 31 ⚓

PSALM 63:1–7

GOD DECLARED IT GOOD

And God saw everything that he had made and that it was very good (Genesis 1:31).

Do you have days when you feel fed up with life—weary of the tedium, the aches and pains, sorrows and problems? Today my swollen sinuses throb, finances aren't great, publisher rejection slips abound, and I've got three loads of laundry to do. But, just the same, there is something still very good about life.

As God saw his universe begin to take shape, over and over he declared it good. When he was finished, he surveyed it all and knew it was very, very good. Of course, eventually we did our level best to ruin creation through the curse of sin. Yet creation was so good to start with, even sin's curse couldn't obliterate its beauty. And in spite of evil, existence can still be fulfilling and meaningful for us.

Life is good. God chose to create you in the beginning, and he selected you as his own child forever. He's allowed you to know him and he's been your companion throughout life. Though maybe you've faced grief or pain in life, some blessings have undoubtedly been sprinkled in. And a good life is not always an easy one. It may be you were specially chosen by God to be formed as his trophy in a furnace of affliction.

LIFE FOCUS: Life is good. Say it aloud and repeat it in the face of hard times. The goodness of life on this planet will begin to break upon you.

FEBRUARY

All Things Become New

⚓ FEB. 1 ⚓

2 Corinthians 3:14–18
To Be Christian Is to Change

We are being changed into his image with ever-increasing glory (2 Corinthians 3:18).

Do you remember the corny things we wrote in the back of classmates' high school yearbooks? We jotted comments like, "You're the greatest," "Keep that cute smile forever," and "Don't ever change." Deep down, we must have known change was inevitable, but maybe we feared the changes that waited around the next bend.

Whether we call it growth, transformation, maturing, or metamorphosis, change is an integral part of what it means to be a Christian. J.B. Phillips translates 2 Corinthians 3:18 this way: "But all of us who are Christians have no veils on our faces, but reflect like mirrors the glory of the Lord. We are transformed in ever-increasing splendor into His own image, and the transformation comes from the Lord who is the Spirit."

Four facts jump out from this verse. First, Christ's Spirit has removed the veil that blinded our understanding of his truth. Second, we model Gods' glory to the world—not as the source, but as reflecting mirrors. Third, we are transformed by a gradual process to the likeness of Christ. And fourth, it is the Spirit of God within us who enables and empowers the changes.

From our point of view, change is not always either desirable or necessary. We may even go to great lengths to retain the status quo. But change that God wants to accomplish in us is always necessary change, and that should make it desirable.

Prayer: Father, help me desire the necessary remodeling you need to do inside me.

⚓ FEB. 2 ⚓

James 1:22–25
Change Isn't Automatic

I'm convinced that God, who began this good work in you, will carry it through it completion on the day of Christ Jesus (Philippians 1:6).

It's important to establish from the beginning a few simple principles of sanctification:

1) Change does not take place in a spiritual vacuum. We need a balanced, accurate flow of biblical instruction about how to think and live.
2) It's possible to be either under- or overfed. If we're underfed, we are naive and misguided Christians. If we're receiving lots of instruction but doing little about it, we may become conceited or lackadaisical.
3) Christian change is usually gradual—a conversion that continues all our lives. Some lessons are learned painfully and may need to be relearned repeatedly before they become habits in our lives.
4) Change takes place in the give and take of daily life. This may involve education gained from difficult experiences and negative people as well as gained from enriching experiences and exemplary individuals.
5) The essence of Christian change is rooted in our motives. As believers, we're to examine the real reasons why we do and say things, that all of it may arise more and more out of unconditional love and a desire to honor Jesus Christ.

Our desired end is often great outward spiritual success. Oswald Chambers reminds us that God's purpose is for this minute—the process is of greatest concern to God. When he sees us faithfully and calmly serving him in the storms, that comprises his ongoing goal.

Prayer: Father, let me replace my grandiose goals with a concentration on the process of inner change.

⚓ FEB. 3 ⚓

MARK 2:15–17
NOT THE RIGHTEOUS, BUT SINNERS

"I've come to call sinners, not people who think they have God's approval" (Mark 2:17).

The African King Lewanika was known as the human tiger. He reveled in inventing new tortures to murder those who offended him.

John Newton was a drunkard, an incessant blasphemer, a lecher, and a pitiless slave trader. What made his evil worse was that he also attempted to lead those around him into the same depravity.

When Nicky Cruz was still a teenager, a veteran social worker claimed that the New York gang leader was the most hardened and hopeless case he'd ever seen.

These three people have at least one thing in common: each eventually bowed before Christ and traded in his old life for a brand new one.

It reminds me of Bill, a brawling alcoholic. For as long as anyone could remember, the haggard loner was known as Old Bill. Then something happened to him. One day he was told about a Savior who loved him and could lift him out of the pit he'd dug for himself. Old Bill was converted, and the transformation was so great that everyone began to call him simply New Bill.

Are you convinced that Christ can transform any human being—no matter how indifferent or how evil? Believe God for that "impossible" individual.

PRAYER: Father, I praise you for old lives made new and for including me in those granted newness of life.

⚓ FEB. 4 ⚓

LUKE 9:51–56

BEING PATIENT WITH NEWBORNS

You were infants in your faith in Christ. I gave you milk to drink. I didn't give you solid food because you weren't ready for it (1 Corinthians 3:1–2).

Joe Medina fled New York City with the police hot on his trail. When he finally stopped running, he found himself in Montreat, North Carolina.

Something unexplainable led Joe to a Bible study led by one of Billy Graham's associates. As Joe left, the leader confronted him. Under sudden conviction by the Spirit of God, Joe knelt and through tears invited Christ into his life.

Joe thought he'd left his past behind, but a part of his past followed him to Montreat. A drug peddler looked Joe up and tried to talk him into a deal. When Joe refused, the dealer turned violent. Suddenly old instincts took over, and Joe struck back. Ripping the knife from the man's grasp, Joe stabbed him with it.

In panic, Joe raced out into the hallway. Then, with a shock, he recalled that he was now a Christian. A different Joe went back and took the injured man to a nearby medical clinic.

By God's grace, charges were not filed against Joe for the felony. In the years following, he grew spiritually by leaps and bounds.

Let's be patient with the mistakes of new Christians and be willing to nurture them with milk in the simple basics of their new life.

PRAYER: Father, make me patient with the failings of new Christians as you have been patient with me.

⚓ FEB. 5 ⚓

2 TIMOTHY 1:1–5, 3:14–15
TRIBUTE TO THE UNKNOWN CHRISTIAN

From infancy you have known the Holy Scriptures. They have the power to give you wisdom so that you can be saved through faith in Christ Jesus (2 Timothy 3:15).

Timothy wasn't a "gospel celebrity." His mother and grandmother had quietly taught him the Scriptures from childhood. Sure, it's thrilling when God draws a hardened criminal to salvation. But, like Timothy, most don't have a glamorized or sensational personal testimony. Many have unassumingly and consistently lived for Christ for almost as long as they can remember, with no decades wasted enmeshed in sin. The awakening and growth of new life in these believers comes as silently as the growth of a plant.

Another group of Christians also deserves great respect. Many lay believers radiantly reflect Christ in the daily rat race of jobs and child care, traffic jams, and tragedies. Even those who are called to full-time Christian service find it difficult to pray, apply biblical principles, and steadily mature in the faith. It seems a greater challenge for office or factory workers who are constantly exposed to distracting pagan influences.

Yet so many just keep on loving God and serving him in ways unnoticed by others.

God is pleased with you today. It doesn't matter how others seem to rate you. There is no question—you are not now, nor will you ever be, considered ordinary to him.

PRAYER: Father, thanks for those who chose you in childhood and have remained faithful. What a great example they are.

⚓ FEB. 6 ⚓

HEBREWS 12:5–11
GOD'S CRUSHERS

We don't enjoy being disciplined. It always seems to cause more pain than joy. But later on, those who learn from that discipline have peace that comes from doing what is right (Hebrews 12:11).

In the book *Seeking Solid Ground*, John Trent tells of an experience that tried his insides. He was serving as an intern in a church, and his supervisor seemed extremely picky and critical. Even little mistakes John made were brought up and pointedly discussed at their weekly meetings. Meanwhile John's blood boiled as the supervisor lectured him long and loudly about each weakness or oversight.

When it came time for John to evaluate the supervisor, he took great delight in listing the man's faults, supposedly in an effort to spare future interns some suffering. He was shocked and humbled to learn later that the supervisor had given him one of the most glowing evaluations ever received regarding an intern. God sometimes allows rather rough fingers to crush us into Christ's image, but the end result is a rare wine.

"God can never make us poured-out wine," writes Oswald Chambers, "if we object to the fingers he uses to crush us. If God would only use his own fingers in a special way—but when he uses someone we dislike or some sort of circumstance to which we said we'd never submit and makes those the crushers, we object. We must never choose the scene of our own martyrdom."

PRAYER: Father, help me to somehow accept those fingers you use to crush out of me what shouldn't be in me.

⚓ FEB. 7 ⚓

HEBREWS 6:1–3

GOD IS STILL THERE

You received Christ Jesus the Lord, so continue to live as Christ's people. Sink your roots in him and build on him. Be strengthened by the faith that you were taught, and overflow with thanksgiving (Colossians 2:6–7).

Many Christians lament that the first excitement of their conversion has died away. They don't sense God's presence today as they did at the beginning. Spiritual laziness or some besetting sin may be suspected as the culprit, and repeated attempts at elaborate spiritual formulas seek to duplicate those golden days of new birth. But in many cases, personal sin isn't the problem.

There's joy and immense security for the young child in the constant aid and encouragement of a parent. There would be cause for serious concern, however, if that child needed the same constant supervision in adulthood.

Those golden moments in the past, which can be tormenting if we erect them into a norm, are both proper and beautiful if we're content to accept them as memories of a new love. Properly bedded down in a past which we don't sadly try to conjure back, they will send up exquisite growths.

It's true, God made some broad, sweeping changes in our lives during those first terrific days of new life. But that doesn't mean the small refinements he's working in us today are any less wonderful. As we sink our spiritual roots deeper, God desires that our faith won't depend so much on ecstatic sensings of his presence as on the absolute reliability of his Word.

PRAYER: Father, thank you for the joys of those golden days after conversion. Thank you, too, for today.

⚓ FEB. 8 ⚓

HEBREWS 11:32–40
THEIR LIGHT STILL SHINES

Through his faith Abel still speaks, even though he is dead (Hebrews 11:4).

When the sun sets below the horizon, its effect lingers. The heavens glow on after its departure. Henry Ward Beecher believed that when a great person dies, the world's horizon is luminous long after the soul passes out of sight. Such Christians cannot merely fade out of this world—everything they've touched reflects a spiritual brilliance. Being dead, their character still shimmers.

Terri Patterson was a talented, witty young mother who always seemed to be busy. Then in 1991, she was diagnosed with cancer. She went into remission after a terrible year of treatments, but was rediagnosed as terminal in 1994. When Terri learned she was dying, she fought past the anger and frustration and refused to give in to bitter cynicism. In fact, she wrote a gospel tract in which she frankly told her story. One part of the tract reads, "My cancer really is terminal, but I don't have to worry about the death penalty of sin. Although this body of mine may die as a result of cancer, my soul will be alive eternally with God. God has successfully treated my sin. If you haven't yet dealt with the sin that, like cancer, will destroy you, please accept God's free gift of salvation today."

Because Terri courageously used her heartbreaking trial to communicate God's love, though she is dead, her beautiful voice still echoes on. Are you leaving behind a legacy that will glow in people's hearts long after you leave this earth?

PRAYER: Father, may your light reflect on through me long after this shell returns to dust.

⚓ FEB. 9 ⚓

1 Peter 2:11–15
Amid a Watching World

Live decent lives among unbelievers. Then, although they ridicule you as if you were doing wrong while they are watching you do good things, they will praise God on the day he comes to help you (1 Peter 2:12).

Shortly before his death, Mahatma Gandhi said, "All about me is darkness; I am praying for light."

Many years earlier, a Christian family had housed the young Gandhi for seven months. At that time, he was evidently open to the claims of Christianity. Months passed and Gandhi observed closely the casual apathy of the family toward God and their reticence to make any sacrifices for the kingdom of God. His interest turned to disappointment. He concluded that Christianity was a good religion but just one more of the many valid religions of the world.

A high school football player was a clean-living Christian. One afternoon the biggest guy on the team walked up to him, grabbed his shirt, and shoved him back against the lockers. "Denny," he yelled, "I heard that you cussed the other day at practice. That true?"

"No way!" squawked Denny. "Somebody must've heard wrong."

"That's good," the tackle said roughly, "cause if I catch you talkin' like the rest of us, you'll answer to me."

Non-Christians are watching us, and they want something genuine and powerful to turn to when they're ready to accept it. Who is watching you these days?

Prayer: God, may those who look for you see you in me today.

⚓ FEB. 10 ⚓

Galatians 6:8–10
Helping or Hiding?

Whenever we have the opportunity, we have to do what is good for everyone, especially for the family of believers (Galations. 6:10).

Paul Rees writes, "If you want a picture of success as heaven measures it, of greatness as God views it, don't look for the blaring bands of Broadway; listen, rather, for the tinkle of water splashing into a basin, while Christ, in a humility that makes angels hold their breath, sponges the grime from the feet of his undeserving disciples."

I heard about a youth worker who committed himself in that way to his high schoolers. He attended their school events, visited them in their homes, and sacrificed the time to really be there for them. To show him their love and respect, some of the students got together and bought him a trophy with the engraving: The World's Second Best Servant.

In stark contrast, Leroy Eims relates an experience when he and his wife had a fish fry in their home for about twenty men. After dessert, one of the guests suggested that they help clean up. As the men organized to wash the dishes and take out the garbage, Eims spotted something he could hardly believe. One of the guys who had eaten the most and enjoyed it to the fullest got up from his chair, walked over to the window, and hid behind the drapes. After the work was well underway, he stepped out, sat down on a couch, and buried his face in a magazine.

Most of us aren't that obvious about avoiding opportunities to help, but do we ever take the initiative to care?

Prayer: Father, your Son was the world's best servant. Give me an added awareness of how to be helpful.

⚓ FEB. 11 ⚓

Mark 1:40–45

The Touch of Acceptance

Then a man with a serious skin disease came to him. The man fell to his knees and begged Jesus, "If you're willing, you can make me clean." Jesus felt sorry for him, reached out, and touched him, and said, "I'm willing. So be clean!" (Mark 1:40–41).

During the summer following my high school graduation, I worked for Tropicana Orange Juice in Florida. I moved into an old home where two other teens lived already. One of the housemates was Buck, an unashamed Christian.

The first evening I was with Buck, he broke the silence with a verbal bombshell: "I was a homosexual," he said, "before I became a Christian."

I didn't know what to say. Feeling intimidated, embarrassed, and somewhat repulsed, I asked haltingly whether Christ had changed him.

"I'm still tempted at times to do wrong," he said, "but I don't do it."

We talked on for a while. Then as I went off to bed, Buck said hesitantly, "Steve, will you shake my hand?"

I felt a sudden fear shoot through me that bordered on panic. But in the next instant, I realized that Buck was simply asking for a symbol of my acceptance—some indication that I didn't consider him some sort of spiritual leper to be observed from afar but never accepted as a friend. I reached out and shook Buck's hand.

Is there someone out there asking for a symbol of your forgiveness or acceptance?

Prayer: Father, help me to accept others as you have accepted me.

⚓ FEB. 12 ⚓

JEREMIAH 17:5–8

SUBMITTING TO DISILLUSIONMENT

My people have done two things wrong. They have abandoned me, the fountain of life-giving water. They have also dug their own cisterns, broken cisterns that can't hold water (Jeremiah 2:13).

We live in a society of disposables. People forsake churches, family members, friends, and spouses. The shrill and whiny reason that resounds over and over again is "They weren't meeting my needs."

Oswald Chambers believed we suffer from illusions because we don't wish to face the facts about human nature. We idealistically look to others to make us happy and complete. In an interesting play on words, Chambers claimed that if we'd submit to disillusionment, it would relieve much of our suffering. When we elevate our love for a human in place of our love for God, we demand of persons and of our church every perfection and the obligation of meeting our inner needs. Then, when we don't get it, we become offended or even downright vindictive. We demand of humans that which they cannot give. "There's only one being," wrote Chambers, "who can satisfy that last aching abyss of the human heart and that is the Lord Jesus Christ. The reason why our Lord is so severe regarding each human relationship is because he knows that every relationship not based on loyalty to him is going to end in disaster."

If we are looking to Jesus as our deepest source of trust and fulfillment, then we can enjoy intimacy with others because we won't be forever demanding from them that which only God can give.

PRAYER: Father, let me not demand from humans that which only you can be in my life.

⚓ FEB. 13 ⚓

GALATIANS 5:16–26
LIVING "UNDER THE INFLUENCE"

If we live by our spiritual nature, then our lives need to conform to our spiritual nature (Galations 5:25).

She swayed and teetered as she tried to walk. With tremendous effort, she reached a streetlight pole and grabbed on to it for dear life. I passed her in my car. Then, on impulse, I turned the car around and went back. The young girl must have consumed an amazing amount of alcohol. I managed to unclasp her hands from the pole and help her into the car. She was almost completely incoherent. When my words finally penetrated her consciousness, she pointed hazily in the general direction of her home. I don't think I'd ever seen anyone so completely under the influence of anything.

The idea in Ephesians 5:18 is that the Spirit of God should exert as much influence in our lives for good as drunkenness does toward reckless abandon. Suppose the most evil, spiritually indifferent person we know gives his life to Christ and encounters some immediate and astounding life changes. We're quick to acknowledge that this is the work of the Holy Spirit, but somehow we're tempted to think that the power that saves is not the same power that sanctifies. However, as we read in Romans 8:9, "If God's Spirit lives in you, you are under the control of your spiritual nature, not your corrupt nature." God offers the identical life-changing power to the long-term Christian as to the new believer. We must daily place ourselves "under the influence" of the Holy Spirit.

PRAYER: Father, don't allow me to be under the domination of anything or anyone except you.

2 Kings 6:15–17

Life from God's Perspective

In the morning, O Lord, hear my voice. In the morning I lay my needs in front of you, and I wait (Psalm 5:3).

Is Christianity hard? That's a difficult question because the same person who said, "Those who want to come with me must . . . pick up their crosses and follow me," also said, "My yoke is easy and my burden is light" (Matt. 11:30).

Christ's perspective is: "Give me all. I have not come to torment your natural self, but to kill it. Then I will make you new." However, we find it frightful and undesirable to hand over ourselves—all our skeletons, our dreams, and our fears. We say we want to remain ourselves, making personal happiness our overriding goal in life, and yet at the same time we want to be "good."

C.S. Lewis believed the most important part of the day for handing life over to God is the moment we wake in the morning. In those fleeting minutes, all our hopes and obligations for the day rush at us like wild beasts. Thus, our first job consists of shoving back those kinds of thoughts and listening to the other voice. Then we can go out seeing life from God's viewpoint. We can stand back from our natural fussings and frettings, periodically coming in out of the cold.

Don't worry if the "wild beasts" still foster panic some days. More and more you can begin letting God work out his daily plans through your life.

Prayer: Father, enable me to give up the attitudes and events of each day to your sovereign control.

⚓ FEB. 15 ⚓

Romans 1:18–25

The Tragedy of Knowledge without Response

They knew God but did not praise and thank him for being God. Instead, their thoughts were pointless, and their misguided minds were plunged into darkness (Romans 1:21).

Some years ago, Dave, my housemate, was a live-in employee in a home for delinquent boys. He developed a friendship with Tim, a troubled kid. Eventually, Dave moved on to other employment, but the boy never forgot Dave's interest and concern.

Recently Tim appeared at the home we rent. He was on leave from Camp Pendleton Marine Base, and he'd come to renew his friendship with Dave.

Tim's is a sad story of an unchanged life. Once I heard him claim that he's taught Bible studies—that leaders marveled at his insights. He knows his Bible and how he ought to live, but he simply will not make a break with the old life. Something about him is simulated and slippery, like a con artist pretending to go straight.

At one time Tim remarked that the girl he was dating was no good for him, but then she became pregnant, and they got married.

Today he wants to sleep on our couch because his marriage is exploding, and he has nowhere else to turn.

Don't let your story be one of an unchanged life. Everything works much better when you live according to the Creator's manual.

Prayer: Father, I don't want to turn you away when you point out something that needs changing in me.

⚓ FEB. 16 ⚓

JEREMIAH 42:1–5, 43:1–4
SKIN-DEEP CHANGE

"You are like whitewashed graves that look beautiful on the outside but inside are full of dead people's bones and every kind of impurity" (Matthew 23:27).

Even after King Saul's rebellion against God, one day he prophesied non-stop with the prophets, then left that place to pursue innocent David. On another occasion, a military captain named Johanan approached Jeremiah with a fellow officer, begging Jeremiah to seek God's mind for them and promising devotedly that whatever God said, they would do. But when God relayed his instructions, Johanan accused the prophet of blatantly lying. Then he led the people to do the opposite. In a different story, we read how King Amaziah started out truly doing what God considered right, but he did it halfheartedly. Then after he defeated Edom, he actually began worshipping their gods.

Sometimes we hear of well-known personalities doing some virtuous act or publicly mentioning their faith in God, and we automatically assume they must be Christians. Then we read of their sensual lifestyles, or we hear their profane conversations, and we're a bit shaken up. We wonder how they could seem so caring or reverent on one occasion and so hardened the next.

Remember, the human mind is the most deceitful of all things. It is incurably evil (Jer. 17:9). There is something in us that loves to be admired—that longs to appear better than we are. Change that's only skin deep isn't sanctification at all. It's a mere spiritual face-lift, and if one looks closely one can spot the stitches and, in time, the ugly reappearing wrinkles. Only God can work lasting change.

PRAYER: Father, deepen your work in me and purify my motives more and more.

⚓ FEB. 17 ⚓

JOHN 9:30–38
EMPATHIZING WITH THE UNWANTED

As the Midianite merchants were passing by, the brothers pulled Joseph out of the cistern. They sold him to the Ishmaelites for eight ounces of silver (Genesis 37:28).

I sat in a restaurant relaxing with John over a cup of coffee. He was in a talkative mood. "They tell me that when I was born I cried all the time," he remarked. "They couldn't find a milk formula I could keep down. I guess I was so much trouble, my parents got sick of me. One of our neighbors offered to buy me, but my ten-year-old sister talked my parents out of the deal."

I couldn't believe what I was hearing. The story sounded too unfeeling to be true. I asked John where his sister was now.

"She's dead," he said sadly. "She had a nervous breakdown when she was seventeen. One day her heart just stopped beating."

"You must really miss her."

"Yes, s-she was a very good person." John sat in silence, brooding over his memory of her.

Finally he said softly, "Not long before my father died, he turned to me and said, 'We should have sold you when you were a baby.'"

My heart ached for John and the devastation of feeling unwanted. I said a few words meant somehow to lift an ounce of John's heavy load.

"Now you know why my Christian friends are so important to me," John said.

And finally I understood.

PRAYER: Father, I want to hurt with those who hurt and understand them.

LAMENTATIONS 3:21–28

THE WISDOM OF SITTING STILL

"The LORD is good to those who wait for him, to anyone who seeks help from him" (Lamentations 3:25).

We exist in a frenetic society. It's remarkable how many products are labeled as instant and how we demand things like instant service and instant gratification. Sometimes we rush decisions. We hurry in and out of jobs and relationships. If hard times come, we fight and squirm and manipulate ourselves out of them as quickly as possible. Meanwhile, in many cases, God is saying, "Surrender yourself to [me], and wait patiently for [me]" (Ps. 37:7).

It's interesting to see what giants of the faith teach about waiting. A.B. Simpson writes, "If we wholly trust an interest to God, we must keep our hands off it; and he will guard it for us better than we can help him. There is nothing so masterly as inactivity in some things and there is nothing so hurtful as restless working, for God has undertaken to work his sovereign will." According to J.R. Miller, it requires the greatest heroism to stand and wait and not lose heart, "to submit to the will of God . . . while the happy, busy multitude goes on and away." Chambers adds, "Never run before God's timing. If you do, you will end up making difficulties that will take years of time to make right. When it's a question of the providential will of God, wait for God to move." "There are times when things look very dark to me," writes George Matheson, "so dark that I have to wait even for hope. A long deferred fulfillment carries its own pain, but to wait for hope, to see no glimmer of a prospect and yet refuse to despair . . . that is the grandest patience of the universe."

Sometimes the wisest work we can do is to wait.

PRAYER: Father, when I'm frantic and anxious, teach me how to patiently wait for you.

⚓ FEB. 19 ⚓

2 CORINTHIANS 1:3–7

HEALED SCARS ATTRACT THE WOUNDED

If we suffer, it brings you comfort and salvation. If we are comforted, we can effectively comfort you when you endure the same sufferings that we endure (2 Corinthians 1:6).

I walked into John's dilapidated home one evening. He was on the phone, sobbing loudly and arguing between sobs. It seemed that he wanted to go along on one of the church high school events, and the youth pastor didn't think it would be appropriate.

You see, John is fifty-nine years old. He lives alone, has no trade, and is socially impaired. He takes a bus at 6:00 A.M. each morning to his part-time job at a fast food restaurant.

Jesus stepped into John's life in 1981. I like to think that John's simple trust in the Savior must be what Christ pictured when he spoke of valuing childlike faith. But John still gets lonely, and his fragile self-confidence wavers precariously when he thinks he's being rejected.

When Christ enters a life, he does not immediately nullify all the negative effects of one's past. There is transformation and healing, but some of the scars may never heal completely. Even in this, God has a purpose. Imperfect people see that we also are defective, and they can admit their need for Christ's embrace without feeling belittled.

Let your battle scars attract the wounded to the Great Physician.

PRAYER: Father, help me realize that even my plain humanness can be used to draw the hurting toward you.

⚓ FEB. 20 ⚓

MATTHEW 25:14–30
RISK FAILURE TO SUCCEED

We want each of you to prove that you're working hard so that you will remain confident until the end (Hebrews 6:11).

God operates with full knowledge that we're sinners and are often full of fear. Instead of despising or bemoaning our weakness, God actually displays within us his greatest power in thunder's stormy crash. Successful Christians are not superhuman—they're not God's special favorites, but are little Christians who face great odds with a persistence born of confidence in a mighty God.

Theodore Roosevelt, America's 26th President, personified persistence. He declared that it isn't the critic who counts—not the one who points out how the strong stumbled or the mighty could have done better. The credit belongs to the one who's actually in the arena, whose face is marred by dust, sweat, and blood; who errs and falls short again and again; who knows the great devotion to a worthy cause; who, at best, knows in the end the triumph of high achievement and, at worst, fails while daring greatly. This person's place will never be with those timid souls who know neither victory nor defeat.

Ruth Graham did not describe a majestic lion or towering grizzly as exhibiting this lesson, but an unassuming little bird:

He sang atop the old split rail
  all while it thundered,
raindrops pelting him like hail;
  and I wondered:
how one small, vulnerable bird,
  defying deafening thunder,
could make itself sweetly heard
  —and still I wonder—

PRAYER: Father, please grant me the courage to defy great odds through the power working within me.

1 TIMOTHY 1:12–16

HE'S CALLING YOUR NAME

I thank Christ Jesus our Lord that he has trusted me and has appointed me to do his work with the strength he has given me. In the past I cursed him, persecuted him, and acted arrogantly toward him. However, I was treated with mercy (1 Timothy 1:12–13).

Picture a little tax man who, according to rumor, would cheat his own mother if enough were at stake. Imagine a woman of darkness possessed by demonic powers. Envision a brutal terrorist who hunts down Christians and has them imprisoned or even slaughtered.

This will be difficult, but now picture Jesus telling the devious tax man that he wants to eat dinner with him. Imagine the woman as the first to whom Jesus appears following his resurrection. Finally, envision Jesus disclosing to the terrorist that he's been chosen to carry God's message to the world.

This is not an ethereal fantasy, for Zacchaeus, Mary Magdalene, and Saul of Tarsus were all real people whom God selected in spite of themselves.

Today you may feel too despicable, too insignificant, or too unspiritual to ever be chosen by God. But the Father may see more in you than you've ever seen in yourself. He knows the person you wished to be even as you wandered the same old rut in life's road. And he knows the person he can make you become as you share his Son's life.

I think I hear a still, small voice calling your name. Can you hear it?

PRAYER: Father, thank you that you don't choose your team the way humans do. Thank you for calling my name.

⚓ FEB. 22 ⚓

PHILIPPIANS 3:10–15

EASY TO PLEASE; HARD TO SATISFY

You will be God's children without any faults among people who are crooked and corrupt. You will shine like stars among them in the world (Philippians 2:15).

Do you ever feel overwhelmed by God's expectations? Are you wearing yourself out trying to please him, yet feeling as if his whip is always poised just above your head?

"In the long run," C.S. Lewis writes, "God will be satisfied with nothing less than perfection. However, he will also be delighted with the first feeble, stumbling effort you make tomorrow to do his will." God's expectations change with our maturity. It is as George MacDonald said, "God is easy to please but hard to satisfy."

The Lord Jesus is constantly moving and working, not from the outside in but the inside out. Oswald Chambers paraphrases Christ: "Jesus says, 'If you are my disciple you must be right, not only in your living but in your motives, in your dreams, in the recesses of your mind. You must be so pure in your motives that God Almighty can see nothing to censure.'" Who can stand in the eternal light in that way? Chambers claimed that only the Son of God can. Jesus Christ declared that by his redemptive presence he can put into anyone his own character and make that person as untainted and simple as a child.

Again, I like the way Lewis puts it: "Christ is beginning to turn the tin soldier into a live person. The part of you that does not like it is the part that is still tin."

PRAYER: Father, let me not fear or grow stubborn as your Son does his remodeling work in my life.

⚓ FEB. 23 ⚓

1 PETER 2:11–12
WITNESS IS A LIFESTYLE

Live as citizens who reflect the Good News about Christ (Philippians 1:27).

I used to sit and talk to Oscar, an eccentric little Jew who lived two doors down. His wife was dead, and his son had killed himself. I often chauffeured Oscar to the corner store to buy his beloved cigars, and I took him to the emergency room once when he gashed his head.

Bob is a man I met at the community pool. When he learned I'm a Christian, he confessed he has a very hard time with the Christian claim that Christ is the only way to God. He asked to read a book I wrote on Bible characters and we've had several good talks since.

I was talking to my neighbor, Jill, the other afternoon, and she mentioned she'd taken her children and some neighbor's kids to Mass on Sunday. The conversation shifted to the church. I mentioned that I believe the Bible, and she blasted me with some impressive anti-biblical info she'd probably picked up in a college anthropology class.

"You know, it's funny," she finally admitted. "I don't believe in God, but I take the kids to church because I want them to receive some moral training. I think the Bible's a pack of myths, but I find church strangely comforting."

These are a few people to whom I've stumblingly tried to be a witness. I am painfully shy and quiet, so I know that if I can do it, you most definitely can. In your world, who knows that you're a child of God?

PRAYER: Father, you know my personality and communication style. Please plan situations in which I can be a witness in some way.

⚓ FEB. 24 ⚓

1 Timothy 4:13–16

Good or Best?

The day will make what each one does clearly visible because fire will reveal it. That fire will determine what kind of work each person has done (1 Corinthians 3:13).

Once upon a time, some people were hired to work all day in a giant apple orchard. They arrived at dawn, but only a few began picking apples.

One man simply stuffed his pockets with the apples and departed. Another worker sat down and philosophized about the advantages of the McIntosh over the common Winesap. Collecting several shiny apples, yet another began juggling them out by the highway, collecting a small crowd of spectators in the process. A young woman competed with the juggler, belting out tunes like, "Little Green Apples" and "Apple of My Eye." Still another volunteer began picking apples, but as he picked them, he gleefully splattered them against the tree trunks.

At sunset, the employer appeared. Most of the workers crowded around him, excitedly describing various things they'd done with the apples. He smiled a little at their enthusiasm, but there was a stern glint in his eye. "I commend those of you who did good things with the apples," he said, "but you may not have done the best thing. I hired you to pick apples because picking apples is profitable. If what you did with the apples was profitable to my enterprise, then, and only then, was it the best thing."

Prayer: Father, show me if I'm doing those things that are most profitable spiritually.

Psalm 119:97–104
Wise Counseling; Biblical Change

I have more insight than all my teachers, because your written instructions are in my thoughts (Psalm 119:99).

Many today believe it is chiefly through psychology that people can heal and change in positive ways. I don't believe that, but I do believe in Christian counseling. Some emotional dysfunction is so severe that many hours must be spent in healing the spirit. However, I'm also convinced that counseling principles should be screened through the Word of God, for it's the Creator who knows best how to fix his creation.

A few possible pitfalls in the sometimes-confusing world of counseling are as follows: (1) Counselors discourage rescuers—that is, those who constantly help people as if they must "save the world." However, if we're not careful, we'll also discourage Christians who devote their lives to serving others as Jesus instructed. (2) Persons are accused of being in denial if they refuse to admit their emotional or spiritual struggles. However, if they admit their struggles, they may suddenly be labeled, obsessed, willfully stuck, or making excuses for failure. (3) In relationships such as marriage, spouses are warned against trying to change their partner. At the same time, spouses are told to be totally flexible and willing to submit to what partners say they need. (4) On occasion, counselors explain away all shame or guilt as only a self-destructive habit; and, in some cases, sin is also minimized or explained away as simply a universal human weakness.

Whether counseling friends casually, or professionally counseling the deeply damaged, only God can give the wisdom and balanced insight to stay true to his eternal principles for human relationship. Ask him for wisdom.

Prayer: Father, give me growing insight into myself and others so I'll have your wisdom to share when opportunities arise.

⚓ FEB. 26 ⚓

1 PETER 3:8–12

ALL TALK, NO ACTION

Everyone must live in harmony, be sympathetic, love each other, have compassion, and be humble (1 Peter 3:8).

This anonymous poem has a message that's meant to jolt us into realizing that our kindness should be expressed with actions, not just words:

I was hungry
 and you formed a debate team
 to debate the pros and cons
 of world hunger relief.
I was imprisoned
 and you crept away busily
 hoping someone would
 somehow find time to visit me.
I was poorly clothed
 and in your mind you disapproved
 of my lack of style.
I was sick
 and you thanked God
 for your good health.
I was homeless
 and you preached about the spiritual shelter of the church.
I was lonely
 and you muttered a quick prayer
 and left me alone.
You seem so content
 so pleased with your Christianity
 but I'm still hungry and
 lonely and cold.

PRAYER: Father, don't let me miss the forest for the trees.

Hebrews 5:12–6:3
Failure Doesn't Demand Regression

We should stop going over the elementary truths about Christ and move on to topics for more mature people (Hebrews 6:1).

Do you remember coming home from Christian camp on a spiritual high? The week at camp had transformed you—people were going to marvel at the new you, and you were going to evangelize your neighborhood for Christ. Two or three weeks later, the excitement was gone. You agonized and prayed, trying to work up the emotions, but you felt you'd totally regressed spiritually.

It's sort of like learning to play the piano. When a kid hits the wrong note, she often goes back, starts at the beginning and tries again—louder. In Christian circles, that sort of thing is called by names like rededication, revival, or renewal. It's a new and louder beginning of Christian commitment. When we've drifted into sin or apathy, we feel we must wallow in contrition for days. Then we work up to a spiritual high, only to lapse again and regress to the elementary principles of our walk with God.

Your self-torturing guilt, rash vows, and repeated rededications can become a vicious circle of spiritual regression. I believe God's intention is that we keep going forward and not start from scratch at every point of failure. The point of failure should become the occasion for immediate confession and restored, ongoing fellowship with God.

The author of Hebrews says to let us go on and get past the elementary stage in the teachings and doctrine of Christ. Let's continue progressing toward maturity, not continually relaying the foundational truths of repentance and faith in God.

Prayer: Lord, may my failures bring a greater determination to progress toward maturity.

⚓ FEB. 28 ⚓

2 CORINTHIANS 4:5–11

THOSE MELLOWED, WEATHERED TROPHIES

As we lovingly speak the truth, we will grow up completely in our relationship to Christ, who is the head (Ephesians 4:15).

There is a small select group of people. They are the ruggedly weathered, beautifully seasoned saints one encounters rarely, and each of us should strive to become a part of their fraternity. Within Christendom, they should be declared a national treasure.

I am struck by how unordinary they seem by human standards. Their tolerant compassion for all, their wisdom in its profound simplicity, their gladness in spending and being spent must represent the best of what it means to be human.

I see an older woman with twinkling, knowing eyes who reminds me that she prays for me every day. I see the fine teacher who cares much more about his learners than about their Bible knowledge or witty answers. And there is that seasoned saint who left behind censorious crabbing long ago, has mellowed well in the stormy tides of life, and now, with patience and compassion, envelops people in the very embrace of Christ.

These Christians are not perfect by any means, yet one gets the feeling that they've matured very nearly as far as a child of God can go in this life.

I love these smiling, caring trophies of God's grace. I see him in their eyes.

PRAYER: Father, continue the hard work of making me into one of your trophies.

⚓ FEB. 29 ⚓

2 CORINTHIANS 4:14–18

THE ULTIMATE BADGE OF COURAGE

I have fought the good fight. I have completed the race. I have kept the faith. The prize that shows I have God's approval is now waiting for me (2 Timothy 4:7–8).

From those whose bodies lit Nero's gardens, to those who calmly sang "Nearer My God to Thee" as the *Titanic* sank, Christians in all ages have been known for the way they die. Yes, there may be fears, but as God's own near the crossing over, there is a peaceful release, almost an eagerness, in their eyes.

A few hours before he died, D.L. Moody murmured triumphantly, "Heaven opens before me. I am not dreaming. I have been within the gates—I have seen the children's faces. It is my coronation day."

On his deathbed, Adoniram Judson said, "Christ is calling me home, and I go with the gladness of a boy bounding away from school."

Premature death is even more difficult to face than death by natural causes. Early death by persecution, injury, or illness merits God's special badge of courage.

Just as my mother died prematurely, so also did Dr. Jane Wheeler of Wheaton College. She wrote to the faculty and students shortly before illness claimed her body: "If the Lord has chosen me to go to him soon, I go gladly. Please do not give me a moment's grief to me. Think of me only happily as I do of you. I do not say a cold goodbye but rather a warm *auf wiedersehn,* till I see you again, by God's power and grace on campus this fall or later in the blessed land."

PRAYER: Father, let me face even the ultimate test with courage.

MARCH

Growing Pains

⚓ MARCH 1 ⚓

ECCLESIASTES 11:9–12:1
FIRST LESSONS

I'm convinced that God, who began this good work in you, will carry it through to completion until the day of Christ Jesus (Philippians 1:6).

It all began when my older brother, David, and I made the decision that the material possessions of others could just as well belong to us. Every summer in the beautiful Blue Ridge mountains of North Carolina where we lived, hundreds flocked to a Bible conference. The plan was really quite simple. He'd enter an empty guest room while I waited outside as a lookout. If a guest walked down the hallway in our direction, I'd whistle so David could hide until the danger was past.

For several weeks, we exulted in the cache of candy, chewing gum, and loose change we'd buried by a tree in the yard. Finally, one day Dad came home with a scowl that told us trouble was brewing. He asked each of us if we had anything to do with the mysterious conference robberies. David denied our involvement emphatically; I admitted it fearfully, and our goose was cooked.

The punishment for our escapade insured that we not only forsook our criminal ways, but we also allowed God to slowly begin his good work in our lives. It has been a long process and one that will continue for the rest of our lives. We can trust him to keep blending his instruction with discipline for our good.

LIFE FOCUS: In the process of spiritual growth, God receives us with full knowledge of our childish foolishness and then begins that patient, lifelong process of making us what we ought to be. Are you allowing the potter to mold you to the image of his Son?

⚓ MARCH 2 ⚓

EXODUS 4:10–17
OVERCOMING FEARS

No fear exists where his love is. Rather, perfect love gets rid of fear, because fear involves punishment. The person who lives in fear doesn't have perfect love (1 John 4:18).

By temperament, some will always be more shy than others. But extreme shyness can make life very painful at times. If allowed to spin out of control, insecurities and fears can render a person relationally paralyzed.

I remember standing in my seventh-grade classroom to recite the Gettysburg Address. "Fourscore and seven years ago . . ." (my voice began to quiver, my fingers clenched my desk) "our f-fathers brought forth on this continent . . ." (my legs shook, my voice quavered uncontrollably) "a nation, conceived in l-liberty . . ." (I went speechless and sat down in utter humiliation).

As a boy, it was terrifying to meet new people, go to a new school or church, take leadership over others, or, God forbid, speak in front of a group. Fortunately, some of the shyness has passed—I teach college classes and church groups; I can reach out to strangers; I have healthy, close relationships; I can say no more easily and deal to some extent with interpersonal conflict. However, some of us will never be social butterflies—the charming conversationalists—and we should be perfectly content with that. If all of us were the life of the party, there would be no one left to listen.

LIFE FOCUS: God can help you overcome fears that paralyze you. His love within you can replace stark fear with a growing confidence in him. Your insecurities may not be connected to shyness, but whatever their source, God is your refuge and your confidence.

⚓ MARCH 3 ⚓

LUKE 17:11–19
REMEMBERING THE MAGIC WORDS

Whoever offers thanks as a sacrifice honors me. I will let everyone who continues in my way see the salvation that comes from God (Psalm 50:23).

Parents know there's almost something magical in words like please and thank you because of how they affect the recipient. When I was a boy, my mother would whisper, "Now, Steve, what do you say?" That was my cue to blurt out a hurried "thank you." How easily we forget to be thankful even to those who deserve it the most.

On September 8, 1860, the Lady Elgin, a crowded passenger steamer, sunk off the shore of Lake Michigan. A student named Edward Spencer was standing on the beach when he saw a woman clinging to some wreckage far out in the breakers. He threw off his coat and swam out through the stormy waters, succeeding in getting her back to shore.

An incredible sixteen times during that day, Spencer challenged the fierce waves, rescuing seventeen persons. Then he collapsed in a delirium of exhaustion from the exposure and exertion. Somehow, he never completely recovered from the physical strain of his accomplishment. With weakened health, he lived out his years in California.

When Spencer died, a newspaper reported that not one of the seventeen people he rescued ever came back to thank him. He risked his life and endangered his health for these individuals, but somehow they overlooked the magic words.

LIFE FOCUS: Someone has said that the most common sin is that of ingratitude. Being thankful is a vital habit we should develop in our lives. Thank God and the people around you each day for who they are and what they do for you.

⚓ MARCH 4 ⚓

PHILIPPIANS 2:1–4
ENCOURAGING OTHERS

We must also consider how to encourage each other to show love and to do good things (Hebrews 10:24).

A Christian athlete tried out for the football team at one of the top football programs in the nation. He was talented but only good enough to play third string. Then an old football veteran watched him quarterback during a practice scrimmage. After the scrimmage, the gentleman walked over to the player. "Boy, I like the way you play. I think you've got some real talent." With that simple affirmation, the quarterback went on to play the sort of inspired football that moved him up to the number one slot.

I attended school at an orphanage for five years. The children there could be tough and obnoxious—some were hardened by a conviction that no one would ever care. They didn't show overt signs of loneliness or fear, but I realize now that they must have been suffering from deep emotional scars. After all, they'd been transferred to the place from the worst possible backgrounds—homes where love and encouragement were rare or non-existent. Tears must have dampened many pillows each night in that dark orphanage.

Even now, many years later, I wonder if any of those children ever found love.

LIFE FOCUS: Genuine love and encouragement can have a profound impact on people. There are thousands of discouraged, hurt people around us who need someone to care. Don't be overwhelmed by the numbers—just begin by encouraging one person.

⚓ MARCH 5 ⚓

EPHESIANS 4:29–32
LEARNING TO COOL IT

Whoever has knowledge controls his words, and a person who has understanding is even-tempered (Proverbs 17:27).

I am pretty laid back and mild-mannered by nature. I don't lose my temper very easily—I don't even like confronting people. But, given the right circumstance, I can be as cruel as anyone.

It was a sweltering afternoon at the orphanage, and a group of us were playing touch football. Tempers grew short and accusations flew as game rules were broken. The leader of the opposing team shouted something crude at me from downfield. Caught up in anger, I shouted, "You motherless baby!" Then I wheeled and walked away. Suddenly I heard pounding feet and ducked in terror as the boy leaped at me. He grazed me and I felt a rush of air as he passed. He was in my face, veins bulging in his neck, screaming vengeance. I was shaken to the core.

Surely I can never tell myself I'm too kindhearted to say things that cut to the soul. James tells us our speech reflects our overall Christian discipline. If I'm controlling my speech, I'm able to also discipline other areas of my life.

LIFE FOCUS: Check your spiritual thermometer. Are you hot under the collar or cooling it in the Spirit? God can cool our hot-tempered tongues when we work with him on the all-important lesson of self-control.

⚓ MARCH 6 ⚓

PHILIPPIANS 4:4–9

EMULATING THE GODLY

Practice what you've learned and received from me, what you heard and saw me do. Then the God who gives this peace will be with you (Philippians 4:9).

One day when no one else was home, I found my mother sitting on her bed gazing out the window, her cheeks shining with tears. I kept asking her what was wrong, but she just shook her head and said nothing. Not long afterwards, I learned that my mother had cancer.

Throughout the next months, I never again saw my mom cry. Whenever I saw her, we held hands, and she smiled and had long talks with me. Then, after a three-year battle, she began to falter. One day she and Dad had their last date in her hospital room. They talked about intimate times—the floods of memories—the future of the family. Later that evening she lapsed into a coma and, hours later, she left us to enter the presence of her greatest love, Jesus Christ.

In retrospect, I think of what made my mother such an amazing woman. I hear her faithful prayers for us. I see her singing choruses with uninhibited joy. I watch her burning her life out in order to make ours comfortable. I hear her wholeheartedly cheering and encouraging people she met. I see her smiling gently through eyes of pain. I sense her unfaltering faith as her time runs out.

LIFE FOCUS: I'm very grateful for mature Christians who consistently translate what they believe into daily living. At any age, we can find another believer to emulate. Is there someone you can imitate as he or she imitates Christ?

Psalm 6
When You Hit Bottom

Don't be surprised by the fiery troubles that are coming in order to test you. Don't feel as though something strange is happening to you, but be happy as you share Christ's sufferings. Then you will also be full of joy when he appears again in his glory (1 Peter 4:12–13).

After my mother died, my dad moved to Columbia, South Carolina, leaving me at a private boarding school in North Carolina. I had no family members close by, and I didn't even realize how desperately I missed the love only a mother can give. As the months wore by, I became listless and discouraged. My relationship with God became crippled with mind-numbing doubt and hopelessness. It seemed as if everybody was happy except me. What scared me most was the horrible sense of restless panic that set in and never seemed to let up. I had hit bottom—I was clinically depressed and no one around me even detected it.

This was before professional Christian counseling became common, and most emotional struggles were treated with only a Scripture verse and an assumption that lack of faith or unconfessed sin was most likely the culprit. In my case, God was especially gracious. With time, the worst symptoms faded away. I became able to face life's ups and downs with some degree of confidence. I will probably always struggle some with depression. The physiological tendency has been passed down through my family tree. Yet, when the darkness closes in, I fly to God as a bird in a storm flies to the cleft of the rock.

Life Focus: Has some tragedy or crisis struck you with great force? You can't imagine any possible way you'll ever see sunlight again? Cast yourself upon the palm of God's mercy. If necessary, find a solid Christian counselor who can help you sort out the despair and see the eternal hope shining underneath. Whatever happens, never, ever give up.

⚓ MARCH 8 ⚓

1 JOHN 4:17–19
DISPELLING DOUBT

You have tested us, O God. You have refined us in the same way silver is refined. You have trapped us in a net. . . . We went through fire and water, but then you brought us out and refreshed us (Psalm 66:10–12).

As I stand at a lectern looking out over a mass of people, my darting glance takes in the classmates, other students, parents and friends, and, of course, faculty.

It's my high school graduation, and it's supposed to be a time of celebration. I've passed the Bible classes, fulfilled academic requirements, and lettered in several sports, but at this moment my mind is a raging cauldron of doubt.

I'd like to speak eloquently to the crowd of the wonderful years of high school and of the great things I hope to accomplish in the future. There have been good times, but my high school years have also been marred with mom's illness and death. As I open my mouth, a glowing testimony doesn't pour out.

"I, um, didn't plan to say this exactly, but, uh, I've got to be honest. My relationship with God isn't going too well. I'm having doubts about him, about his Word, and even about my salvation. I'm not giving up, but I'm crying out to God to help me. Tonight, I ask you to pray for me. I claim the verse that says, 'You have tested us, O God. . . . We went through fire and water, but then you brought us out and refreshed us'" (Ps. 66:10, 12).

There was no immediate supernatural intervention . . . no great rush of exhilaration. But, step by step, out of the fog of confusion and disillusionment, God brought submission and a fuller understanding of himself.

LIFE FOCUS: God needs to show us what we are without him before he will show us what we can accomplish with him. Eventually, through the tough times, he will bring us out into a place of spiritual refreshment and abundance. It isn't magical—just a revealing of himself and a gradual stabilization of our ups and downs.

1 CORINTHIANS 9:24–27
TIMES OF TOUGHENING

So I run—but not without a clear goal ahead of me. So I box—but not as if I were just shadow boxing. Rather, I toughen my body with punches and make it my slave so that I will not be disqualified after I have spread the Good News to others (1 Corinthians 9:26–27).

DECEMBER 18: I'm perspiring like crazy, my muscles are cramped, my hair is matted, and I can't get any sleep in this hot, stuffy car. I'm traveling on a thirty-hour trip down to Monterrey, Mexico, to take part in a missions crusade. During the next two weeks, we will attempt to saturate the city of Monterrey with the gospel.

DEC. 21: Spent all day selling Christian books door to door. It's hard to remember my lines in Spanish. There's no telling what the nationals think I'm saying.

DEC. 23: Beans again! We barely sold enough books and Bibles today to pay for our food. Have to pray for a better day tomorrow.

DEC. 25: I never expected to spend Christmas doing mission work. Had three doors slammed in my face this morning. Does wonders for the old self-confidence. One woman did seem interested in Christ, though.

DEC. 27: I'm increasingly frustrated with the language barrier. I feel insecure about telling these people that their beliefs are all wrong and that we have the only truth.

DEC. 29: Finally getting used to sleeping on a cement floor. We've now held evangelistic meetings and canvassed about two-thirds of the city with Bibles and Christian books. These people seem so hungry for the literature.

JAN. 1: Heading back home. What a good experience! Closest thing to New Testament evangelism I've ever encountered. Thanks, Lord.

LIFE FOCUS: Spiritual toughening comes as we discipline ourselves to endure in his power what we cannot take in our own strength.

⚓ MARCH 10 ⚓

Romans 14:10–13
Resisting Legalism

Why do you criticize or despise other Christians? Everyone will stand in front of God to be judged (Romans 14:10).

I thought I was a fairly open-minded Christian. Then my brother and I started an area Bible study one summer and a couple of smokers began attending. They listened attentively with cigarettes lodged between their lips. The room became hazy with smoke and my attitude became huffy with indignation. I complained to my brother and he rebuked me soundly for my legalism.

He was right. I nurtured a sort of spiritual conceit because of all the external things I wouldn't do. I never listened to rock and roll, I wore my hair short, I never went to movies, I wouldn't play cards—and the list went on. I was smug in the realization that I was spiritually superior to all those "worldly" Christians around me. Those in my circles rarely even spoke to non-Christians, and, with us, it became a habit to smugly flex our spiritual muscles, showing off our ultra-strict lifestyle. But I don't think we impressed God at all.

As Yancey says, legalism can be spiritual show-offism: it breeds the hypocritical ignoring of hidden sins, it addicts us to competition for holiness, and it lowers our view of God to a morality grader and nothing more.

Life Focus: God's law must be obeyed, but it doesn't make us holier and we don't gain extra divine approval if we add laws. More isn't holier in this case. By grace, the Holy Spirit can enable us to fulfill God's clear moral guidelines for life and godliness and to drop man-made rules.

⚓ MARCH 11 ⚓

LUKE 18:1–8
PRAYING THROUGH

Pray in the Spirit in every situation. Use every kind of prayer and request there is. For the same reason be alert. Use every kind of effort and make every kind of request for all of God's people (Ephesians 6:18).

Praying through is a good expression from the past that means persisting in prayer until God comes through. Prayer is hard work. Sure, there are euphoric moments of hearing God speak or sensing his unmistakable presence. But many times we don't feel like praying, and when we bow, the words do not flow like a verbal river.

We may become discouraged and think we're merely wasting our time. But the sense of ineffective prayer may be easily explained. First, sin must be confessed so our fellowship with God isn't blocked. Second, we should be specific about our prayer needs. F. B. Meyer writes, "It is far better to claim a few things specifically than a score vaguely."

How can we know when a prayer is answered unless it is clearly asked?

Third, it would not only boost our faith but honor God if we kept a prayer list with a column for his answers. Isaiah 12:4–5 emphasizes the wonderful things God has done for us, but we probably forget our past prayers and his answers every day.

Fourth, we shouldn't neglect to worship and praise God when he grants a request, even if he doesn't do it the way we imagined. Worship is the only gift we can give to God that he hasn't first given us.

LIFE FOCUS: Prayer is hard work but it's also the most important thing we can do. Longfellow was undoubtedly right when he wrote, "More things are wrought by prayer than this world dreams."

⚓ MARCH 12 ⚓

ROMANS 1:14–17
SHARING CHRIST

Don't be afraid of those who want to harm you. Don't get upset. But dedicate your lives to Christ as Lord. Always be ready to defend your confidence in God when anyone asks you to explain it (1 Peter 3:14–15).

"Hey, Preach, you gonna save my soul?"

"Yeah, Rev, I know this pretty blond I could set you up with. Maybe you could save her soul and have a little fun!" (Laughter)

I was working one of those unappealing summer jobs one settles for during college days. My two partners constantly ridiculed my Christian convictions. They could twist almost anything I said and use it to accuse me of wrongdoing. Many times it seemed like only Satan, the great accuser, could twist my words so ingeniously. Needless to say, I often wanted to quit that job.

Imagine my surprise when, near summer's end, one of the guys began asking questions about Christ. Then one day he expressed an interest in giving his life to Christ. He reached out his hand toward Christ, hesitated, seemed to teeter on the edge of commitment, and then he backed away.

At times like this it's important to remind ourselves that only the Spirit of God can actually convince a person of a need for salvation. Our responsibility is simply to share the message, leaving the results to God.

LIFE FOCUS: Though in the end there may be scorn, indifference, or misunderstanding, we should be ready to explain our uniqueness in Christ to those who ask the reason for our hope. Some will be searching for him.

Genesis 39:7–12
Resisting Temptation

There isn't any temptation that you have experienced which is unusual for humans. God, who faithfully keeps his promises, will not allow you to be tempted beyond your power to resist. But when you are tempted, he will also give you the ability to endure the temptation as your way of escape (1 Corinthians 10:13).

I was driving down the street with a teen in the car, but my mind was definitely not on the traffic signals. She had just given me a warning that hit me like a load of bricks.

"Steve, you'd better watch out for Jessica. She told me she's got plans for you, and I know you wouldn't want to fall for that."

Maybe the saddest aspect of the situation was that the girl in my car was a non-Christian, and she was warning me about a girl under my charge in the church high school group.

I drove in silence for a minute, jumbled thoughts racing through my mind. As a single youth pastor, I had experienced the typical crushes girls sometimes have on their leaders, but I'd never faced a situation like this. I realized at the same time that many a Christian worker has ruined his or her life and ministry by falling into similar temptation.

When confronted, Jessica admitted a plan of seduction. With many embarrassed pauses, she told of her involvement in a sex club at school in which immorality was habitual. Purity had no real meaning to her anymore.

We're surrounded by temptations of various kinds. We live in a society where it's much easier to give in to temptation than to resist. But the power to resist is available.

Life Focus: God hasn't established biblical guidelines on moral conduct in order to deprive us of good things. Can you trust your Creator to know what's best? Will you submit to his commandments?

⚓ MARCH 14 ⚓

1 TIMOTHY 4:12–16

FAILING SUCCESSFULLY

We know that all things work together for the good of those who love God—those whom he has called according to his plan (Romans 8:28).

"The elders have decided to terminate your youth pastorate." I sat in stunned silence as the chairman of the elders opened our conversation with these words.

Finally I asked softly, "What are the reasons for the decision?" He attempted to explain, but my mind was too numb with shock to take it all in.

Though I knew my enthusiasm for youth work was ebbing a bit, it had been a good year. We had more than doubled the attendance of our youth group, two teens had gone on a mission trip to Europe, several kids had become Christians, and a number were really beginning to grow in Christ.

My mind snapped back to reality as I heard, ". . . and so, even though things are going OK, we feel your focus seems to be shifting away from youth ministry. We honestly believe God has a greater mission in mind for you."

In a sense one could say I had failed. I had not fulfilled my function to the complete satisfaction of my superiors, and yet I believe God had fulfilled certain purposes in my ministry. It had been a pleasant, beneficial experience for all concerned, and a solid foundation had been developed for the youth ministry of a young church. This was my opportunity to let God turn negative happenings in my life into something positive for his own glory.

LIFE FOCUS: God can take what seems a failure and make it a spiritual success. When it seems he isn't rewarding our trust with clear direction and provision, he is still leading with an unseen hand in the background.

⚓ MARCH 15 ⚓

1 JOHN 4:7–12
FOCUSING ON RELATIONSHIPS

A friend always loves, and a brother is born to share trouble (Proverbs 17:17).

It's important to realize how much we really do need each other. Solomon wrote: "Two people are better than one because together they have a good reward for their hard work. . . . Though one person may be overpowered by another, two people can resist one opponent" (Eccles. 4:9,12).

Workaholism, health problems, busyness, even entertainment can distract us from developing intimacy with people. I went through a period in which I was so anxious about trying to survive that I let family relationships slide and my friendships stagnate. I was trying to be productive and perhaps leave some sort of a legacy, but I didn't realize that when all is said and done, it's our relationship with God and loved ones that really make life worth living.

If you're a Type A personality or you tend to be very task-oriented, your temptation may be to view planned family reunions as boring or long conversations with friends as a waste of valuable time. But it's through those lazy summer barbecues and those long telephone conversations that deep, trusting relationships are grown and cemented.

LIFE FOCUS: Of course it's wrong to sacrifice productiveness for a life of idle chatter. But it's imperative that you make time for God and for those you care about.

⚓ MARCH 16 ⚓

1 SAMUEL 19:1–5
RISKING VULNERABILITY

Jonathan became David's closest friend. . . . Saul told his son Jonathan and all his officers to kill David. But Saul's son Jonathan was very fond of David, so he reported to David, "My father Saul is trying to kill you" (1 Samuel 18:1; 19:1–2).

I worked as a youth pastor for six years. They were good years during which a number of teens became committed to Christ. I could organize staff, teach the Bible, lead singing, and establish personal rapport . . . but I sensed a weakness. I was sometimes too sensitive about what kids might think of me.

I guess I feared rejection. If a high schooler turned down an invitation to get together, I sometimes took it personally. If a kid was moody or rude, I found it hard to just write it off as immaturity. I also pictured many teens as too shallow to have a really meaningful relationship with adults.

I'm becoming more vulnerable in relationships. I'm able to admit my weaknesses more easily. I've come to realize that it's better to risk my love than never to have loved at all. After all, Jesus made himself vulnerable to twelve disciples, one of which betrayed him to his death. Christ was willing to lay himself on the line for the sake of the ones who would, in the end, be faithful.

LIFE FOCUS: Are you willing to spend vital time with individuals—people who may let you down, take you for granted, make unfair demands, or even reject you at some point? Are you willing to make yourself vulnerable enough to have a spiritual impact on others as they see both your strengths and your frail insides?

⚓ MARCH 17 ⚓

LUKE 19:1–10
LOVING THE UNLOVABLE

Be happy with those who are happy. Be sad with those who are sad. Live in harmony with each other. Don't be arrogant, but be friendly to humble people (Romans 12:15–16).

In high school, Kay was a gorgeous cheerleader. She was popular and fun-loving. At college she lived life in the fast lane. Besides cheerleading, partying, dating, and working part-time, she spent a little time studying. Drugs and alcohol gave the artificial lift she needed to continue life at this feverish pace. Then suddenly something snapped in that pretty body and Kay suffered a complete breakdown.

She used to pedal her bike over to my office at church. She sang to me and drew crude pictures with crayons. Her mind had reverted to that of a six-year-old. Quite overweight, she was no longer the beauty she once was.

At times I saw Kay as a nuisance, yet I knew she needed someone to listen and care. She'd talk about her father's indifference and her brother's cruelty, of her childish dreams and hopes. Sometimes she'd just sob out her pain and desperation.

King David once befriended a "useless" cripple. What's more, that cripple was the grandson of a man who had spent years hunting David down to kill him. David invited the cripple, Mephibosheth, to the palace and treated him as an honored son for as long as he lived. What a remarkable brand of love.

LIFE FOCUS: Is there an unlovable person in your life that you can begin loving today? As you reach out, God will supply the supernatural love.

⚓ MARCH 18 ⚓

DANIEL 6:1–10
FOLLOWING THROUGH

The other officials and satraps tried to find something to accuse Daniel of in his duties for the kingdom. But they couldn't find anything wrong because he was trustworthy. No error or fault could be found (Daniel 6:4).

When I attended a Bible school in Germany, a young instructor from England taught us the book of Luke. Some of the courses in that school were somewhat unstructured and few assignments or exams were given. However, this particular instructor gave us homework assignments. I didn't take the assignments very seriously and handed some in late, others not at all. It wasn't until the teacher sternly reprimanded me that I realized how lackadaisically I was behaving. I apologized, but, from then on, the man seemed to have lost trust in me.

In Acts, missionaries Paul and Barnabas planned a return visit to cities where they'd started churches. Barnabas wanted to take John Mark along, but Paul drew the line. After all, John Mark had deserted them on a previous mission trip. He hadn't learned to follow through on his commitments. Apparently he was a good starter but lacked the quality of enduring to task's end.

It's interesting to note, however, that Mark did develop perseverance in years following. In Paul's last letter before martyrdom, he wrote to Timothy, "Get Mark and bring him with you. He is useful to me in my work" (2 Tim. 4:11). In striking contrast, Paul wrote in the verse immediately preceding, "Demas has abandoned me. He fell in love with this present world" (2 Tim. 4:10).

LIFE FOCUS: Can people look to you as a consistent Christian example? Can others depend on you to follow through on commitments? Faithfulness is a rare quality in our world, but it's a trait the Spirit can develop in us.

⚓ MARCH 19 ⚓

PHILIPPIANS 3:7–11
BECOMING LIKE CHRIST

These things that I once considered valuable, I now consider worthless for Christ. It's far more than that! I consider everything else worthless because I'm much better off knowing Christ Jesus my Lord. . . . I threw it all away in order to gain Christ (Philippians 3:7–8).

What is becoming like Christ all about? Sanctimonious, self-righteous believers may think they're the most like Christ, but it could be they're actually the least like him. I've found that unassuming, humble Christians with a compassionate spirit are those who remind me most of Jesus.

But sometimes we fear going deeper in our spiritual growth toward Christlikeness. We'd just as soon maintain a shallow brand of Christianity. It's safer to maintain a faith which touches only the surface of God's intentions for us. Maybe we're afraid that the enjoyments of life will be swallowed up in our quest for holiness. We fear Christians will call us fanatical, and non-Christians will discount us as strange.

Some think that the dedicated Christian can't joke around with non-Christians, enjoy arts and entertainment, read exciting novels, or play a wild game of touch football. I believe we can legitimately relish many of these enjoyments of life. However, the maturing Christian will reflect Christ in the fun or the mundane events of life, as well as in activities such as prayer or worship.

When I was learning to swim as a boy, I ventured into the deep end of the pool. As I stroked sluggishly to the other side, I faltered and went underwater. Only my fingers were visible, but suddenly a lifeguard's hand reached down and pulled me to the pool's edge.

LIFE FOCUS: Though it can be scary, we need to venture into the deeper waters with God. Staying in the shallow end may be safer, but one doesn't win any races there.

⚓ MARCH 20 ⚓

1 TIMOTHY 1:12–17

AMAZING GRACE!

"You say, 'I'm rich. I'm wealthy. I don't need anything.' Yet you do not realize that you are miserable, pitiful, poor, blind, and naked" (Revelation 3:17).

Last night I preached at a rescue mission. As I scanned that huge crowd, a wave of sadness swept over me. I saw men dressed in drab, washed-out grays, greens, and blacks. Some dozed while others just sat, staring vacantly into space. I saw their choppy beards, their sunken eyes, and looks of haunted hopelessness on their ravaged faces. These men were some of the casualties of society. For a host of different reasons, they had failed to meet the requirements for success. And finally, hardened and embittered by repeated failure, they had resigned from life. In a sense, they were living carcasses—dead minds waiting for their bodies to follow suit.

With stark realization I understood anew that "there, but for the grace of God, go I." It wouldn't have taken much—a lousy home life, failure in school, rank poverty, a devastated self-image, the wrong set of friends . . .

You and I are not somewhat successful because of our inherent superiority to society's dropouts. We are not exempt from failure, nor are we invincible in the face of tragedy.

LIFE FOCUS: In the face of undeserved success, has your heart ever overflowed with thankfulness to God for his graciousness? It's good to remind ourselves now and then concerning who we are and to whom we owe everything. But for the grace of God, where would you be?

⚓ MARCH 21 ⚓

LUKE 5:4–8
THE WILLING HEART

If you are willing and obedient, you will eat the best from the land (Isaiah 1:19).

I feel like a nobody today. I wonder what it would be like out there serving on God's front line instead of working in a very small corner of the vineyard.

Whenever I feel as if God could not possibly appreciate ordinary folks like me who sin too well and fail too often, I leaf through my Bible to the familiar passages about good old Peter, impulsive, outspoken Peter—the guy who so often could stick both feet in his mouth and not even realize it.

Jesus was patient with Peter. The craggy, hulking fisherman would start walking on water and then panic. He'd declare the deity of Christ and then rudely rebuke him. He'd adamantly reject a foot-washing and then beg for total cleansing. He'd claim a martyr's allegiance for Jesus and then swear he never knew him. He'd follow Jesus faithfully and then ask what his great rewards would be. And yet, while on earth, Jesus counted Peter as one of his closest and most trusted friends. You see, beneath that rough-hewn exterior, Peter had a soft and pliable spirit. In a word, Peter had a willing heart.

LIFE FOCUS: We need to realize that Christ is not looking for bright halos; he is looking for tender hearts that are willing—willing to trust and submit and be changed. God knows the sort of deceitful rascals we are, but he also knows what he can make of us.

⚓ MARCH 22 ⚓

HEBREWS 10:24–25
DEALING WITH LONELINESS

The God who is in his holy dwelling place is the father of the fatherless and the defender of widows. God places lonely people in families (Psalm 68:5–6).

I am a bachelor and, of course, I'm not getting any younger. As the years go by, now and then I sense those deadening tentacles of loneliness close in, and time alone with God doesn't always leave me feeling warm and embraced.

What is it like to be one of the multi-million single adults in our nation? It means hiking alone through silent forests, humming softly to keep yourself company. It means eating countless meals in dingy restaurants until all the food tastes the same. For some it means trying desperately to pay the bills while being both a mother and a father to young children. Or it may mean working late into the evening, knowing there'll be no smile welcoming you back home.

God designed people to need people. We wish loneliness was an emotion that didn't exist, but if we didn't feel lonely at times, we may not seek to develop meaningful relationships. Loneliness isn't a pleasant emotion, but it can be a good motivater for friendship.

LIFE FOCUS: If you're lonesome, don't isolate yourself in a shell of sadness and self-pity. In contrast, don't rush into unhealthy relationships just so you can have companionship. Reach out to the family of God and allow them to love you. God has a special set of friends for you. Just ask him to help you be a friend to others.

MARCH 23

1 KINGS 17:8–16

FAITH IN HIS FAITHFULNESS

"First, be concerned about his kingdom and what has his approval. Then all these things will be provided for you" (Matthew 6:33).

"Lord, I'm beginning to run a little short again. You know I have bills to pay, and my part-time teaching salary doesn't go very far. The money I got for the oil painting is earmarked for next month's utilities, and I need to get the car repaired with the paycheck for that writing project. Sometimes I get so busy trying to survive that I forget you're my only secret to survival."

There's an old story about a king who gave his son an annual allowance. Eventually the father realized that about the only time his son really came to fellowship was the day he received the yearly allowance. So the king modified his plan and gave his son day by day what he needed. Then the son visited his father every day.

Hopefully, our love for God is mature enough that we maintain intimacy whether we have pressing needs or not. But I wonder how many of us would remain close to him if we never experienced need. C.S. Lewis writes, "'We have all we want' is a terrible saying when all does not include God. We find God an interruption. As St. Augustine said, 'God wants to give us something, but cannot, because our hands are full—there's nowhere for him to put it.'"

Thank you, God, for periods of need because they press me to a daily dependence on you. In the wilderness you instructed your people to take only enough manna for each day's provision. So, in my life, I am trusting you each day for necessities. I know you'll never fail or forsake me.

LIFE FOCUS: Do you ever thank God for a need? It can be your opportunity to witness his love and his power on your behalf.

⚓ MARCH 24 ⚓

1 Peter 3:8–11
Maintaining Relationships

"If you are offering your gift at the altar and remember there that another believer has something against you, leave your gift at the altar. First go away and make peace with that person. Then come back and offer your gift" (Matthew 5:23–24).

Growing up, my older brother, Dave, and I were probably as close as two brothers can be. He's a born leader and I'm a follower, so in the early years he had a strong influence in my life.

When I hit adulthood, Dave maintained his tendency to take charge (by his own admission, he can be pretty dominant). My health also affected relationships. As I felt worse physically, I withdrew from others. My relationship with Dave gradually spiraled downward. He'd criticize things about me and try to give advice, and I'd respond by ignoring him or bristling. This would only make him more stern and overbearing.

Finally, I wrote Dave a long letter, mentioning things that had hurt me and attempting to explain why they'd been painful. I tried to take some responsibility for the rift in our relationship—I'm sure I didn't take enough. My brother took the high road. He accepted responsibility for things he'd said and done and apologized with humility and class. I will always love him for that.

Since that time our relationship has been much closer. There have been a few times we needed to clarify things or even apologize, but the friendship is healthy and growing.

Life Focus: Don't allow relationships to suffocate through too much control or die for lack of attention. Mutual respect and love will build deep relationships that can bend under stress, yet not break.

⚓ March 25 ⚓

1 John 3:19–21
Understanding Guilt

Whenever our conscience condemns us, we will be reassured that God is greater than our conscience and knows everything (1 John 3:20).

I was driving back from some church event in a caravan. When we arrived at the church parking lot, one guy said something like, "You really drag race in that car of yours." I called him a day or so later and said, "Do you remember when you mentioned I was speeding when we came back from that church event?" There was sort of an awkward pause—then he said, "Not really. Why?" I explained and apologized, leaving him mystified.

There's such a thing as false guilt—guilt that's unwarranted, sometimes originating from an oversensitive conscience or guilt trips levied on us by others. God seems to have freed me from this unreasonable, plaguing guilt, but it took some time. When I'd recognize the oppressive feeling, I had to reject it and refuse to let it grow . . . refuse to go confess things that left people wondering what I was talking about.

Of course, there's true guilt—a definite knowledge we've done something God has outlawed. When the Holy Spirit's genuine prodding convicts our hearts, we should never ignore that or explain it away.

Life Focus: Appropriate guilt prompts us to confess sin, but "guilt trips" are oppressive and inaccurate. We shouldn't allow trumped up guilt to overwhelm us with its dark power.

⚓ MARCH 26 ⚓

1 CORINTHIANS 13:1–7

TRUE GREATNESS

I may have the gift to speak what God has revealed, and I may understand all mysteries and have all knowledge. I may even have enough faith to move mountains. But if I don't have love, I am nothing (1 Corinthians 13:2).

I once knew a Christian leader who was well known and quite respected in some circles. At one point I failed to measure up to his expectations. It was actually a rather insignificant issue, but instead of approaching me, he poured out his disapproval to my father. When I went to apologize to him, he wasn't gentle and constructive in his criticism. He left me discouraged and wounded. Delving into my personnel files, he tried his best to find faults. Then he cornered me and began describing my various personal weaknesses he'd discovered.

Another man served as our staff counselor at camp one summer. He wasn't well known and his resume was somewhat brief. But his apartment was always open to staff and whenever we had a break, we went there to relax and talk. He sent us notes of encouragement in the camp mail, and he made the effort to become a friend. He could joke with us, but he could also teach us. He could cheer us, but he could also confront. I will always look at him as a true man of God.

LIFE FOCUS: Greatness in God's sight is not measured by sensational accomplishment or a vast following but by humble holiness and self-sacrifice. Are you gauging spiritual greatness by the right standards?

⚓ MARCH 27 ⚓

2 CORINTHIANS 12:6–10
HELPLESS DEPENDENCE

[Christ] told me, "My kindness is all you need. My power is strongest when you are weak." So I will brag even more about my weaknesses in order that Christ's power will live in me (2 Corinthians 12:9).

I stuck a pill in my mouth and swallowed hard. I didn't want to take more medication but I was so miserable. In a few minutes I'd be attempting to teach eighty young campers, and I wanted to communicate clearly and warmly.

I'd suffered from acute allergies since childhood, but as I hit adulthood, they became much worse. I felt as if I had a perpetual head cold, complete with throbbing head, sinus irritation, sore throat, dulled senses, and listlessness.

Yet, through the years, this physical condition has forced me to depend on God even more as I've sought to serve him. Though unwelcome, this has been, in a sense, a blessing in disguise.

The apostle Paul endured a "thorn in the flesh" to prevent him from exalting himself. Paul knew that when we draw praise and honor to ourselves, we forfeit our spiritual power and effectiveness. For this reason, he actually welcomed insults, distresses, persecutions, and troubles, because in his acknowledgment of weakness he gained access to the valve of God's compensating power in his life.

You may also face a humbling weakness, and, in this life, it may never be removed. Try to think of it as a channel through which God can show the world his sufficiency through you.

LIFE FOCUS: Out of our weakness shines forth God's power. There is no limit to what God can do with a person, as long as he or she will not touch the glory.

⚓ MARCH 28 ⚓

LAMENTATIONS 3:21–26
LEARNING TO WAIT

Surrender yourself to the LORD, and wait patiently for him (Psalm 37:7).

One of the greatest tensions in the Christian experience involves knowing when to move forward and when to wait on God. John Miller believed that though we sometimes miss out through over-waiting, we miss most through not waiting for God. He writes, "Much trouble in life comes out of our restless, sometimes reckless, haste." It takes special wisdom to either wait or move at appropriate times.

Sometimes the Christian who often holds back and waits is criticized by fellow-believers for being too mystical and cautious. It's true that some may use waiting on God as an excuse for their laziness or fear, but over and over in Scripture we are reminded to wait.

We praise spiritual exploits, but sometimes it takes greater courage to wait and not lose heart, to submit to God's will, to be quiet as others prosper, and to trust until God brings light. This patience trusts though we feel forsaken, it continues praying though there's no voice in reply, it believes God is awake and caring, though life drags on in utter sameness, it waits patiently in the thick darkness.

LIFE FOCUS: At times, I've tried to make things happen, manipulate circumstances to my liking, or even fulfill spiritual goals in my own way. Almost inevitably, I've seen the doors slam in my face, and I have to assume that God was saying, "Wait on me. I'll do this in my way and in my time." Are you willing to wait?

⚓ MARCH 29 ⚓

ACTS 16:22–25
LAUGHING IT OFF

A cheerful heart has a continual feast (Proverbs 15:15).

When asked to name the most important quality on the mission field, one veteran missionary answered, "I think it's the ability to see the lighter side of life and to be able, at times, to laugh at oneself."

One day I hurried to my office at church to pick up some things I urgently needed. To my surprise, I found someone had locked the door, and I was without my key. I quickly forced the lock, and in the process I scratched up the doorway.

The following Sunday, the elders were in an uproar because they'd discovered someone had broken into my office. The pastor took me aside and asked worriedly, "Steve, do you have any idea who'd do this terrible thing?"

Thoroughly embarrassed, I muttered, "Yes, I have a good idea who it was." He kept grilling me, but it wasn't until later that I could bring myself to admit to him that I was the mysterious criminal.

Today I can laugh about that story, but I know how easy it is to take mistakes and humiliations too seriously at times. I've had to learn that without a sense of humor the problems and embarrassments of life can be seen in exaggerated proportions.

LIFE FOCUS: When we know God, there are never any bad days—just different kinds of good days. But life is messy, and as long as we're human, we'll embarrass ourselves. It sometimes helps to laugh in the face of your human foibles and fiascoes

⚓ MARCH 30 ⚓

JAMES 3:13–18
SHOWING GENTLENESS

A servant of the Lord must not quarrel. Instead, he must be kind to everyone. He must be a good teacher. He must be willing to suffer wrong. He must be gentle in correcting those who oppose the Good News (2 Timothy 2:24–25).

Jesus was gentle. He hugged children in his arms, conversed quietly with women, shed tears over wayward Jerusalem, and showed mercy toward outcasts. He could be mild without his strength being threatened.

There is a harsh brand of Christianity that hurls out condemnation like whiplashes and lectures glibly about the immature distrust of those who shrink from trials. However, the person who has suffered much doesn't do this, but is very tender and gentle. F.W. Robertson states that if we would pass through life with the delicate tact that doesn't inflict searing wounds, we must be content to pay the price of a costly education—like Christ, we must suffer.

Why is gentleness so vital for Christians? First, it negates many unattractive traits. How can gentleness coexist with violence, harsh anger, offensiveness, irritability, impatience, or pushiness?

Second, gentleness does not repel—it draws people into our friendship and trust because they feel safe and secure in our presence. There's no fear that with a stony silence or sudden outburst we may cut deep and leave people bleeding.

LIFE FOCUS: Someone once said, "We must die before we are turned into gentleness, and crucifixion involves a breaking and crushing of the self." Have you begun dying to that ugly side of self?

⚓ MARCH 31 ⚓

TITUS 2:1–6

BEING TEACHABLE

Silver hair is a beautiful crown found in a righteous life (Proverbs 16:31).

A wise man gave some great advice. "While you're young," he said, "spend much time with your elders that you may gain their wisdom; and when you grow old, spend time with youth that you may maintain a bright, fresh outlook on life."

I've been fortunate in having received much training at my father's feet. He instructed me in family devotions, taught me in Sunday school, preached to me in churches, and, in addition, he taught me in high school, college, and even seminary. I'm very grateful for all he contributed to my education, as well as my spiritual growth.

In our society, age groups are often rigidly separated, and there's little meaningful interaction between young and old. Yet the Bible seems to present a different picture. In Titus 2 we read that older women should teach young women how to develop a Christian lifestyle, and young men are to be instructed by their elders (Titus 2: 3–6).

In Bible times, the older men and women were accorded special respect, and people paid heed to their experiential wisdom. Unfortunately, today seniors are sometimes ignored when it comes to advice or teaching.

LIFE FOCUS: I challenge you to find a mature man or woman you highly esteem. Glean from that person the loving wisdom and guidance he or she has learned through the decades. Mature people can make great mentors.

APRIL

Reflecting the True Light

⚓ APRIL 1 ⚓

ACTS 2:16–21
BE MY WITNESSES

"You will receive power when the Holy Spirit comes to you. Then you will be my witnesses." (Acts 1:8).

Through the generations, we've developed a strange concept of witnessing. We hear people say, "We went out witnessing at the mall" or "Stacy is such a great witness." What we mean is, we tried to briefly present the Good News to mall shoppers. Or we imply Stacy is especially skillful and bold at explaining to people how to become Christians.

The word for *witness* in the New Testament is *martureo*, which means having direct, experiential knowledge of something. This knowledge may be expressed in words or reflected through a deep inner conviction. Of course, if one chooses to make potentially explosive knowledge public, there is always the possibility of severe unpleasantness. Ultimate danger for the Christian can result in martyrdom—a form of that root word martureo.

Authentically, witnessing is not an activity we go out and do periodically. We are in God's witness box every hour of every day. Whether we're explaining the Good News to a new acquaintance or reflecting Christ's love to a Christian friend, we are living epistles known and read by all. "A holy life will produce the deepest impression," writes D.L. Moody. "Lighthouses blow no horns; they only shine."

Christians are witnesses of the most remarkable reality ever known. This month we will attempt to gain greater understanding of what that means.

PRAYER: God, just as lawyers speak of placing their key witness on the stand, teach me how to be a key witness on your stand.

All of April's devotional entries were written by Tony Fortosis.

⚓ APRIL 2 ⚓

JOHN 10:34–42

UNFLAMBOYANT FAITHFULNESS

John didn't perform any miracles but everything John said about this Man is true (John 10:41).

Have you heard a preacher or evangelist proclaim a "health/wealth gospel"? Such a preacher promises that if we only believe, God will not only heal any illness but will heap on us material prosperity. The only thing holding us back, he declares, is our own lack of faith—God wants us to demand the good life.

The Bible and church history don't support this claim. John the Baptist, for example, preached to crowds while dressed in camel hide. He munched grasshoppers for lunch, not prime rib. And when he was arrested, Jesus made no appeal on his behalf. John was finally led from his dark prison cell to a chopping block to be beheaded. Though Jesus did miracles, he did none for John. Yet John was a dynamic witness, pointing to Jesus as Christ and honoring the Lamb of God.

The Lord calls us to gut-level faithfulness, serving and honoring him. This is really a better way than wowing crowds with spectacular miracles. We need to show our love for God in the everyday events of life. Admittedly, the Christian church burst in on a dark world with a glorious display of signs and wonders. The newborn, fledgling church needed special manifestations of God's power during those early years of her existence. However, our God places the highest premium on daily faithfulness that powerfully proclaims the truth about our blessed Redeemer. The greatest work of the church is our persistent day-in and day-out testimony of Christian living.

PRAYER: Father, keep my eyes not on the spectacular, not on my own power, but on my Redeemer. May I be faithful each day.

⚓ APRIL 3 ⚓

JOHN 3:1–3

QUEST FOR FULFILLMENT

"I came so that my sheep will have life and so that they will have everything they need" (John 10:10).

I grew up in the Orthodox Church, but I read deeply about other religions, looking for answers. I tried to get recognition through education, a prestigious job, and nice things. My whole existence seemed a strange quest for fulfillment.

Then I met Anne. I had dated other women, but none of them impressed me like this one. Her face radiated an unselfconscious joy. She was poised and peaceful. I realized she took her Christianity seriously. She was sensitive to the needs of others and lived the life she professed.

We had gone to a Christian rally one evening, and during the invitation Anne left me to assist those who had gone forward. I sat and imagined what she was telling these people.

Later, as we sat in a restaurant, she turned to me with a smile. "Tony, do you love Jesus?" she asked. "Is he very important to you?"

"Well, Anne," I said. "There's a place for God in life, but there are things I want to do and see. Right now that's very important to me."

Tears misted her eyes, but she said nothing. I lay awake that night. All I could hear were her pointed statements. All I could see were the tears of disappointment. She had quoted a verse that began to scare me: "It is appointed unto men once to die, but after this the judgment" (Hebrews 9:27 KJV). In that dark night, I cried out to God for forgiveness. I poured out my longings to him, and the peace I had long sought came quietly and filled my heart.

PRAYER: Father, I praise you for drawing me to yourself.

⚓ APRIL 4 ⚓

MATTHEW 9:27–30
FAITH OR MENTAL ASSENT?

"What you have believed will be done for you!" (Matthew 9:29).

What does it mean to believe? We often attach a meaning to the word that's distinctly different from what the Scriptures suggest. We may think of believing as an intellectual acknowledgment to a proposition, mental acceptance of a theory, agreement to a theological idea, but with no committed obedience of the will. To many people, this is faith. Remember, even Satan "believes"—that is, he recognizes Jesus as the Son of God, but he has never trusted Jesus as his own redeemer (James 2:19).

The early church understood a different meaning for belief. To them, it meant relying on and clinging to, with complete dependence. True Christians made a total surrender of all they were and looked to Christ as life itself. When they agreed to baptism, they realized this public step could eventually mean their death in Roman arenas. They did not merely assent to the dependability of the bridge—they crossed it, knowing there was no going back. They did not merely agree to the strength of a new foundation—they built their entire lives on it.

We need to recover the true meaning of faith in Christ. Faith means saying, "Jesus, I trust your deity enough to receive your forgiveness and give over my life and everything I hold dear to you forever."

PRAYER: Father, let me understand true biblical faith and be able to communicate it effectively as you give me opportunities.

⚓ APRIL 5 ⚓

MATTHEW 5:14–16

AN IMAGE PROBLEM

If it is God's will, it's better to suffer for doing good than for doing wrong (1 Peter 3:17).

We have an image problem in our society. When a Christian falls, especially a highly visible leader, some members of the media splash it all over the headlines. Christians are then labeled as religious hypocrites, Bible thumpers, or some other negative label. These comments build a convenient stereotype to support an already anti-Christian bias.

Often we are our own worst enemy. When church members fight, wounding leaders and lay people; when we tolerate corruption and moral compromise; when we diminish the truth of Scripture; when our lifestyles come across as mean-spirited, self-serving, judgmental, then the Christian community gets what it deserves.

We're called to make a difference in the world. We're to reflect the Spirit of God by demonstrating a faith that is attractive, authentic, and persevering. We must not retreat into evangelical enclaves, or the caricatures of Christianity will proliferate.

We'll never completely escape critical comment. A positive image, however, is possible when we live out our faith consistently and conscientiously. If that happens, when Christians are associated with hypocrisy and bigotry, people will say, "Hold on. I know some Christians, and that isn't always true."

PRAYER: Father, let me be an unclogged channel that positively portrays you in my thoughts, speech, and actions.

⚓ APRIL 6 ⚓

2 CORINTHIANS 10:3–6

A MIND UNDER GUARD

Brothers and sisters, keep your thoughts on whatever is right or deserves praise: things that are true, honorable, fair, pure, acceptable, or commendable (Philippians 4:8).

Paul calls us to examine the state of our thought life, for as we think in our hearts, so we are. As Paul parades each thought category before us, let's take a test. Are my thoughts . . .

- *Truthful?* Do I desire my thoughts to be all true and nothing but the truth with no convenient omissions or additions, even if it hurts?
- *Noble?* Are my thoughts superficial and careless, or are they worthy of the king? Do they honor God?
- *Right?* Are my thoughts just and fair, considerate of others before myself? Am I forgiving and humble?
- *Pure?* Do I reject thoughts of lust, of immoral fantasies, of dishonest ideas?
- *Lovely?* Is my mind cleared of bitterness, selfishness, harshness, and slander?
- *Admirable?* Are my thoughts positive, constructive, helpful, self-sacrificing?

To protect the critical bastion of the mind, God has given us the resident Holy Spirit to stand guard as a sentinel. Thus alerted, when a wrong thought enters our minds, we need to reject it in the power of Christ.

PRAYER: Father, it seems like I grieve your Spirit so often. Give me your mind that I may think your thoughts.

⚓ APRIL 7 ⚓

MATTHEW 18:1–4

TRAIN UP A CHILD

Then [Jesus] said to them, "I can guarantee this truth: Unless you change and become like little children, you will never enter the kingdom of heaven" (Matthew 18:3).

My father wasn't a Christian. As a member of the Greek Orthodox Church, he was hostile and displeased that his son and daughters had become Protestant believers. My sister tried the direct approach to persuade him to Christ, but it boomeranged. He forbade us to say anything to him or to the other members of the family about our newfound faith. We prayed for years for his conversion, but nothing seemed to happen.

In the meantime, God gave children to my wife and me. Our boys attended a Christian school. We taught them courtesy and Christian virtues. My dad loved his grandchildren. Whenever he was with them, he couldn't help but notice their attitudes, good manners, and the standards they'd been taught. He compared them mentally with the grandchildren of his friends.

As years passed, he grudgingly admitted that our brand of Christianity had made a difference in his grandchildren. As he softened he began to ask questions. He took a liking to Billy Graham, and at age seventy he watched a crusade on television one evening. His heart was ready to commit to Christ. The angels had new cause to rejoice that night.

PRAYER: Father, thank you that you can even use a child to lead people to your Son.

⚓ APRIL 8 ⚓

MATTHEW 21:12–16

OUT OF THE MOUTHS OF BABES

"From the mouths of little children and infants, you have created praise" (Matthew 21:16).

It was recess at a Christian school. Heather, a second-grader, was ashamed of the freckles that covered her face, so much so that her mother considered taking her to a dermatologist for help. David, a young classmate, heard about Heather's hang-up. He walked up to her on the playground. "Hi Heather. You know what? I think freckles are beautiful."

Heather frowned. "What do you mean?"

"Well, freckles aren't ugly 'cause God made 'em, and God can only make beautiful things."

On another occasion at the playground, a group of kids surrounded a boy named Joey. "We don't like you," they said. "We're not gonna play with you anymore."

"That's OK," said Joey. "I'm never alone 'cause Jesus is still with me."

As adults, we may underestimate what children can learn from the Bible. Christ's ministry was profound yet, at the same time, understandable to children because he often applied truth in ways they could grasp. Let's teach the next generation the simple truths of God's Word so they'll be ready to stand for truth in their own generation.

PRAYER: Father, use me as an example to children of the truth of your Word. Don't let me underestimate what children can learn about you.

⚓ APRIL 9 ⚓

MATTHEW 25:31–40
NO LITTLE PEOPLE

"Whatever you did for one of my brothers or sisters, no matter how unimportant they seemed, you did for me" (Matthew 25:40).

In God's kingdom, there are no "little people"—no insignificant second-class citizens. All are valuable.

I retain a vivid picture in my memory. It was commencement at a Christian college. President McQuilkin was leading the solemn procession. Unknown to him, dear friends were seated in the audience—a missionary couple with their four-year-old son. Suddenly, to the embarrassment of the couple, their son darted out into the aisle. Wrapping his arms around the president's legs, he said, "Dr. McQuilkin, it's Donny, it's Donny!"

Dr. McQuilkin stopped with a smile, knelt down to embrace the boy, and said, "I'm so glad to see you, Donny. I'm looking forward to seeing you and your parents after commencement."

Donny returned to his parents. The president stood up and continued his march in the procession.

I recall going to L'Abri to study with Dr. Francis Schaeffer. I had many needs as an inexperienced school administrator, not the least of which was a legalistic spirit which needed to be replaced with accepting love. Dr. Schaeffer, though extremely busy, invited me to walk with him in the Alps. That afternoon, he poured truth into me that revolutionized my life.

To Schaeffer and McQuilkin, there were no "little people."

PRAYER: Father, teach me to understand that there should be no conceited hierarchy among Christians. We're all equal in Christ.

⚓ April 10 ⚓

Luke 15:11–24
Come Home

"'My son was dead and has come back to life. He was lost but has been found'" (Luke 15:24).

Jesus' parable of the Prodigal Son is a powerful message of the compassion and forgiveness for us in the Father's heart.

The story is told of a young man who had a stormy falling out with his father. "Dad, I'm outta here!" he yelled. "And I hope I never see you again."

"OK, if that's what you want," said his father brokenly.

Three years passed. Finally the boy headed back home on a train. A Christian sat next to him, and sensing his pain asked if he could help. The young man related the blow-up, his deep regret and change of heart, and his decision to come home. He'd written his mother asking that they tie something white around a tree out front if they were willing to see him again. "We're coming into town now," he continued, "and you can just see my house from the tracks—it's up on a hill. I can't look. Would you look for me?"

The Christian peered out the window, then suddenly said, "Take a look." All around the yard were sheets and pillow cases, and his parents stood waving a tablecloth. When the train slowed, the son leaped from it and ran for the hill. He was home.

God is on Calvary's hill waving great sheets in the wind, saying, "Come home. I will forgive."

Prayer: Father, I praise you for your loving invitation to return to your arms. Teach me also to love the prodigals in this world.

⚓ APRIL 11 ⚓

ROMANS 11:17–22

GOD IS A CONSUMING FIRE

Look at how kind and how severe God can be. He is severe to those who fell, but kind to you (Romans 11:22).

It's popular to think of God as a mild, over-indulgent, grandfatherly being. We hear much about God's goodness but little of his sternness.

Though it's terrifying, there are accounts in the Bible in which God strikes humans down. For offering strange, unlawful incense to God, Nadab and Abihu met fatal judgment (Num. 3:1–4). For carelessly handling the ark, Uzzah died (2 Sam. 6). Ananias and Sapphira lost their lives for lying blatantly (Acts 5:1–11). Corinthian believers died for partaking of communion unworthily (1Cor. 11:17–34).

Suppose all those living a lie fell dead in the next church service. We recoil and reject such a thought, but we need to realize that these Scriptural accounts are still a warning to us. Thomas Carlyle writes: "The Christian must be consumed with the infinite beauty of holiness and the infinite damnability of sin." When we consider the sacrilegious way many speak of God and sacred truth, it's vital that we emphasize the holiness as well as the goodness of God.

Even God's sternness comes from a caring heart. He disciplines those he loves and punishes everyone who is truly his child (Heb. 12:5–6). Therefore we shouldn't trifle with our Heavenly Father.

PRAYER: Father, guard me from irreverent familiarity with your holiness. Let me see sin as you see it.

⚓ APRIL 12 ⚓

JEREMIAH 8:18–22
THE BALM IN GILEAD

Is there no balm in Gilead; is there no physician there? (Jeremiah 8:22, KJV).

Vance Havner tells about a young boy who sat in church one Sunday and heard the soloist sing "There Is a Balm in Gilead." At lunch the boy asked curiously, "Dad, where's Gilead and why'd they drop that bomb on it?"

We shouldn't be too surprised at the boy's misunderstanding. Hardly a day goes by without news of terrorist bombs exploding, injuring and killing innocent people. Nuclear warheads in various countries still pose a threat of potential world holocaust. A frightened world trembles as modern technology churns out more bombs than balm.

There is no lasting hope for the person who has no healing salve for the heart. Yet there is a balm in Gilead, and the Great Physician's hands are ready to apply his healing touch to our wounded, hurting spirits. Though the world lives in fearful dread, God's children can know perfect calm.

Our assurance of safety is based on rejecting the fear of those who can kill the body but can't destroy the soul. There is a sure way to live in peace. We can hide from God's judgment by hiding in his merciful palm. It's a place where God can apply his soothing salve to wounded hearts.

PRAYER: Father, keep me from fear of earthly dangers. Please spread soothing balm when my heart surrenders to fear.

⚓ APRIL 13 ⚓

LUKE 11:32–36
CHANGE BEGETS CHANGE

"If your enemy is hungry, feed him. If he is thirsty, give him a drink. If you do this, you will make him feel guilty and ashamed" (Romans 12:20).

I was away from home and family working on my doctorate at Duke University in the '60s. Another Christian student and I were belittled for our Christian faith. Once my friend's room was broken into. Beer cans were stacked around the room and pornographic pictures plastered on the walls and ceiling.

On my dorm floor, a group of medical students would go out drinking late at night. After midnight they'd pound loudly on my door and shout obscenities. I'd lie in the dark praying, but with growing resentment in my heart.

I was home one weekend wondering what to do. During my quiet time I read Luke 6:27: "'Love your enemies. Be kind to those who hate you.'" Love those jerks? I couldn't stand them, but I prayed God would not only change my attitude but maybe even the attitude of my dormmates.

I brought back a box of my wife's chocolate chip cookies and took them across the hall to the ringleader. He looked shocked to see me at his door. "My wife baked a batch of cookies and I thought maybe you'd like some." Struck speechless, he took the box, mumbling something I assumed was a thank you. The bashing on my door and the obscenities stopped from that day on. I think it was God's way of changing me in order to change others.

PRAYER: Father, help me look past my anger and to exercise your love.

⚓ April 14 ⚓

Job 2:3–10

Humility Tested in Adversity

"The Lord has given and the Lord has taken away! May the name of the Lord be praised" (Job 1:21).

In our walk with God, we must hold on to his blessings loosely lest we make idols of them. Grady Spirer, a professor at Gordon College, had been blessed in many ways. After ten years of work on his dissertation, he was poised to finish it and receive his doctorate. Then somehow his copy at the college was destroyed. Shortly thereafter, his house burned down, and the only other copies went up in smoke. In response, Spirer quoted Job, "The Lord has given and the Lord has taken away. Blessed be the name of the Lord."

Job was the envy of his day. He had material possessions beyond description and his sons and daughters were his unfailing pride and joy. Among the many great in the East in that day, some consider Job the greatest. Then God permitted all of it to be ripped from his grasp.

Job's wife sneered at his clinging faith, but Job wasn't about to turn on God. Though he wavered and wallowed in doubt and fear, in the end he stood firm in humble acceptance of his tragic losses, never dreaming that God would restore great blessing again.

True love and faithfulness have no hidden, self-serving agendas. God loves us with no strings attached. We should love him in the same way.

Prayer: Father, teach me to love you through each loss or trial that may come my way.

⚓ APRIL 15 ⚓

HEBREWS 13:5–7

GO ON

God has said, "I will never abandon you or leave you." So we can confidently say, "The Lord is my helper" (Hebrews 13:5–6).

God never promised that our pilgrimage to the Celestial City would be either easy or pleasant. Yet we have the promise of God's strength, the wisdom to enable us to solve puzzling life dilemmas, his smile of compassion, his reassuring Word, and the knowledge that we are actually more than conquerors through him who loved us and gave himself for us.

During a time of testing, God gave me this simple poem:

The menacing breakers rose high,
Poised themselves and crashed;
Retreating to gather new strength,
They flung their wrath upon me,
Battering, tearing, tugging, retreating;
Watery tentacles
Like some treacherous octopus,
Reached out to hold me under;
They were draining me of strength;
Life was ebbing into darkness,
My frenzied eyes saw nightmares,
My soul cried out for help:
What can I do? Is there no hope?
A strength beyond me heard,
A hand of hope reached out;
Tho' waves continued their assault,
The peaceful shore was nearer than before;
The ocean swells nudged me closer;
Soon my weary feet touched sand,
And underneath, a solid Rock.

PRAYER: Father, teach me to keep my mind on you, keeping in step with your direction, encouraged and strengthened by your Spirit.

⚓ APRIL 16 ⚓

2 Timothy 3:10–17

God's Word Works

Every Scripture passage is inspired by God. All of them are useful for teaching, pointing out errors, correcting people, and training them for a life that has God's approval (2 Timothy 3:16–17).

From its beginning, the Bible has been under attack as well as subtle undermining. Insidious doubts are planted in hearts. But God's Word works! It is eternal truth—invaluable and eternally unfading.

This Word is useful or profitable as an authoritative guide for our eternal good in these vital ways:

- Teaching involves doctrine that explains the path to forgiveness and eternal life and the standards for living a life acceptable to God.
- Rebuking points out errors and shines the holy light of God upon the cold, dark recesses of our human ways, thus reproving us for reckless love of self, money, pleasure, and our cool indifference to God's standards.
- Correction speaks of resetting the direction of a person's life.
- Training in righteousness speaks of instruction in integrity and moral discipline. This means living a life within God's biblical parameters. We can imagine the chaos of a football game played without sidelines or goal lines. What some non-Christians view as puritanical repression is to us the discipline of a growing freedom from sin. Christians who are following the instructions of the Bible can honestly say, "God's Word works."

Prayer: Father, give me a willing, teachable heart to follow the instructions of your Word.

⚓ APRIL 17 ⚓

MATTHEW 23:13–24
MAJORING ON THE MAJOR

"How horrible it will be for you, scribes and Pharisees! You hypocrites! You give God one-tenth of your mint, dill, and cumin. But you have neglected justice, mercy, and faithfulness" (Matthew 23:23).

Jesus indicted the Pharisees more than any other group. These religionists put the emphasis on an empty religious form but neglected the greater matters. Jesus challenged them to put first things first without neglecting the rest.

This is still a common deficiency in religion. Spiritually we may be very prim and proper on the surface, but inwardly we may be dry and dead, like the inside of a frigid tomb. Showing mercy and treating people fairly takes time, and it can be messy. People don't always plan their crises to match our schedules.

It's easy to stuff our lives with so many activities that we no longer have time to nurture our spirits. If we feel we're rich in material things and need nothing, our surface contentment may mask a very real spiritual malnutrition. On the other hand, it's also possible to be so busy in spiritual endeavors and in reaching the lost that we neglect the biblical imperative to grow in knowledge and wisdom.

God wants us to go for his best. Let's not allow our mint, dill, and cumin to become the enemy of justice, mercy, and faithfulness. Jesus promises a special blessing if we genuinely hunger and thirst for righteousness. His Word can fill us. How's your appetite?

PRAYER: Father, show me how to align my goals with the major aspects of the Christian life that will most glorify Christ.

⚓ APRIL 18 ⚓

REVELATION 3:1–6
IN NAME ONLY

"I know what you have done. You are known for being alive, but you are dead" (Revelation 3:1).

I was reared in a nominal Christian home that held membership in a nominal church. Like the church at Sardis, many people in our church seemed to be Christian in name only.

The church at Sardis had a reputation of being alive, but was dead. Its works were empty in the sight of God. It was an organization all right, but not a living organism. There was no satanic persecution there because the church posed no threat to the Prince of Darkness. Sardis was evidently a busy church with lots of activity. People were going through religious exercises, but they were bypassing God's program, purpose, and goals.

Satan scores greater victories in the blind misdirection of nominal churches than he does with outright hostility. Many join churches without actually being redeemed and indwelt by God's Spirit.

Yet John writes that even in the Sardis church, was a small group of true believers. They had work to do, for the best antidote to the deadness of nominal Christianity is a vibrant witness from real, transformed Christians. I came to Christ and embraced him as my Lord and Savior because I met a real believer whose life radiated the sweet aroma of Jesus Christ.

PRAYER: Father, put me in vibrant contact with individuals who need to receive eternal life and truly know Christ as Savior and Lord.

ACTS 26:24–29
GOD'S HIDDEN AGENDA

"Let your light shine in front of people. Then they will see the good that you do and praise your Father in heaven" (Matthew 5:16).

When I was a high school principal, one year our baseball team was pretty weak. In a game with one of the strong schools in town, the Falcons were soundly beaten 14–2.

One of the Falcon players took the loss especially hard. "Coach," he said, "we prayed and then we got slaughtered. How come?"

The coach grinned. "Ted, when we pray, we can't know whether God will let us win or lose. What counts is to play hard and clean for Christ and leave the rest to him."

Ted walked away shaking his head.

After practice a few days later, Coach Weeber asked the team to sit down for a few minutes. Pulling a paper out of his pocket he said, "I want you guys to hear this letter I received today:

> Dear Coach,
>
> A few days ago our school baseball team defeated your team on the scoreboard rather handily. My son is one of the players. I watched the game and was very impressed with the sportsmanship of your players. I was ashamed of our boys. They used profanity, were crude in their remarks, unsportsmanlike in their actions, and lacked grace in victory. Your team handled themselves like true gentlemen. We may have won the game on the scoreboard, but your school won the game that really counts. I am not a Christian, but I believe you brought honor to the God you represent."

PRAYER: Father, show me your agenda when I get shortsighted.

⚓ APRIL 20 ⚓

1 CORINTHIANS 1:20–30
THE WEAK THINGS

God chose what the world considers ordinary and what it despises what it considers to be nothing—in order to destroy what it considers to be something (1 Corinthians 1:28).

"In Christ's body," writes Paul Brand, "a teacher of three-year-olds has the same value as a bishop, and that teacher's work may be just as significant. A widow's dollar can equal a millionaire's annuity. Shyness, beauty, eloquence, race, sophistication, none of these matter. . . . The church Jesus founded is more like a family in which the son retarded from birth has as much worth as his brother the Rhodes scholar."

I was invited to meet with some of my former students at a college reunion. They reported their success in a whole gamut of careers. The last student to share was Ellen, the daughter of missionaries. We remembered her as a naive, silent student, often made the butt of jokes by classmates.

Ellen said, "Remember me? Timid Ellen. When I graduated, I felt weak and scared. I hung onto the Lord for all I was worth. I learned to pray as never before and to know God in a special way. Jesus has me by the hand, and I cannot fail."

A holy hush settled over the room. The Spirit of God had spoken to us through Ellen. I asked her if she would pray. Seldom have I heard a prayer like hers. Jesus was so real to her. We felt his presence in the room as she worshipped and interceded for us all. God's strength is shown most perfectly in human weakness.

PRAYER: Father, let me not try to overpower others with my strength, but to show forth your greatness even through my weakness.

⚓ APRIL 21 ⚓

1 JOHN 1:5–10

WALK TOWARD THE LIGHT

As ye have therefore received Christ Jesus the Lord, so walk ye in him (Colossians 2:6 KJV).

The medical profession often prescribes walking as an appropriate exercise for the sedentary, the overweight, and those with blood pressure problems. Some don't like walking. They find it boring because they'd rather be "doing something." They may not realize that walking can actually burn off more calories than sprinting back and forth across a tennis court.

The Bible speaks of the spiritual walker. The Christian life is set before us more as a walk than any other image. We're called to walk in newness of life, to walk in love, in the light, in truth, by faith, and in the Spirit. We're to walk worthy of the Lord, even as he walked. It is more than a baby step. Some take a step of faith, but don't continue with a walk of faith. Some are frozen in place, while others are in a frenetic dash in all directions.

Walking permits us to be reflective. It's the proper pace to think through wise decisions about where and how to walk—keeping in step with Jesus. Two can't walk together unless they are unified. So, we must be in agreement with our royal companion.

Enoch's spiritual biography includes three brief descriptions: First, he walked with God, second, he pleased God, and third, God took him home. The greatest of all walkers is like Enoch—a pleaser of God.

PRAYER: Father, teach me how to walk in step with your Spirit, not lagging behind and not jumping ahead.

⚓ APRIL 22 ⚓

2 CHRONICLES 6:7–10
GOD'S CHOICE LEADERS

The LORD's eyes scan the whole world to find those whose hearts are committed to him and to strengthen them (2 Chronicles 16:9).

God does not choose leaders like the typical high-powered CEO. God looks for those through whom he can firmly show himself. It's not what we can do for God, but what he can do through us. A professional personnel director is not needed to find God's choice leader. God can reveal the right person, and the distinguishing mark is that the leader's heart is right toward God. This doesn't mean absolute perfection, of course, but a whole heart devoted to pleasing the Lord.

In a human sense, Israel's army had soldiers who were skilled, brave warriors—capable, perhaps, of meeting Goliath in battle and of leading the people. However, God was searching Israel for a humble person whose heart was totally committed to Jehovah. In David, the shepherd boy, God found his man.

Leaders like David are in short supply. There are plenty of candidates who sell their charm, education, and talents. Their resumes may be long and just as impressive. However, they may not meet God's qualifications. Instead, they may be showing off their own abilities. God is out to reveal himself through the humble, faithful, and dedicated. Richard Cecil, an eighteenth-century Anglican, writes, "It is always a sign of poverty of mind when men are ever aiming to appear great; for they who are really great never seem to know it."

PRAYER: Father, work in me. Give me a heart that is singularly devoted to honoring you, not myself.

⚓ APRIL 23 ⚓

1 KINGS 18:20–19:3

THE DEADLY DS

Frightened, Elijah fled to save his life (1 Kings 19:3).

Meet Elijah, one of God's best prophets, a man of deep faith and believing prayer. Look in on his confrontation with evil King Ahab and his 450 perverse prophets on Mount Carmel. Watch as Elijah challenges these Baal priests and prays to Jehovah for victory. God responds with crackling lightning that obliterates the sacrifice. The priests are slain, and another miracle occurs—God sends rain after a long drought.

With adrenaline flowing in his veins, Elijah sprints into town. By this time, he's exhausted, and his defenses are down. The evil Queen Jezebel counterattacks, promising to murder Elijah.

His upward look of faith now becomes a horizontal terror. Elijah is disappointed that God hasn't eliminated Jezebel; and, discouraged, he runs for his life. Thus, he stumbles into the third deadly D—disillusionment. He cries, "I'm the only one left, and they're trying to take my life." Depression sets in, and the frightened, exhausted prophet crumbles into despair, wailing, "Take away my life!" He's holed up in a cave, totally demoralized.

It is then that God says, "There are yet seven thousand others who are loyal to me. You're not alone, Elijah." Then God gives him refreshing rest and food.

It wasn't a time for a withering lecture about weak faith and spineless fear. It was a time for encouragement.

PRAYER: Father, guard me against a driven lifestyle. Guard me from the downward spiral of the deadly Ds.

⚓ APRIL 24 ⚓

HEBREWS 3:12–15

THE MINISTRY OF ENCOURAGEMENT

Encourage one another every day while you have the opportunity (Hebrews 3:13).

Satan was having a garage sale. His salable were displayed, each with a price tag: Malice, Greed, Lust, Pride, Envy. One item was showcased under a spotlight and carried a very high price tag. The label read, *Discouragement.*

Someone asked Satan, "Why such a high price?"

With a malicious leer, he said, "With this weapon, I can kill a person's spirit and leave him hopelessly groping for light."

The antidote to this deadly weapon is encouragement—the act of inspiring others with renewed courage, spirit, or hope. Affirming words are often a verdant, refreshing oasis in a vast, dreary desert of defeat. It's far more important to affirm people for who they are than for what they may accomplish. We can do this without detracting from the significance of the latter.

The world is full of people who are cynical about others' ideals, who pour cold water on others' optimism or put them down, making them feel inadequate. They make this a part of every relationship, but God has called us to lift and cheer. Many times an expression of praise or thanks or a note of appreciation can keep someone going just when they're desperate for a boost.

PRAYER: God of all comfort, teach me to be an encourager with sensitivity and effectiveness to hurting ones you send my way.

⚓ APRIL 25 ⚓

2 CORINTHIANS 12:1–10

ENCOURAGED SO AS TO ENCOURAGE

"My kindness is all you need. My power is strongest when you are weak" (2 Corinthians 12:9).

The most effective encouragers God uses have something in common: they have experienced suffering. Christ experienced the pain of rejection, ridicule, physical attack, betrayal, and the agony of the cross. Therefore he has empathy for us. Our pain is meant to make us empathizers with those in the body of Christ who hurt. Those who have endured to stings of life are the choicest counselors God can use.

I grew up in a multi-ethnic community where we were a minority. Consequently, we were hounded a bit. I would sometimes be bullied and beaten on the way to school and again on the way home. Running the gauntlet was a demeaning experience. But God used it to develop in me a sensitivity to the underdog or the downtrodden.

For a number of years, I struggled with the assurance of my salvation. As a result, the Lord has sent my way students who are plagued with a lack of assurance. My wife's death from cancer gave me a ministry of support for cancer victims.

When a part of our body is hurting, other parts should come alongside to compensate. God's plan is to carry this principle to the body of Christ. We who are strong should bear the burdens of those who feel beaten down.

PRAYER: Father, keep me sensitive to the needs of the hurting so I'll come alongside and help for your glory.

⚓ APRIL 26 ⚓

PROVERBS 18:20–24

HOPE TO THE HOPELESS

The tongue has the power of life and death, and those who love to talk will have to eat their own words (Proverbs 18:21).

God's encouragers give hope to those labeled as hopeless. My sixth grade teacher picked on me and put me down again and again. I tried to do my best, but it was never good enough. Finally, I rebelled and it only made matters worse. At the end of that painful year, she indicted me to my seventh grade teacher, Mrs. Schmoyer, as a hopeless student.

Mrs. Schmoyer, however, was wise and gentle. She took me aside on the first day of school and said, "Tony, I know you had a rough year. I want you to know that the slate is clean. I'll do my best to help you succeed. I think you'll do well."

Because of her acceptance and encouragement, I did my best. I didn't want to disappoint Mrs. Schmoyer. It was a turning point in my education.

During my wife's terminal illness, many stayed away, probably because cancer is scary. They sent pious platitudes or little sermons, but they carried no comfort. One friend, who'd gone through tough times of his own, logged four hundred miles a week driving up from a neighboring state to see us. His coming into our home was like sunlight bursting through dark clouds. His smile and caring words strengthened us. True encouragement is often costly, but it's a witness that restores hope to those who feel hopeless.

PRAYER: Father, may I accept and care for others the way you've accepted and cared for me.

⚓ APRIL 27 ⚓

JAMES 3:6–10

IT TAKES TWO TO TANGLE

A hothead stirs up a fight, but one who holds his temper calms disputes (Proverbs 15:18).

I placed the blistering letter back on my desk. An angry parent had unloaded a torrent of sarcasm and caustic criticism on the school and on me as principal. I passed it wordlessly across the desk to my assistant.

He scanned the contents and exploded, "You're not going to let her get away with this, are you, Tony? Blast her out of the saddle."

I was fighting resentment too, but I managed to squeak out, "No, Paul. The lady isn't thinking straight. Let's pray about it."

Paul sputtered, "But she needs to learn a lesson."

We bowed together: "Lord, you have something to teach us through this attack. Guide this woman and teach her whatever she needs to learn too. Give us the ability to accept and forgive. In Jesus name."

A week passed. Paul saw me in the hall. "Did you answer that letter yet, Tony?"

"No, I just haven't felt the freedom to write."

The next week I saw Paul in the hallway and handed him a letter from the woman. It read:

> Dear Dr. Fortosis,
>
> Please forgive my angry letter. I was wrong in writing it. Everything had gone wrong that week. The flu was getting me down, and my son's letter of complaint [against the school] struck me with negativism. My emotional outburst was unwarranted, and my letter was an inappropriate way to express weaknesses in the school. I apologize.

PRAYER: Father, keep a firm grip in my tongue when I'm tempted to give a tongue-lashing.

⚓ APRIL 28 ⚓

ISAIAH 6:1–8
"LISTEN UP"

I heard the voice of the Lord, saying, "Whom shall I send? Who will go for us?" (Isaiah 6:8).

During my years in Christian school classrooms, students often asked, "How can I discover God's call?" There's considerable misunderstanding about a call to Christian ministry. Some are tempted to charge out like gangbusters; others wait for supernatural signs or a special feeling within.

God's call to his people has three facets:

First, there's a command from heaven. "'Go, make disciples of all nations'" (Matt. 28:19). Whatever our work or profession, the call is the same. No audible voice or exhilarating feeling is needed. God's command is clear.

Second, there's a call from outside. The need is the call. A lost world is all around us. Our neighborhood as well as the world overseas has crying needs. If we are willingly serving where we are, God will give us his specifics. God won't make our guidance difficult and mysterious.

Third, there's an inner urgency. When we willingly submit our hearts to the Lord and obey his call, under the control of the Spirit, the love of God is sent out from our lives, and the love of Christ urges us on to please him—to make him known. When we're filled with the experiential knowledge of his love, the people whose lives we touch will sense that love too.

PRAYER: Father, stir up the gift within me and use me to know you better and to make you known.

⚓ APRIL 29 ⚓

PROVERBS 28:10–13

REPENTANCE BRINGS PEACE

Whoever covers his sins does not prosper. Whoever confesses and abandons them receives compassion (Proverbs 28:13).

While serving as headmaster of a boarding school, I received a letter from an alumna:

> Dear Sir,
>
> After I graduated from the school, I experienced a lot of guilt, and there are a couple things I need to clear up. I've confessed what I did to God but I feel I should also confess to you.
>
> First of all, I cheated in all my subjects. Of course, with the cheating came irresponsibility in my studies. Secondly, I stole money. When the girls went to town on the school bus, I collected the fares, taking only a portion so it wouldn't be missed. I rationalized my stealing since I used it for my "needs."
>
> I ask forgiveness and for your prayers. What a load's been lifted from me! I'm clean before God. I hope you can share my peace and joy. Please let me know how I can make restitution for what I did.

This courageous letter, signed "Love in Christ," portrays how sin breaks off our relationship with Christ and robs us of joy and peace. Repentance, however, brings peace and restoration.

PRAYER: Father, search my heart and know me. Point out how I need to change. I'm open to repentance as I need it.

⚓ APRIL 30 ⚓

MALACHI 3:10–16
THE DIVINE LISTENER

Then those who feared the LORD spoke to one another, and the LORD paid attention and listened. A book was written in his presence to be a reminder to those who feared the LORD and respected his name (Malachi 3:16).

The Bible says that God's eyes ceaselessly roam the earth in search of those whose hearts are perfect toward him. Malachi preached to a careless people who didn't think God heard them or knew their heart attitudes. But God was listening and he knew that only a small remnant were actually faithful to him. These reverenced God, they were nourished on his Word, they fellowshipped around the Scriptures, and their names were engraved in God's Book.

God is the divine listener. Even as we human parents sometimes find ourselves innocently eavesdropping on our children's conversations with each other, our Heavenly Father listens in on ours. What are our conversations like? Gossipy and slanderous? Judging and critical? Whiny and grumbly? There are exceptions—John Bunyan overheard godly women talking about the Lord, and it turned his heart heavenward.

It is awesome to stop and realize that God himself listens to us. He hears us talking to ourselves on the way to work and talking all day to anyone who'll give us an ear. This should motivate us to monitor our conversations more and try to make more things we say worth saying.

PRAYER: Father, may the words of my mouth and the thoughts of my heart be acceptable in your sight.

MAY

The Roots of Our Faith

⚓ MAY 1 ⚓

2 PETER 1:16–19
OLD TIME RELIGION

When we apostles told you about the powerful coming of our Lord Jesus Christ, we didn't base our message on clever myths that we made up. Rather, we witnessed his majesty with our own eyes (2 Peter 1:16).

Humanly speaking, traditional Christian faith is well beyond the scope of logic and scientific possibility. We believe in talking serpents and donkeys, seas parting down the middle, and fire shooting from heaven upon demand. We believe that God's Son became a human being for a time, that he died—actually sacrificed his life—then revived and zoomed back to heaven. One of these days, he will suddenly appear in the clouds and propel us like helicopters into the sky to be with him forever.

Yet we speak of this faith of our ancestors as old time religion. What we seem to mean by that phrase is that this mind-boggling faith has been the tenacious, rock-solid bulwark of thousands of saints through numerous generations.

Has the Christian faith changed? No, traditional faith still focuses on the redemption of sinful humanity through Jesus Christ, the Son of God. In an interview, Billy Graham said, "Theology never changes. Man's heart stays the same. And there have been no additions to the Gospel that was preached in the first century." We follow a long line of dignified, weathered old saints who were just radical enough to believe it too. We will look back this month to the roots of an old time religion that is somehow still as fresh and vibrant as it was when Christ first emerged from that dark tomb.

LIFE FOCUS: Our Christian heritage is rich, and the rarefied air where great old saints trekked comprises an education we can sink our teeth into. Prepare for a learning experience.

⚓ MAY 2 ⚓

EPHESIANS 2:1–10

CHRIST: TRUE AND AGELESS FOUNDATION

God is rich in mercy because of his great love for us. We were dead because of our failures, but he made us alive together with Christ (Ephesians 2:4).

"Islam says that Jesus was not crucified; Christianity says he was," writes Alistair Begg. He continues, "Judaism says Jesus was not the Messiah. Christianity says he was. Hinduism says God has often been incarnate. Christianity says God was incarnate only in Jesus. Buddhism says that the world's miseries will end when we do what is right. Christianity says we cannot do what is right. The world's miseries will end when we believe what is right."

Our faith is based on substitutionary animal sacrifices that led eventually to a human sacrifice of God in human flesh. This is not the stuff of a religious fairy tale. The Bible never presents a faith that is easy or cozy or entertaining. C.S. Lewis pondered which faith gives its followers the greatest happiness. "While it lasts," writes Lewis, "the religion of worshipping oneself is the best. If you want a religion that makes you feel really comfortable, I certainly don't recommend Christianity. There must be a patent American article on the market which will suit you far better, but I can't give you any advice on it."

If you want a religion which says that enough gallant deeds may win you some points with God, then don't turn to Christ. If you want a faith that glorifies yourself and makes your desires king, then Christ is definitely not for you. If you're ready to trust in Christ—to die with him on that mountain—then he's ready with open arms.

LIFE FOCUS: Our Christian faith is definitely not a faith that can be tossed in the pot with all other world religions. It is unique because it came from the very mind of God.

⚓ MAY 3 ⚓

Romans 3:1–4

Resting on God's Honesty

God is honest, and everyone else is a liar (Romans 3:4).

The true source of the Bible has been debated over the centuries. People have taken all manner of positions from literal inerrancy to fable, from an indifferent shrug of the shoulder to a firm, unwavering conviction that the book is without error, God's revelation to us. Everything pivots on this, for if the Bible is not God's Word, the whole edifice crumbles.

We believe the Scriptures in entirety are inspired by the Holy Spirit, and there are sound reasons for this faith. The Bible has proven remarkably resilient to attack. It's core message not only transforms the human being, but the book has proven amazingly accurate historically, archaeologically, and internally. The Bible is its own best argument.

"God is honest, and everyone else is a liar," writes Paul. God's truth is not always easy for us to understand now. Some enigmas clear up as one grows in faith. Others may continue to confuse. But we need never apologize for simple faith. Brilliant scholars have spent lifetimes with the Bible, probing deeply into its treasures—becoming more convinced all the time of its authenticity. We must take the book for what it claims to be and rest our faith on God's integrity, for he is the God who cannot lie.

Life Focus: If the Bible is a lie, it is the most heinous, deceitful fraud ever conceived upon the human race. Yet we rest in the faith that it is true because the person who is the main character is a God of unimpeachable integrity.

⚓ MAY 4 ⚓

Matthew 13:53–58
Over-Familiarity with Truth

He didn't work many miracles there because of their lack of faith (Matthew 13:58).

Among some, there is a biblical over-familiarity that breeds a sort of contempt. Our Lord was not received in his hometown of Nazareth because to them he was just a hometown boy, and what could he know? They thought of Jesus as just a carpenter's son who lived down the street. Though they were astonished at his teaching and his works, he could do little because of their unbelief.

There's danger in the familiar. It's a blessing to be reared in a Christian home and in a Bible-believing church. But there are also dangers. One can live so close to God's Word that familiarity breeds unbelief.

Once when teaching Bible in a Christian high school, I sensed the students were bored with the Scriptures. They could parrot back the facts, but there was a superficial attitude toward truth. To touch their need, I asked two radical-looking friends to visit the class unannounced and play the devil's advocate. When the guests arrived, they began to fire some questions about the students' faith—what they were doing to handle need in their world, how they were living out their faith. It was quiet in the classroom as the Holy Spirit jolted apathetic hearts. The students realized faith grows on the cutting edge of life's realities.

Life Focus: No matter how thoroughly you know the Scriptures, ask the Lord to keep your heart open to fresh insights.

—Tony Fortosis

⚓ MAY 5 ⚓

Mark 8:38
Good Company

If the people are ashamed of me and what I say in this unfaithful and sinful generation, the Son of Man will be ashamed of those people when he comes with the holy angels in his Father's glory (Romans 1:16).

Buechner describes a holy moment depicted in one of Rockwell's best known paintings. An elderly man with raincoat and umbrella pauses at the door to look back. Another peers over a newspaper, and two teens stare in dazed fascination. Outside, the rain pelts a dim, monotonous city; but, inside at that moment the silence is fathomless. The watchers are gazing at something they've all but forgotten. They could be watching creatures from another planet—a wrinkled woman and a gawky young boy saying grace in a drug store sandwich shop, unashamed and oblivious to whoever might be looking.

The Apostle Paul had many reasons to not only be ashamed but afraid to reflect his faith to others. He'd been a star student in Old Testament studies, trained by dignified Pharisees who spat on those poor Christians with their "ridiculous" message of forgiveness through a seedy impostor whose radical message ended with his death on a Roman crossbeam. Yet, once converted, this Paul went everywhere spouting the crazy message even in the face of beatings and stonings—recklessly unashamed, totally devoted to this Jesus whose love had so captivated him that Paul was eventually beheaded for love.

The old woman and the boy were in good company.

Life Focus: We should never be ashamed to show, even in small ways, that we are those people called Christians.

ROMANS 8:5–8

STOP CATERING TO SELF

Those who live by the corrupt nature have the corrupt nature's attitude. But those who live by the spiritual nature have the spiritual nature's attitude (Romans 8:5).

A vivid descriptor of self-centered people is that they're full of themselves. This does not always denote a completely treacherous or perverted existence. It does refer to whatever is involved with the natural self-life, as opposed to a Christ-centered life.

When I was first approached with the age-old gospel message, my first reaction was to imagine how empty life would be without drinking, gambling, and night clubs. The pastor who was sharing the truth with me just smiled and ignored my protests. He could have argued with me until doomsday, but he knew my attitude would change if I let Christ in.

It is possible to stop blatant sins and to be as separated from overt evils as the Pharisees, yet still follow after selfish goals. An individual out to be a "big time" preacher is living to satisfy the desires of the old nature as truly as a teenager who is drunk at two in the morning.

The secret is found in our text. The Lord calls us to yield our whole selves to him. When we respond to him with love, we will replace self-seeking habits with spirit-led patterns. A natural-minded person cannot see the joy of yielding to the Spirit. Giving up an activity or two won't do it. The answer is in becoming genuinely Christ-centered—motivated by love and a longing to please him.

LIFE FOCUS: Our hearts were created for God. True joy will spill out when we replace self-centered living with Christ-centered living.

—Tony Fortosis

⚓ MAY 7 ⚓

LUKE 6:21–23

THE RAGGED SEAMS OF GREATNESS

Make us rejoice for as many days as you have made us suffer, for as many years as we have experienced evil (Psalm 90:15).

Adoniram Judson is known today as a great missionary to Burma. During the nineteenth century, the nation seemed totally indifferent to Christianity. But finally Judson glimpsed a breakthrough, and Burmese began showing a growing interest in Christianity. His eventual completion of a Burmese translation of the Bible also helped initiate spiritual awakening.

Yes, there were triumphs in Judson's ministry, but gazing up through the ragged seams of his life, we see a vulnerable humanness which strikes at our hearts. For over a decade, his ministry was almost completely fruitless. Suspected of being an English spy, Judson was jailed in a death prison for almost two years. Five of his children died. His first and second wives died of disease, and Judson himself died of fever, leaving a third wife to grieve. After the death of his first wife, Nancy, Judson became clinically depressed. He built himself a small hut and lived as a complete recluse. Digging himself a grave, he morbidly kept vigil there daily. "God is to me the Great Unknown," he mourned, "I believe in him, but I find him not."

Then, with no psychologist but God, gradually Judson began to heal emotionally. As months passed, his faith was restored. Understanding love and prayer from fellow missionaries and native converts helped him to begin relating with others again. This outstanding missionary was great because of what God brought him through.

LIFE FOCUS: Don't imagine you're the only Christian God has ever trusted to go through heartrending tragedy. Others have passed through the fires with honors, and you can too.

⚓ MAY 8 ⚓

ECCLESIASTES 5:1–7
STAYING TRUE TO COMMITMENTS

When you make a promise to God, don't be slow to keep it, because God doesn't like fools. Keep your promise (Ecclesiastes 5:4).

A teen at camp rededicates his life to Christ around a bonfire, only to revert to old habits as the spiritual euphoria wears off in the face of familiar old temptations. Maybe you've known of believers who trudge down the aisle every year at the same special meetings, making the same weary commitments again. Have you made promises to God, only to renege on them in the strain of daily distractions and pressures?

In generations past, it seems as if people knew commitments were inexorably linked to character. If you promised to do something, come hell or high water, you tried to do it. Have we changed? We can be so weak, so easily drawn away from promises we make with such bravado. Yet we must never give up—never stop making commitments. Jesus knows us through and through. No doubt he's grieved over our broken commitments, but I'm sure he wouldn't tell us to make no more.

In a sense, the Christian experience can be seen as an ongoing series of commitments. Some of these promises will be kept for a lifetime. Others we will have to make repeatedly. However, it's important to realize how seriously our Lord takes them. We should think hard and pray much before and after we make a commitment to him. Knowing how God looks on our promises should motivate us to take them more seriously ourselves.

LIFE FOCUS: God will forgive you for past promises you've broken. Trust him to help you stay true to spiritual commitments.

⚓ MAY 9 ⚓

Job 29:12–22

What's So Great about Job?

The Lord asked Satan, "Have you thought about my servant Job? No one in the world is like him! He is a man of integrity: He is decent, he fears God, and he stays away from evil" (Job 1:8).

We would be hard pressed to find anyone in the Bible whom God praises more highly than Job. Yet have you ever looked to see just what it was in Job that God treasured so much?

We find a description of Job's lifestyle in chapter 29. He took the initiative to help the poor and orphans, brought joy to widows, helped the blind and disabled, gave to people in need, defended strangers, gave wise counsel, and fought injustice in every form. These were hardly high-profile "soapbox" ministries. Rather, most of this description involves quiet, behind-the-scenes care for the disadvantaged. God was glorified far and wide as a result of Job's merciful activities (vv. 7–11).

Once upon a time, the church was the primary arm of assistance for the needy. Then society transferred most of that responsibility to the government and social agencies. But there are still many ways we can show compassion for people in need. It's obvious that the government hasn't met all the needs of the poor, sick, lonely, lost, and impaired, nor does the government communicate the love of Jesus. Even if your church doesn't seem interested in these people, maybe there's someone to whom you and Jesus can find ways to express love.

Life Focus: Ask the Lord to bring one hurting person across your path. Be ready to show compassion to him or her.

⚓ MAY 10 ⚓

1 CORINTHIANS 6:19–20

GOD, THE MASTER BUILDER

Don't you know that you are God's temple and that God's Spirit lives in you? (1 Corinthians 3:16).

For centuries artisans have used skill and ingenuity to build magnificent cathedrals, many of which have taken decades to erect and, at least originally, were planned in honor of a magnificent God. Now tourists flock from one cathedral to another, awestruck by the architecture, the murals, the intricate carvings and sculptures. Meanwhile on worship days, some of these superstructures are dead inside, with only a pitiful smattering of hopeless parishioners. The original intent was noble, but is even a fraction as much time and money spent in building the true temples as in building these mortared ones?

The true temples of God are not constructed by human hands. Stephen, martyr of the early church, declared, "The Most High doesn't live in a house built by humans." Quoting the prophet Isaiah, Stephen explained that whatever we may try to build for God consists of matter he himself created! (Acts 7:48–50).

God wants us to concentrate on building and beautifying a different kind of temple. When Jesus said, "I will build my church," (Matt. 16:18) he was referring to converted saints, and Paul added that we are actually God's temples because his Spirit lives inside us. The church of the living God is a miraculous spiritual edifice, yet we are self-centered enough to limit his presence to the dimmest and darkest rooms in our lives. Calamy, a London Puritan, declared, "God is a guest that requires the upper rooms, that is, the head and the heart."

LIFE FOCUS: Are you giving him the upper rooms of your life?

ROMANS 6:16–22

CONTENT, YET NEVER SATISFIED

Now you have been freed from sin and have become God's slaves. This results in a holy life and, finally, in everlasting life (Romans 6:22).

In our society, we find two sorts of perfectionists. The first kind sees people in extremes—utterly good or utterly bad—leaving no room for real Christians, who are in many ways bad, yet being conformed to the good. This perfectionist demands too much of frail humanity and expects more than most can produce. He or she blames and blusters, finding few, if any, who can live up to the monumental expectations.

Jesus did say, "Be perfect as your Father in heaven is perfect" (Matt. 5:48). In other words, you must be spiritually mature or complete in righteousness. We cannot expect anything of ourselves, but we can expect everything of God. As we're receptive to him, he's ready to produce in us the desires and actions that please him. Thus, the second kind of perfectionist accepts his or her great imperfection, yet sets an ongoing goal of fulfilling God's standards by the power that works within.

How do we prevent spiritual stagnation? By always seeking out avenues for new growth—by moving on from issues like salvation and baptism to Christian character and serving in love. We develop wisdom as we make God's Word a working principle of our daily lives. As we walk morally in the light, we will enjoy close fellowship with other believers and with Christ. Christ will gradually produce in us his holiness.

LIFE FOCUS: Though on this earth we'll never be completely satisfied with our spiritual state, we can consistently live contentedly in Christ.

⚓ MAY 12 ⚓

PSALM 131:1–2
MORE SPIRITUAL THAN GOD?

O LORD, my heart is not conceited. My eyes do not look down on others. I am not involved in things too big or too difficult for me (Psalm 131:1).

"One of the blunders religious people are particularly fond of," writes Frederick Buechner, "is the attempt to be more spiritual than God." This tendency is often reflected in a censorious attitude toward those around us, both Christians and non-Christians. Athananius, the Bishop of Alexandria, believed that "the truly humble Christian does not inquire into his neighbor's faults; he takes no pleasure in judging them; he is wholly occupied with his own." Some may claim that enthusiastic loyalty to God is what prompts judgment of others. Yet Nettleton, a New England evangelist, states, "Zeal without prudence will defeat its own end. Zeal, untempered with love and compassion for souls, will soon degenerate into harshness and cruelty of manner and expression."

It seems as if the sons of thunder were attempting to be more spiritual than God when they angrily asked Jesus if he'd like them to call down fiery destruction on a city who'd turned him away. Jesus hushed them with the warning that they had no idea whose spirit their sentiment really reflected. When Peter tried to lecture Jesus against his pessimistic prediction of his own ugly death, Jesus saw Satan's slithery shadow in Peter's superior outburst. The tragic truth that examples such as these seem to bear out is that in our attempts to appear more spiritual than God we may find ourselves actually miming Satan's dark aspirations. And that is downright scary.

LIFE FOCUS: What nerve it takes for us to self-righteously imply that we're on par with God in any way under heaven.

⚓ MAY 13 ⚓

PSALM 135:5–13
GOD'S APPOINTMENTS

I know that the LORD is great, that our Lord is greater than all the false gods. The LORD does whatever he wants in heaven or on earth, on the seas or in all the depths of the oceans (Psalm 135:5–6).

David declared confidently to God, "My future is in your hands" (Ps. 31:15). Based on this principle, Sir Walter Raleigh stated that the smallest accident, which may seem to us as occurring by chance, is caused by God to affect something else. Yes, and often to affect things of the greatest earthly importance, either presently or many years later, when God's original act may be either unconsidered or forgotten.

I was on my way to Lancaster, Pennsylvania, via Philadelphia on a plane that arrived so late in Philly that I missed the connecting flight. It was midnight and I was scheduled to speak early the next morning. My only recourse was an expensive taxi ride to Lancaster.

Though I was nervous and exhausted, the taxi driver and I began conversing. I discovered a Christian who'd turned his back on God and was desperately in need of instruction and encouragement. After an hour-long discussion, the driver said he thought his midnight fare was sent by God to restore his Christian commitment. My body was wiped out as we finally pulled up to the convention site, but my heart was singing.

Our timetable must be turned over always to our divine manager.

LIFE FOCUS: God won't waste opportunities or lead us aimlessly toward dead ends. As we look for his hand behind the scenes, we will see sovereign situations that achieve his good purposes.

—Tony Fortosis

⚓ May 14 ⚓

2 Peter 3:8–12
God Hasn't Forgotten

Think of the kind of holy and godly lives you must live as you look forward to the day of God and eagerly wait for it to come (2 Peter 3:11–12).

Thomas Browne, seventeenth century writer, mused that many Christians in his day speculated about the enjoyment of living in a past age. In contrast, Browne stated that the uncertainty of future times had tempted few to wish they could live then. "And surely he that hath taken true altitude of things," writes Browne, "and rightly calculated the degenerate state of this age, is not likely to envy those that live in the next; much less three or four hundred years hence, when no man can comfortably imagine what face the world will carry."

We now live in that age which Browne anticipated with such apprehension. We don't know how seventeenth-century believers would have reacted to the current state of things. But we do know that perilous times seem to be snowballing, and life in the twenty-first century does not seem to promise a brighter, new tomorrow. This is a world of AIDS, homosexual marriages, mothers killing their children, and new prisons bursting at the seams—intricate alarms, double-bolted doors, and millions slaughtered in places like Rwanda, Bosnia, and Zaire. Has God finally given up and moved on to other, more promising projects? No, but in his infinite heart, a panoply of surging emotions are growing: his grief for the innocent, his protective love for his own, and a thunderous gathering of rage against the wicked.

Life Focus: Take hope. Though deep darkness settles in around us, God has not forgotten. He's on his way.

⚓ MAY 15 ⚓

ROMANS 6:1–16
PLANNING TO SIN

Should we sin because we are not controlled by laws but are controlled by God's favor? That's unthinkable! Don't you know that if you offer to be someone's slave, you must obey that master? (Romans 6:15–16).

A supposed Christian approached a leader with a dilemma. "I'm very attracted to a woman I've met," he said. "It just seems like we're made for each other. Now, if I leave my wife for this woman, God will forgive me, won't he?" In another case, a friend confronted a professing Christian with the wrongness of sleeping with various women he dates. "I never said I wasn't a sinner," he bristled abruptly.

These are blatant examples of abusing God's grace. Centuries ago, Paul blasted this distortion head-on when he declared, "Should we continue to sin so that God's kindness will increase? That's unthinkable! As far as sin is concerned, we have died. So how can we still live under sin's influence?" (Rom. 6:1–2).

In the field of law and order, much is made of whether a crime is premeditated or not. A planned crime receives a much stiffer penalty than one that's unplanned. Do we Christians ever plan our sin? Our first impulse may be a resounding no. It's true that most sin is not anticipated—temptation comes and we fall because we're not prepared and we don't resist in Christ's power. Yet humans are just devious enough to set ourselves up in a place, or with a person, or in a situation that we know spells trouble. "Nothing darkens the soul," writes Evans, "like indulged sin."

LIFE FOCUS: Sin won't finally be wiped out until our bodies are made like Christ's. But we make a dark mockery of grace, especially when we plan our sin.

⚓ MAY 16 ⚓

PSALM 116:5–14
LEARNING TO RECEIVE

How can I repay the LORD for all the good he has done for me? I will take the cup of salvation and call on the name of the LORD. I will keep my vows to the LORD in the presence of all the people (Psalm 116:12–14).

King Jehoash of Israel visited Elisha as the prophet lay dying. Elisha instructed him to shoot an arrow out the window. "That is the arrow of the LORD's victory, the arrow of victory against Aram," said the prophet. "Take the arrows," continued Elisha, "Stomp on them" (2 Kings 13:17–18).

The king looked at him strangely, then awkwardly stomped on the arrows three times. "You should have stomped five or six times," said the prophet sternly. "Then you would have completely defeated the Arameans" (2 Kings 13:19).

God wanted to give the king a more resounding victory, but Jehoash may have felt self-conscious about God's simple instructions. In effect, he stopped halfway and received half of what God intended.

Some Christians find it very difficult to receive thankfully and fully what God wants to give. "Let us not dally with God," writes Milton, "when he offers us a full blessing—to take as much of it as we think will serve our ends and turn him back the rest upon his hands, lest in his anger he snatch all from us again." At times we are like the proud homeless who may angrily snap, "I don't take charity." However, we must remember that God never patronizes or condescends. He's the ultimate gentleman.

LIFE FOCUS: What he gives we need, and he intends for us to take and use it fully, graciously, and thankfully.

⚓ MAY 17 ⚓

HEBREWS 6:9–12
PLODDING FOR GOD

He will pay all people back for what they have done. He will give everlasting life to those who search for glory, honor, and immortality by persisting in doing what is good (Romans 2:6–7).

He was an impoverished English cobbler, as plain and ordinary as one of the old shoes he hammered together. He muddled through jobs slowly, completing them only out of a bulldog determination. “I can plod,” he said. “I can persevere in any definite pursuit. To this I owe everything.”

William Carey was thirty-two years old before he even became a missionary. His wife fought the idea all the way. When they arrived in India, seven years passed without a single convert. Then the Careys’ five-year-old son, Peter, died and the precarious sanity of Carey’s wife finally snapped. She lived thirteen more years in psychosis.

Much of Carey’s ministry consisted of Bible translation. Thus, it was devastating when volumes of his translation work were wiped out in a warehouse fire. But instead of giving up, the little man accepted this from God and began all over again.

As decades passed, Carey and other veteran workers also had to humble themselves toward brash new missionary recruits and a partisan mission board. Throughout his long career, this mild-mannered man waded through struggles and tragedies that would have wiped out most of us. Yet when twilight fell and the shadows lengthened on a tumultuous ministry, he was still plugging away—always plugging.

LIFE FOCUS: Like William Carey, nothing may seem outstanding about you as a Christian. You may be reserved, methodical, and unexcitingly ordinary, yet God can use your life as surely as he used a fiery Martin Luther or a dynamic Charles Spurgeon.

⚓ MAY 18 ⚓

1 CORINTHIANS 3:10–15
METICULOUS FOR QUALITY

If what a person has built survives, he will receive a reward. If his work is burned up, he will suffer the loss (1 Corinthians 3:14–15).

Philip Yancey tells of a trip to Venice where he attended a chamber concert in a grand hall decorated with fifty-six Tintoretto canvases. He was "surrounded by reminders of the glory that can be achieved only through laborious human effort: the care of a master violin maker, the long hours of practice by the ensemble, the meticulous brushstrokes covering every surface of the walls." This stood in stark contrast to our day, when it seems as if the cheap and the instant are priorities.

Behavioral scientists performed an experiment in which individual children were placed in a room with a marshmallow. "You can have one marshmallow now," announced the scientist, "or you can wait while I run an errand and then have two marshmallows when I return." For these four-year-olds, it was agonizing—some covered their eyes or ran around the room in resistance while others gave in and just ate the lone treat.

As Christians, we're like those children at times. We're unwilling to wait or work for what would inevitably be much more gratifying, not only to God, but also to us. We're often unwilling to devote the discipline and time needed to become fully mature. Solid maturity never comes quickly.

LIFE FOCUS: It takes time for God to paint a lily and grow an oak; we must plow and sow, wait and work until God's deepest purposes are completed in us.

⚓ MAY 19 ⚓

PSALM 95:1–7
ABSORBED WITH GOD

Come, let's worship and bow down. Let's kneel in front of the LORD, our maker, because he is our God and we are the people in his care, the flock that he leads (Psalm 95:6–7).

To worship is to attribute true worth to one who deserves it. Worship is that which rises from Spirit-controlled believers through the Son to the Father.

When my first son was a little boy, he would often interrupt me in my study with questions and needs. One day, after a long string of interruptions, I asked impatiently, "David, what do you want this time?"

"I don't want anything, Dad," he replied. "I just want to be with you." I believe we bring delight to the Father when we simply bask in his presence and enjoy him alone.

It was so cold one winter evening, moisture crackled in the air. Wending his way home, a man heard a metallic clang and glimpsed a shivering puppy with a tin can tied to his tail. Without a word, he removed the can, and tucked the mangy pup inside his coat.

Arriving home, he set the pup near the crackling fireplace and gave him hot bread and milk. The ragged tail wagged slightly.

A month passed and the animal regained his strength. One evening as the man sat by his fire, he saw the dog staring at him adoringly. The dog hadn't come into the room to beg for food or even to be petted. He wanted nothing but to lick the hand of his benefactor in gratitude and love. This is worship.

LIFE FOCUS: Worship is the absorption of the heart, not with its needs or even with its blessings, but with God himself. This should become more of a focus in our lives.

—Tony Fortosis

⚓ May 20 ⚓

Galatians 6:1–10

Every Mile Has Meaning

We can't allow ourselves to get tired of living the right way. Certainly, each of us will receive everlasting life at the proper time, if we don't give up (Galatians 6:9).

A young college graduate found his first steady job. When asked how he liked it, he said, "It's OK, except that it's so daily." He was entering the world of the daily routine, the grind, the mundane experience of a work-a-day world.

Jesus encouraged us to request our daily bread and said we're to take up our cross daily. The early Christians continued daily in prayer, and the Lord added to the church daily. Paul exclaimed, "I face death every day" (1 Cor. 15:31) and Christians are told to exhort one another daily.

We're reminded by the greats that Christian character shows up best in ordinary, daily life. Faber writes, "The fragrant woods and painted flowers are not half so beautiful as a soul that is serving Jesus out of love, in the wear and tear of common, unpoetic life." "Do not wait for some ideal situation," an anonymous writer adds, "some romantic difficulty, some far-away emergency; but rise to meet the actual conditions which the providence of God has placed around you today."

Life is not a sprint, but a marathon that winds mile after mile across life. Every mile has meaning, every hill and valley has purpose. We try to do our best, whether inspired or not. "If you make a god of your best moments," writes Chambers, "you'll find that God will fade out until you do the duty that lies nearest."

Life Focus: Most of life is made up of the routine, and perhaps the greatest test of Christian faithfulness is the ability to consistently live out the faith in tedium, whether others are aware of it or not.

⚓ MAY 21 ⚓

PSALM 145:14–21
OUR IRON LUNG

The LORD supports everyone who falls. He straightens the backs of those who are bent over. . . . He fills the needs of those who fear him. He hears their cries for help and saves them (Psalm 145:14, 19).

John Berridge, a 1700s evangelist, writes, "Truly, my friend, your cross is just the same with my own. I am not able to walk a step without a crutch. The wood of it comes from Calvary. My crutch is Christ; and a blessed crutch he is. Oh, let me lean my whole weight on Thee whilst I am walking through the wilderness."

Back in college days, I recall a non-Christian accusing Christians of being weak and dependent—of using Christ as a crutch. A friend admitted, "Jesus isn't just my crutch; he's my iron lung."

A psalmist writes, "God is our refuge and strength, an ever-present help in times of trouble" (46:1). David cried, "I went to the Lord for help. He answered me and rescued me from all my fears" (Ps. 34:4). Jesus said, "You can't produce anything without me" (John 15:5). And Paul states, "At the right time, while we were still helpless, Christ died for ungodly people" (Rom. 5:6).

In the rough and tumble world of the rugged individualist, admission of vulnerability or need is considered inexcusable. One doesn't dare reveal the chinks in one's armor. Yet God says the direct opposite—his own must finally humble themselves enough to admit need and helplessly depend upon Christ for life and all that pertains to it.

LIFE FOCUS: When it comes to depending on Christ, don't worry about wimpiness. Sometimes it takes more courage to admit need than it does to play the silly game of macho self-sufficience.

⚓ MAY 22 ⚓

1 PETER 1:1–5
ATONEMENT BELOW; HEAVEN ABOVE

We have been born into a new life that has a confidence which is alive because Jesus Christ has come back to life. We have been born into a new life which has an inheritance that can't be destroyed or corrupted and can't fade away. That inheritance is kept in heaven for you (1 Peter 1:3–4).

In reading about giants of the faith, two topics appear predominant: the atonement of Christ and the anticipation of heaven. J.H. Evans writes, "The great secret of all happiness is knowing the way to the cross." These saints seem overwhelmed by Christ's love. "O thou Loving One, thou deservest to have me all," writes John Bunyan. "Thou hast paid for me ten thousand times more than I am worth." John Berridge declares, "O heart, heart!" The vainest, foolishest, craftiest, wickedest thing in nature. Yet the Lord Jesus asks me for this heart, woos me for it, died to win it! O wonderful love! Adorable condescension!"

Of heaven, John Angell James writes, "Christian, why weepest thou? Heaven is opening before you! The last tear of earth will soon be wiped away amid the first smile of heaven, and that smile will be eternal." These equated a focus on heaven with a close walk with God. Whitefield writes, "We do not live up to our dignity till every day we are waiting for the coming of our Lord from heaven." Hewitson says, "I find that to say, Come quickly, is the result only of close walking with God." M'Cheyne adds, "You will be incomplete Christians if you do not look for the coming again of the Lord Jesus." And of that final triumph, Powerscourt cries, "What a thunderclap of hallelujah when all the prayers of all saints for our poor world, long, long laid up, shall all be answered in one event!"

LIFE FOCUS: It seems as if the Christian whose underlying focus is on the death of Christ for sin and on the life with Christ forever cannot go wrong.

⚓ MAY 23 ⚓

1 SAMUEL 2:6–8

NO CHANCE

The Spirit said to Philip, "Go to that carriage, and stay close to it." Philip ran to the carriage and could hear the official reading the prophet Isaiah out loud. Philip asked him, "Do you understand what you're reading?" The official answered, "How can I understand unless someone guides me?" (Acts 8:29–31).

The Bible teaches that God is constantly moving in the millions of intricate encounters of life with life. "Never let us say of anything, it happened by chance," writes Basil, a first century bishop. "There is nothing that has not been fore-arranged, nothing which has not its own special end, by which it forms a link in the chain of appointed order."

It appeared that Joseph's childish pride finally caught up with him when his brothers sold him into slavery. But many years later Joseph himself told his brothers, "Even though you planned evil against me, God planned good to come out of it. This was to keep many people alive" (Gen. 50:20). Moreover, it seemed as if charm and beauty had won Esther the queen's throne in ancient Persia. But when her fellow Jews were endangered, her uncle said, in effect, maybe divine power has placed you in your royal position for just such a time as this.

On the way to some important ministry, Amy Carmichael's cart broke down. After a very long delay, the party finally reached a town and, near some palms, Amy met a woman who seemed prepared, and waiting for someone to tell her of Jesus. James Graham, missionary to China, missed his boat upriver to preach in scheduled evangelistic meetings. Frustrated, he headed back home. On the way, he encountered a despairing Buddhist monk who opened his heart to the Good News explained by this white-faced giant, eventually founding a Christian church himself. It seems old Basil was right.

LIFE FOCUS: Look for God's fingerprints in the daily events of your life. He leaves them everywhere.

ZEPHANIAH 3:11–12

FAITHFULNESS, NOT FAME

Those who are wise will shine like the brightness on the horizon. Those who lead many people to righteousness will shine like the stars forever and ever (Daniel 12:3).

Some Christians go down in the annals of history as spiritual giants to admire and imitate. Others are obscure and their lives seem to fade into oblivion. Yet God keeps different records. Faithfulness matters far more to him than fame, and many of the truly great may never grab a headline.

When Kansas farmgirl Maude Cary arrived in Morocco as a missionary, she was perceived as proud, giddy, and overly aggressive. In fact, after only two years of service, Maude was evaluated as unsuitable and advised to return to the United States.

Though quite discouraged, Maude stayed on in this stubbornly Muslim nation. Difficult times came and went, and after over twenty-three grinding years, things became even more challenging for her. Only one other missionary remained with her to staff Gospel Missionary Union stations. A few more arrived later, but it was definitely a skeleton staff that kept the ministry going throughout World War II.

As Maude aged, chronic health problems limited her to teaching at the language school and orienting new recruits. However, at age seventy-one, she was given a mission in a new city.

Finally at age seventy-seven, Maude retired. A small obituary appeared in a local paper some years later. It mentioned a funeral which only a few attended. Two sprays of flowers and hardly any tears marked the death of a very old woman. Maude Cary had stepped up to the reward stand.

LIFE FOCUS: There will be some great surprises on the final day when shining thousands who few knew and none applauded lay their glorious rewards before the King.

⚓ MAY 25 ⚓

2 SAMUEL 21:1–10
RARE LOYALTY

Loyalty is desirable in a person (Proverbs 19:22).

Rizpah, one of King Saul's concubines, bore him two sons. Then Saul died on a Philistine battlefield, and Rizpah became a grieving widow. She didn't realize, however, that her grief had only begun.

During his reign, King Saul tried to annihilate the Gibeonites, with whom Israel had a long-standing peace treaty. After Saul was killed, the Gibeonites cried out for justice. "If you'll turn over seven male descendants of Saul for execution," they said, "justice will be satisfied." The two sons of Rizpah and five sons of Saul's eldest daughter were handed over and hanged on a hilltop on the eve of barley harvest.

The breaking of Rizpah's heart was almost audible. She realized the Gibeonites had no intention of burying the bodies. So she trudged up the mountain, spread sackcloth on a rock, and began a silent vigil. Days were horrible as Rizpah beat the vultures away from her sons. Nights were even worse as the exhausted woman tried to keep wild animals at bay. The bodies blackened and decayed, the stench was revolting, but Rizpah continued her loyal vigil. As spring rains came, David heard about Rizpah's amazing act of love, and he finally had the shrunken bodies buried in dignity (2 Sam. 21:1–14).

When I was a boy, we lived near a Christian high school, and the school nurse became a friend. Then I reached high school and my mother contracted cancer. I'd show up at the school clinic late at night, desperately needing to talk and pray, and the exhausted nurse never turned me away. Many years have passed, and this wondrous woman still writes and prays for me faithfully. She's a descendant of the lovingly loyal Rizpah.

LIFE FOCUS: There is something so rare in unfailing loyalty that it moves and inspires us to love and admire the loyal.

⚓ MAY 26 ⚓

MATTHEW 6:5–8

DOWN-TO-EARTH PRAYER PROBLEMS

The Spirit also helps us in our weakness, because we don't know how to pray for what we need (Romans 8:26).

It's easy to be overwhelmed by the myriads of books about prayer and reports of great saints who spent multiplied hours each day in their prayer closets. I was refreshed to find very honest, down-to-earth prayer challenges from Amy Carmichael, a missionary who knew God intimately. In her books, she addresses struggles such as doubts, distractions, and speechlessness.

Distractions are described by Carmichael as a "thousand invisible enemies who fill the air and crowd between us and our Lord." This lack of focus results in the sort of thing some ancient saint experienced: "I pray giddily and circularly, and returne againe and againe to that I have said before, and perceive not that I do so." In times like these, Carmichael suggests turning a psalm or hymn into a prayer—using structure to chase away distractions.

We all recall prayers we don't believe God answered, and, in down moments, we may be tempted to wonder if our prayers rise to God at all. Carmichael declares that we must boldly fight through these whispering spiritual foes, using the sword of God's Word.

Sometimes we can't find words, and maybe we're not always meant to find them. "Words fail us at times," writes Carmichael. "I've been greatly comforted . . . that we are not heard for our much speaking."

Don't be afraid of silence; don't fear to listen for God.

LIFE FOCUS: Try not to overcomplicate prayer. We may not need to read multitudes of books on prayer as much as we need to simply overcome basic obstacles with which most of us struggle.

⚓ MAY 27 ⚓

HEBREWS 9:11–14
THE LIFE IS IN THE BLOOD

Realize that you weren't set free from the worthless life handed down to you from your ancestors by a payment of silver or gold which can be destroyed. Rather, the payment that freed you was the precious blood of Christ, the lamb with no defects or imperfections (1 Peter 1:18–19).

An agnostic woman I knew was appalled by the violence and blood in the Bible. It's true; the book isn't all that warm and fuzzy. Some may try to avoid the violent parts, but even Christ's life ends in a brutal scene of gore and blood.

In reality, though, blood is not gross in itself. First, it is priceless and indispensable to human existence. Doctors agree with Bible authors that blood is the life stream of the body (Deut. 12:23). No part of the body can live without this red fluid. Second, blood is the body's cleanser, taking oxygen to the extremities and returning with wastes to be purified. Figuratively, through Christ it is also the soul's cleanser (1John 1:7). Third, blood protects the body against infection and neutralizes harmful bacteria; similarly Christ's blood protects us from Satan's great power (Rev. 12:10–11). Fourth, blood nourishes us by distributing vitamins, enzymes, hormones, etc. to tissues and organs. Symbolically, Jesus said that if we ingest his flesh and blood, we'll be nourished forever (John 6:54).

I had a professor in college whose son, Mark, was a hemophiliac. If he was bruised or gashed, the boy could literally bleed to death. My instructor misted over as he told of a time when Mark was two and was minutes from death from loss of blood. As an emergency transfusion was given, the boy's immediate visible reviving gave his father a movingly indelible lesson about the life-giving blood of Christ. There is wonder-working power in that blood.

LIFE FOCUS: That liquid life-stream of the body somehow takes on immense significance when one realizes that it bled out of God Incarnate until his broken heart had no more blood to give. And he did this for you and me.

⚓ MAY 28 ⚓

1 CORINTHIANS 12:14–26
FISHING FOR COMPLEMENTS

If the whole body were an eye, how could it hear? If the whole body were an ear, how could it smell? (1 Corinthians 12:17).

He was a frail, quiet man, hesitant and stuttering. No one looked up when Philip Melanchon walked into a room, and unlike E.F. Hutton, when he spoke, few listened.

In his book, Chuck Swindoll brings out the great contrasts between Martin Luther and his close friend, Philip Melanchon. Luther was a powerful leader—dynamic, vigorous, larger than life. Yet without a tempering, he could be stubborn, overbearing, even coarse. Melanchon's love of order, his moderation, and his superior scholarship reined in Luther's impulsiveness, and his writings won for the Reformation the support of the educated.

In the familiar Romans 12 and 1 Corinthians 12 passages, the church is compared to a human body. Each part of the body crucially complements every other part. Even the parts that seem hidden and unimportant have a vital function, and if these were missing, we would be less efficient and effective as humans.

If we Christians only spend time with those of our own personality and gifts, we duplicate efforts, under- or overwhelm others, compete unnecessarily, tire of sameness, and do incomplete work. God has given varied personalities and gifts to us so we can strengthen and temper one another in the quest of reaching our potential.

LIFE FOCUS: Try to gather around some friends and associates who complement you rather than duplicate you.

⚓ MAY 29 ⚓

Hebrews 13:1–3

Conquer by Love

Love never stops being patient, never stops believing, never stops hoping, never gives up (1 Corinthians 13:7).

Christ said all would recognize his future followers by their love. Aristides observed early Christians and declared, "They are eager to do good to their enemies. . . . And when they see a stranger, they take him into their homes and rejoice over him as a very brother. . . . And if they hear that one of their number is imprisoned or afflicted on account of the name of their Messiah, all of them anxiously minister to his necessity. . . . And if there is among them any that is poor and needy, if they have no spare food, they fast two or three days in order to supply the needy their lack of food."

In the context of encouraging peace and kindness in place of revenge, Paul writes, "Don't let evil conquer you, but conquer evil with good" (Rom. 12:21). Justin, a church father, substantiates the fact that the early church tried to exemplify this: "He [Jesus] challenged us to lead everyone away from shamefulness and pleasure in evil by patience and kindness. We can, in fact show that many have been transformed in this way who were once among you. Either they were conquered by the sight of their neighbors' patient life, or they were convinced by noticing the extraordinary kindness and patience of some defrauded traveling companions, or they were overcome by encountering and testing this attitude in people with whom they had business dealings." Do people still recognize us Christians today by the way we love?

Life Focus: More can always be conquered by love than by hate.

⚓ MAY 30 ⚓

JOHN 15:18–25
HATED FOR THE NAME

"If the world hates you, realize that it hated me before it hated you. If you had anything in common with the world, the world would love you as one of its own . . . I chose you from the world, and that's why the world hates you" (John 15:18–19).

Devoted Christians have never been voted most popular. A few outsiders flutter toward their light, but most move away. Some attack with a rage that's truly blind and often destructive.

A bitter diatribe from historian Minucius Felix reflects the public sentiment in Roman times: "Their [Christians'] alliance consists in meetings at night with solemn rituals and inhuman revelries. . . . They recognize each other by secret signs and signals. They love one another before being acquainted. Everywhere they practice a kind of religious cult of lust, calling one another 'brother' and 'sister' indiscriminately. [They] venerate an executed criminal. . . . Their feastings are notorious. . . . All single acts correspond to the will of all."

As humans, we long to be loved. That's why it's hard for us to accept Christ's warnings that we'll be hated by the world. Church father Tertullian knew it was actually the name of Christ that stirred such rage. He writes, "The Christian never has to suffer for any other affairs except those of his own sect, which during all this long time no one has ever proved guilty of incest or any cruel act. It is for our singular innocence . . . for the living God that we are burned to death. It becomes evident that the entire crime with which they charge us does not consist in any wicked acts, but in the bearing of a name. . . . Again and again it is the name that must be punished by the sword, the gallows, the cross, or the wild beasts."

LIFE FOCUS: We tend to recoil in hurt and shock when outsiders belittle our Christian beliefs or despise us for our moral lifestyle. But, all along, Jesus said it would happen, and he acknowledged they'd do it because we bear his name.

⚓ May 31 ⚓

2 Corinthians 5:1–10
Be Heavenly-Minded

We are confident and prefer to live away from this body and to live with the Lord. Whether we live in the body or move out of it, our goal is to be pleasing to him (2 Corinthians 5:8–9).

Enslaved blacks in America wrote many spirituals—songs that expressed deep, anguished emotions about their sufferings and their hope in Jesus. A primary theme of these songs is heaven. John MacArthur tells of a visit he made to impoverished Christians in an isolated town near Siberia. They begged him to teach them what the Bible says about heaven. As they listened, many wept with joy.

Affluent Christians with few hardships are often not especially interested in heaven. They may accuse believers who focus on heaven as being too heavenly-minded to be of any earthly good. MacArthur, however, sides with great old saints such as Puritan Richard Baxter: "A heavenly mind is a joyful mind; this is the nearest and truest way to live a life of comfort, and without this you must needs be uncomfortable. There is no man so highly honoreth God, as he who hath his conversation in heaven; and without this we deeply dishonor him."

Don't worry about being called home early and missing out on life's best joys or of feeling out of place in heaven. Life in Christ's presence will burst with pleasure. MacArthur writes, "Heaven will seem more like home than the dearest spot on earth. It is uniquely designed by a tender, loving Savior to be the place where we will live together for all eternity and enjoy him forever."

Life Focus: It is the Christian whose greatest focus is entering heaven with joy who will now be of most earthly good.

JUNE

Monday Morning Christianity

James 1:22

Epistle of Practicality

From James, a servant of God and of the Lord Jesus Christ. To God's faithful people who have been scattered. Greetings (James 1:1).

James must have been quite a guy—here he was, the half-brother of Christ, but he wasn't out blowing his own horn. He called himself a servant of Christ. That's surprising, because John tells us quite candidly of the unbelief of Jesus' half-brothers (John 7:5). Maybe there was unbelief once or a sibling rivalry, but after the resurrection, everything changed.

Apparently, James was also a remarkably devout Christian. His nickname was camel knees because supposedly he had calluses on his knees from praying whenever he wasn't preaching.

James' epistle was written about A.D. 45–50. Though he specifically addressed his Jewish counterparts scattered among the gentiles, his letter concerning Christian living is also addressed very clearly to us.

And talk about gut-level spirituality! No pious platitudes, no dead theories, no anemic exhortations. Just a down-to-earth, practical, go-out-and-live-it brand of Christianity. James was aware that we live in an imperfect world, and we are imperfect people, in need of extensive reconstruction.

Life Focus: As the half-brother of Christ, James could have been a prima donna name-dropper, but instead he exhibited humility. We should follow his example.

⚓ JUNE 2 ⚓

ROMANS 5:12–15

DOWN-TO-EARTH, HONEST-TO-GOD SAINTHOOD

Sin came into the world through one person, and death came through sin. So death spread to everyone, because everyone sinned (Romans 5:12).

There was once a group of children who were taught about Adam and Eve for the first time. After the story, the teacher asked for prayer requests. A little boy raised his hand and said worriedly, "Let's pray for that guy who's wife gave him the poison apple." Mixing truth with fancy, the child was worried for Adam, but he was way too late to help. When Adam sinned, a lot of things went haywire in our world in a lot of ways.

And one thing you will learn about James is that he does not see a God-cursed world through rose-colored glasses. He's the totally earnest, brutally honest type of guy who'd be willing to tell any emperor alive that he's wearing not a stitch of clothing.

We have to hand it to James; he breaks through all the spiritual smoke screens, all the term paper padding, all our spoiled whinings and smacks us in the face with the bold-faced truth. What's more, he doesn't even apologize for his directness. In five short chapters, James outlines the Christian lifestyle.

We would sometimes rather have a stimulating discussion on the glories of heaven or on the timing of the rapture than go the extra mile with a cantankerous neighbor. But the Christian experience is to be lived out there in real life, slogging through mud, lifting up the fallen—slipping ourselves but getting up and moving on.

LIFE FOCUS: Be careful not to either become too discouraged about your imperfections to want to change or to have the sort of inflated idea of your own spirituality which resists positive change.

⚓ JUNE 3 ⚓

PHILIPPIANS 2:17–18
HAPPY IN HASSLES

My brothers and sisters, be very happy when you are tested in different ways (James 1:2).

For all his practicality, James stumps us momentarily with his philosophy of life. He starts out with a real winner: "My brothers and sisters, be very happy when you are tested in different ways." The New Testament word for test or trial is *peirazo*, which means to prove something worthy of a standard. God examines us under the pressure of difficulties to see how we are suited for his service. But what is this about maintaining our joy? It sounds a little like Jesus' statement, "When you are persecuted, leap and dance for joy, for great is your reward in heaven" (Matt. 5:12, author's paraphrase.)

How outlandish can you get? Sure, I once heard of a guy who was always happy, but he also grinned smugly as he claimed to be Napoleon Bonaparte. Is James saying we should be tickled pink because the car broke down in the middle of the freeway on a Monday afternoon during rush hour? I don't think so. He seems to be saying that we're to rejoice because of a process which results in a finished product. The finished product is spiritual toughness, and the process involves any situation in our lives which tests our faith in Christ—in his love, in his sufficiency, in his ability.

LIFE FOCUS: Next time Murphy's Law kicks in, by an act of the will ask God to use the hassle to make you more like him.

⚓ JUNE 4 ⚓

JAMES 1:3–4

A REMINDER EVERY HOUR

You know that such testing of your faith produces endurance. Endure until your testing is over (James 1:3–4).

Do trials in themselves sanctify us? No. Any benefit lies in our response to the difficulties: Do we whine or win? Do we give up or hang in? Do we boil over or triumph over?

Bushnell claimed that a Christian needs a reminder every hour—some defeat, surprise, adversity, peril—to be agitated so that all remains of selfishness will be sifted out. This does not mean we're to lose our unique individuality, nor the preciousness of personality. It simply refers to that egocentric, sin-loving side of self which must be daily crucified with Christ.

James reminds us that the crown of life is promised to those sufferers who love God. Love is a funny thing. We will go to amazing lengths and will endure great inconvenience for someone we love. Fenelon, French spiritual counselor in the king's court, said that when a sufferer reaches a sweet calmness of attitude, smiling at adversity, no longer begging for immediate deliverance, then patience has accomplished its perfect work. If I love God, I can endure the trials he allows, knowing that he only allows them with a glorious end in view.

LIFE FOCUS: Is there a chronic problem in your life that has humbled you? How have you managed to endure it? In what way has it affected you as a Christian?

⚓ JUNE 5 ⚓

JAMES 1:5–8
TRUST FOR WISDOM

If any of you needs wisdom to know what you should do, you should ask God (James 1:5).

Go ahead! Memorize the Bible from cover to cover. Then go out and face the large and small problems of life. It won't do you any good without wisdom, because wisdom tells us what to do with knowledge. Knowledge says God answers prayer; wisdom says to pray consistently and expectantly. Knowledge says people need encouragement; wisdom says to refresh and motivate others. Knowledge says sin is destructive; wisdom says to demonstrate an alternate lifestyle.

If our lack of wisdom makes us appear foolish to one another, how must we appear to God? But as James writes, God doesn't dole out wisdom grudgingly, with a harsh scolding attitude. He's longing to develop his wisdom in our lives, if we will only express the desire to learn.

Sometimes we sound like wishy-washy, wind-tossed waves: "God, I don't know why I'm asking you this—but do you think, just maybe, there's an outside chance you might be able to develop a slight bit of wisdom in my life?"

Obviously, that isn't an example of brimming faith. At least it indicates evidence of the mustard seed faith which asks, though it senses the tremble of doubt. However, if we're double-minded—totally irresolute in our trust—then we need to develop the stability which undivided loyalty to God can bring.

LIFE FOCUS: Ask God for more wisdom. If you're sincere, he won't ignore a request for such a crucial quality.

1 PETER 1:6–7

GOING FOR THE GOLD

Blessed are those who endure when they are tested (James 1:12).

Our Heavenly Teacher sometimes puts us through that old school of hard knocks. An Olympic trainer cannot be Mr. Nice Guy. If he's soft and easygoing with his young protégé, it will mean disappointment: no medal, no glory, no success; only groans as the crowd turns away after the gymnast falls off the balance beam, or the runner is lapped in the 1500 meter run, or the diver does a belly flop in the competition.

God trains us for excellence, but he isn't a heartless slavedriver. Though God places a yoke on our necks, it's a yoke of love. A teacher read to her class the text, "My yoke is easy . . ." (Matt. 11:29–30).

"Who can tell me what a yoke is?" she asked.

A boy replied, "A yoke is something they put on the necks of animals."

Then the teacher asked, "What is the yoke God puts on us?"

A little girl replied, "It's God putting his arms around our necks."

But when trials come crowding in, sometimes it doesn't feel like God is holding us. How do we prevent bitterness from rearing its ugly head? First, we realize God's yoke is a yoke of love. Second, we remind ourselves that God's allowing the trial for our highest good. Third, we decide to love this God and to accept the disciplines of one who was willing to face head-on the same tests we face.

LIFE FOCUS: Today thank God that he's training you to be the best you can be through his Spirit.

⚓ JUNE 7 ⚓

JAMES 1:13–15
TAKING RESPONSIBILITY

When someone is tempted, he shouldn't say that God is tempting him (James 1:13).

Sin doesn't creep up behind us and wipe us out in one fell swoop: "It happened too fast, God. I was just walking down the sidewalk, minding my own business, and suddenly, before I knew it, *wham!* The temptation overcame me, and I accidentally sinned." Nope.

As James explains, first I allowed myself to be caught up in some immoral desire. Then I allowed myself to be lured away from God's truth. Next, I put myself in a place of vulnerability, and finally, I fell flat on my face. The last thing on my mind was the stark fact that sin is the number one cause of death in our world.

A summer camp speaker tells of a gorgeous young girl at a youth camp. She was nicknamed "Shark Bait." It was a demeaning nickname for a girl who the boys described as sweet and seductive. Well, she baited her hook, all right. Several boys contracted syphilis from her that summer.

Adults may think smugly, "Irresponsible kids! Whatever's happened to the morals of today's young people?" But we are all capable of falling at any moment, and we must never forget it.

LIFE FOCUS: Sometimes we have the nerve to blame God for our falls, but God is incapable of sin, and he'll never tempt a person to do what his Son died to destroy.

⚓ JUNE 8 ⚓

James 1:16–18
God Isn't Fickle

The Father doesn't change like shifting shadows (James 1:17).

God is not the author of evil—he is the source of all good. James 1:17 reads, "Every good present and every perfect gift comes from above." Of course, we perceive most gifts as coming to us from people, not God. God does give us gifts through people, but did we expect an angel to appear and encourage us in our hour of need? Did we really think Christ would stage a special intergalactic appearance just for our benefit?

In this age, God usually uses people to express his love through, give his gifts through, and manifest his character through. The only problem is that we are fickle and he is not.

God is the creator of the heavenly lights: the stars and planets vary in brilliance, the moon waxes and wanes, and the sun casts shifting shadows. But God himself is never subject to variation or eclipse. His character does not change, and he exercises his will based upon eternal principles. It was out of the goodness of God's will that he chose to call out from the human masses a people to be his own very special possession. James and his Christian contemporaries were the first fruits of God's new orchard—the first specimens, the first children of God's family. They were the guarantee of the sure expansion of God's new kingdom which dwells in our very bodies.

Life Focus: You are greatly treasured by God today, and his tender compassion isn't unstable and fickle like ours.

⚓ JUNE 9 ⚓

JAMES 1:19–21
KEEP YOUR COOL

Everyone should be quick to listen, slow to speak, and should not get angry easily (James 1:19).

A person who can't stop talking makes a poor listener, and an angry talker is even worse. That's the trouble with big talkers—some won't listen, other talkers want equal time, conflicts develop, and bitter anger can result. We spew out words indiscriminately. We allow anger to grow and fester in our hearts. We may even stop our ears while declaring concern for those begging to be heard. To the person of anger, God says, "Don't be quick to get angry, because anger is typical of fools."

A little poem our grandparents used to quote says it pretty well:

A wise old owl sat in an oak,
The more he saw the less he spoke,
The less he spoke the more he heard,
Let's try to imitate that bird.

Sir Walter Raleigh writes, "Speaking much is a sign of vanity; for he that is lavish in words is a niggard in deeds. Restrain thy anger, hearken much, and speak little." If we were as ready to listen as we are to speak, perhaps we'd be scratching where people itch, instead of raising angry welts in all the wrong places. Our world could sure use more loving listeners.

LIFE FOCUS: When's the last time you sat and listened attentively while someone unloaded heartaches? Now's the time to try it.

⚓ JUNE 10 ⚓

Psalm 119:97–104
Becoming Bible-Literate

The person who continues to study God's perfect teachings that make people free and who remains committed to them will be blessed (James 1:25).

Some believe we live in a post-Christian era. That's debatable, but surveys do show that many are sadly lacking in Bible literacy. Some of the incidents reflecting this lack of Bible knowledge are amusing, but they should motivate us to teach the Bible to more people.

In New York City, a Sunday school teacher asked a child, "Who defeated the Philistines?" "If they don't play the Mets," the boy replied, "I don't keep track of 'em." In another classroom, a teacher asked, "Why do you suppose we no longer offer burnt offerings to God?" A pupil answered, "Air pollution?"

Of course, throughout the Bible are challenges to be thankful, but even many Christians are either not aware of this or they choose not to practice it. An elderly gentleman was invited to dinner in a home where giving thanks before dinner wasn't practiced. After watching the man bow his head before dinner and speak in hushed tones, the young son asked his mother, "What did Mr. Bryan just say to his plate?"

Because of the biblical famine among the Israelites before the captivity, the prophet Hosea writes: "How can the Lord feed them like lambs in and open pasture?

Life Focus: A commitment to God is a commitment to listen intently to him regularly. It's a commitment to encourage other believers in our lives to know God's book and do his Word.

⚓ JUNE 11 ⚓

EPHESIANS 5:8–13

A FAITH THAT WORKS

[A] person may say, "You have faith, but I do good things." Show me your faith apart from the good things you do. I will show you my faith by the good things I do (James 2:18).

Paul writes, "We know that people don't receive God's approval because of their own efforts to live according to a set of standards, but only by believing in Jesus Christ" (Gal. 2:16). In contrast, James writes, "You see that a person receives God's approval because of what he does, not only because of what he believes" (James 2:24).

On the surface, these verses appear to reflect a stark contradiction. For this reason, Martin Luther James' letter an epistle of straw. However, James seems to be fervently pointing out the difference between a true active faith and a faith that has mental knowledge without trust and commitment to Christ as Lord. He declares that even demons mentally acknowledge and tremble at truths about God, but this doesn't demonstrate saving faith. Machen states that it was as clear to Paul as it was to James that people who had been saved by faith could not continue to live unholy lives. Now there was a new nature within, brought by the indwelling Spirit of God.

James holds that those who are born of God are certain to resemble their Father. He also declares that one lone sin is enough to condemn us before a holy God. If James believed we can actually become godly, yet one sin is enough to ruin us, he had to believe that Christ's atonement is the only answer, and through that atonement comes the possibility of a godly life.

LIFE FOCUS: The reality of Christian faith is reflected through daily behavior, both in public and in private.

JAMES 1:22–25

LET YOUR WALK MATCH YOUR TALK

Do what God's word says. Don't merely listen to it (James 1:22).

A man wakes up and stumbles to the bathroom. He groans as he sees the tough stubble, the dark bags under his eyes, the hopeless tousle of greasy hair. Then, as we watch, he just shrugs his shoulders and shuffles back into the bedroom to dress for work. Imagine the stares and amused mutterings he'll receive from onlookers as he stumbles his way through the day looking like something that crawled out from under a rock.

We study God's Word; we underline it; we take notes on it; we even memorize famous passages. The Bible shows us how much we really need to clean up our act, but then we walk out into real life and dismiss it from our minds.

More than any other book in history, the Bible is a "how to" book that really works. But it doesn't work by osmosis; the instructions must be followed before desired results occur. One characteristic of Christians reared in the church is that we often know far more than we do. We pride ourselves on our exposure to seminars, Bible studies, sermons, and conferences, but we seem happily oblivious to the gap between knowing God's truth and living it out. It's those who intently study God's liberating Word and then try to practice it in the marketplace who shall be greatly blessed in their deeds.

LIFE FOCUS: A Christ-professed faith must be backed up by a Christ-possessed lifestyle. The person who has works but no faith is a lost philanthropist; and the person who claims faith but has no works is a hypocrite.

⚓ JUNE 13 ⚓

ISAIAH 50:4

A SPIRITUAL THERMOMETER

If a person thinks he is religious but can't control his tongue, he is fooling himself. That person's religion is worthless (James 1:26).

Did you know there's a way to take our spiritual temperature? Picture an old time doctor attending a patient. He usually examines the tongue and places a thermometer under it to check the temperature. A tongue check is also a way to see if someone is spiritually sick. If a person appears to be quite spiritual, and yet has little control over the mouth, this person's faith is vain and futile. It is crucial that we develop an open quietness of spirit. John Love, cofounder of the London Missionary Society, writes, "Stillness of spirit is like a canvas for the Holy Spirit to draw his various graces upon."

Uncontrolled talkers may intimidate others with their grandiose religious jargon and their ceaseless religious activity; but if you're around them long enough, you will begin to hear the caustic opinions and see the ugly habits by which they spiritually damage others right and left.

What, then, is pure genuine spirituality? It means controlling our words, caring for those in real need, remaining morally unstained. Our words are to be characterized by restraint, our works are to be characterized by compassion, and our will is to be characterized by moral purity—this necessitates personal discipline, outward love, and inner integrity. This is what it takes to be truly spiritual.

LIFE FOCUS: Do you just appear spiritual, or are you genuinely living out what God has begun inside you?

JAMES 2:1–4

DON'T PLAY FAVORITES

My brothers and sisters, practice your faith in our glorious Lord Jesus Christ by not favoring one person over another (James 2:1).

C.S. Lewis boarded a train after a long, tiring walk. A wealthy old lady in the first class compartment was startled by his unkempt appearance.

"Have you a first-class ticket?" she asked haughtily.

"Yes, Madam," Lewis replied gently, "but I'm afraid I'll be needing it for myself."

Snobbery's ugly, and snobbery is the result of prejudice. In the New Testament, partiality is expressed with a word which means giving special respect to others on the basis of their position, rank, popularity, or wealth, instead of intrinsic qualities. Etymologically, prejudice started out as a neutral word, simply meaning judgment formed beforehand. Yet so often did people form harsh judgments that the word became negative; now it invariably denotes unfair favoritism.

Shortly after the Civil War's end, a black man entered a fashionable church in Richmond, Virginia. At the appointed time, the man walked down the aisle and knelt at the altar to receive communion. Shock and anger rippled through the congregation. Suddenly a distinguished man stood, walked forward, and knelt beside him. Captured by his spirit, others followed him to the altar. The distinguished gentleman was Robert E. Lee.

LIFE FOCUS: Guard yourself from prejudice. Spiritual prejudice is the ugliest of all, because it's such a blatant contradiction of the very God it claims to represent.

JAMES 2:5–7
LIFTING THE DOWNTRODDEN

You show no respect to poor people (James 2:6).

Remember Robin Hood? Like James, Robin Hood detested the injustice and oppression of the rich. He beat them at their own game, and ended up taking some of their wealth and dispensing it to the poor.

In Deuteronomy 15, God actually decrees that the Hebrews make sure there are no poverty-stricken Hebrews. And God cries through Isaiah, "How can you crush my people, and grind the faces of the poor into the ground?" (Isa. 3:15). Many Scriptures testify to God's very special compassion for the poor and downtrodden. In some cases, He intervenes by protecting the defenseless, providing for the destitute, freeing the captive, and giving hope to the crushed.

Robin Hood did that too, but when he pointed at sin, he also had to point right back at himself. In order to aid the poor, he stole, killed, and deceived. God is the only legitimate "Robin Hood." He is the creator of humankind and is absolutely, unquestionably perfect. Therefore, when he takes the part of the needy, whatever he does in their behalf is unimpeachable, for his acts, as well as his motives, are always utterly pure and right.

LIFE FOCUS: Rich people as well as poor can be greedy and selfish. But God forbids that we Christians have that reputation. If God's heart breaks for the needy, how wrong is it for a child of God to hoard or fritter away that which the Lord heaps on us so generously?

⚓ JUNE 16 ⚓

James 2:12–13

Whom Sin Condemns, Mercy Wins

No mercy will be shown to those who show no mercy to others. Mercy triumphs over judgment (James 2:13).

One day I watched a beautiful woman being interviewed on a TV talk show. She described her experience of posing for *Playboy* magazine. Reflecting innocence, she smiled sweetly and declared a fervent love for God, exclaiming that the centerfold photos had set her free spiritually.

During the interview, the woman judged a reputable Christian leader a phony. Only God knew who was truly the phony at that moment. And here's where I must be very careful because my first impulse is to judge this woman and throw mercy out the window. But the warning of James 2:13 stops me cold.

Jesus said we would be judged by the standards we use to judge others. James underlines the teaching and then adds a curious phrase: Mercy triumphs over judgment. Jesus represented pure holiness and always stood for righteousness from the heart, but he was also known far and wide for his deep spirit of mercy. I think one of the toughest challenges in the Christian life is hating sin the way God hates it and still showing mercy in the face of it.

Life Focus: The greatest illustration of the balance between judgment and mercy would have to be Calvary: God's holiness required judgment, his love overflowed mercy, and God's Son reconciled the two. And God is the only and final judge.

⚓ JUNE 17 ⚓

JAMES 2:14–19

THE GREAT PRETENDERS

My brothers and sisters, what good does it do if someone claims to have faith but doesn't do any good things? Can this kind of faith save him? (James 2:14).

It is said that Adolf Hitler showed a tattered Bible to some deacons, declaring that he drew strength for his great work from the Word of God. But claiming faith in Christ and living without him is hypocrisy.

Speaking of hypocrisy, apparently even gentle dogs may become guilty of killing livestock. The killing is always done under cover of darkness, the marauding dog tries to tempt other dogs to take part. But the culprit is not above incriminating participants and the dog will assume during daytime hours an unusually genial and friendly air.

We are each capable, like that dog, of fooling others. Over and over the Bible emphasizes living out the life we profess. Jesus says, "So you will know them by what they produce" (Matt. 7:20). John writes, "We must show love through actions that are sincere, not through empty words" (1 John 3:18). Peter admonishes, "Live decent lives among unbelievers" (1 Peter 2:12). Jude condemns those who "use God's kindness as an excuse for sexual freedom" (1:4).

Absolutely anyone on earth can claim a faith in Christ they do not possess. Some seem to consider it a kind of macabre game to hoodwink folks into believing they're part of the family when all the while they may be "crucifying Jesus afresh, and putting him to an open shame."

LIFE FOCUS: Pious claims are nothing but a voice print, if they do not convert into footprints.

⚓ JUNE 18 ⚓

JAMES 2:21–26
FAITH COUNTS FOR RIGHTEOUSNESS

You see that a person receives God's approval because of what he does, not only because of what he believes (James 2:24).

These are James' strongest words as related to the faith/works issue. It is the closest he comes to preaching salvation by works. He chooses a few examples, one of which is Abraham's offering of his son as a human sacrifice.

In verse twenty-two, James writes, "You see that faith was at work with Abraham's actions, and by these actions the integrity of his faith was fully proved" (NEB). The word meaning ìto work withî brings out the point that Abraham's faith was assisting him by enabling him to perform deeds that were pleasing to God. And the word some translate "perfect" actually means to consecrate or make complete. So Abraham's faith was not made perfect through his deeds. This means, rather, that his faith reached its goal of completeness as it was activated in his daily life.

Thus, Abraham's trust in God found its highest expression in good deeds, and these deeds were a natural outflow of Abraham's growing friendship with God. He believed God actively, and it was counted for him as righteousness. You see, God has decreed that faith alone saves, but faith that saves is not alone; for just as body and spirit support each other in human life, faith and works support each other in spiritual life.

LIFE FOCUS: God can complete in us the work he's begun as we allow our faith to be activated through good works.

⚓ JUNE 19 ⚓

JAMES 3:1–2

TEACHERS ARE ACCOUNTABLE

Brothers and sisters, not many of you should become teachers. You know that we who teach will be judged more severely (James 3:1).

I like the way Moffatt translates verse one: "My brothers, do not crowd in to be teachers, knowing that we shall be judged with special strictness." There is a saying: "Those who can, do. Those who cannot, teach." The saying may be somewhat debatable on the secular front, but for teachers of the Bible, it should not even be a possibility. God demands that his instructors be growing examples of the lifestyle they teach.

Certainly the Scripture, "To whom much is given, much is required," should apply here. From these God grants knowledge, training, and experience, he expects wisdom, discipline, and consistency. We often do not hide and watch to find salvation's fruit in new Christians. We place the inexperienced saint in the spotlight; then believers cringe and unbelievers turn away as the professed Christian stumbles face-first into a moral pothole.

It is not in God's interest to end up with a world full of spiritual pygmies. That's why it is essential, as Arthur Pink writes, "not only that we begin right, but that we continue right, because a persevering attendance to Christ's instructions is the best proof of the reality of our profession."

LIFE FOCUS: Don't forget the special responsibility of setting an example you have if you present the Word of God to others.

⚓ JUNE 20 ⚓

JAMES 3:3–6
THE SMALL ORGAN THAT MOVES THE WORLD

The tongue is a small part of the body, but it can brag about doing important things (James 3:5).

A horse is controlled with a relatively small bit, a ship is steered with an extremely small rudder, and a mere spark may set a vast city aflame. Even so the tongue is small but can wreak great havoc. In 1871, a cow kicked over a single lantern somewhere in the city of Chicago. That flickering flame became a raging conflagration which very rapidly, consumed 17,450 buildings, covering an area of three square miles.

A paraphrase of James 3:6 reads, "The tongue is like a fire; it proves itself a very world of mischief, thus contaminating the whole body. It sets on fire the cycle of our natural life with a flame fed from hell."

Can words really be like a fire in their power to destroy? Hundreds of poison-pen letters were written to the inhabitants of Robin Hood's Bay, a village on the east coast of England. All were abusive and vulgar, accusing the townspeople of unspeakable atrocities including prostitution, infanticide, and incest. For long decades these notes caused great heartache, and the spreading hate forced some to even move away.

LIFE FOCUS: It only takes a few careless seconds to let our tongues run away from us. If we can consistently control our speech then we are mature, and we have the capability of controlling all our human desires.

JAMES 3:7–12

WHAT'S WORSE THAN STICKS AND STONES?

People have tamed all kinds of animals. . . . Yet, no one can tame the tongue (James 3:7–8).

How many people have died because of annihilating words long before their bodies ceased to function? On his deathbed, Aaron Burr told a friend that the words "They said . . . " have broken more hearts than any other. A young woman found dead by her own design had an unfinished suicide note containing just those two devastating words: "They said . . . "

When my little brother was a carefree six-year-old, he broke a man's window and my dad brought the colleague to our house for an apology. My brother sauntered up and Dad said, "Son, do you have something to say to Mr. Morrison?" Chris looked him over and with an impish grin blurted, "I'm gonna throw dirt on you, you monkey."

Slander is sort of like throwing dirt on someone. In fact, we use some vivid colloquialisms which bear witness to that: mudslinging, smearing, trashing—all synonyms for staining reputations.

There was a child who was learning the Lord's Prayer and tried to pray it in family devotions. As he came to the part about trespasses he said boldly, "And forgive us our trash baskets as we forgive those who trash basket against us." If he'd been referring to sins of the tongue, he couldn't have been more accurate.

LIFE FOCUS: As we've heard, the most untamable creature in the world has its den just in back of the teeth. And like a restless snake as it strikes or a death-dealing poison, we must realize our words can absolutely kill.

⚓ JUNE 22 ⚓

James 3:13–18
Two Kinds of Wisdom

Do any of you have wisdom and insight? Show this by living the right way with the humility that comes from wisdom (James 3:13).

We may think we're pretty clever and intelligent, but we should show by our good conduct that our deeds are done in the humility which wisdom produces. If we harbor a root of bitterness or envy in our hearts, we are being arrogant and defying the truth. This wisdom is counterfeit and is not from above. It comes from this world—from our lower nature. Wherever there's jealousy and rivalry, there is disorder and every vile deed. Whenever you see Christians competing for attention, affection, or position, realize there's a tragedy in the making. If they don't come to their senses and stop, heartbreak is usually left in its wake. Instead of fighting for what we think we should have, why not ask God for what is best? Often we have not because we ask not.

James 3:17 describes the wisdom from above as first pure-hearted, then peace-loving, reasonable, compliant, full of helpfulness and kind actions, free from partiality and insincerity. I would have expected a description full of high-powered words like, "Wisdom is knowledgeable, efficient, decisive, disciplined, and beyond all reproach." Instead, most of the words seem to profile a person who is, above all, flexible, merciful, and caring. I don't know about you but when it comes to this brand of wisdom, I've got a long ways to go.

Life Focus: Are you blindly competing with other Christians or has wisdom developed in you a desire to assist others in their pilgrimage?

⚓ JUNE 23 ⚓

MATTHEW 9:10–13

ORDINARY CHRISTIAN LIVING

God opposes arrogant people, but he is kind to humble people (James 4:6).

Sometimes we are tempted to over-spiritualize life. Oswald Chambers writes that drudgery is the touchstone of spiritual life. We look for great spiritual quests, but Christian experience is humbling, often carried out in shadowed routine. Jesus was so much in the ordinary world that religionists called him a glutton and a drunkard. Reality culminated in a Messiah shrouded in filth and congealed blood. At that point, his life seemed a failure to everyone else but his Father. But out of that sickening life tragedy burst glory beyond description.

In the book Run with the Horses, Peterson emphasizes the down-to-earth nature of true Christian experience when he says that biblical faith rejects fiercely and unhesitatingly any conduct or thinking that diminishes our ability to function as human beings in time and space. Biblical faith everywhere and always warns against siren voices that lead people away from specific and everyday engagement with the weather and politics, dogs and neighbors, shopping lists and job assignments. No true spiritual life can be distilled or abstracted out of this world of chemicals and molecules, paying your bills and taking out the garbage.

LIFE FOCUS: It is often when non-Christians see us stumbling through ordinary duties with an unconscious reflection of Christ that they are drawn to us like moths to a light.

⚓ JUNE 24 ⚓

PHILIPPIANS 3:7–11

KNOWING THE INVISIBLE

Come close to God, and he will come close to you (James 4:8).

It's hard to accept the fact that getting to know God is much different than getting to know another human. R.C. Sproul voices it well: "I rejoice in God's wisdom and in His everlasting power. It is his persistent invisibility that saddens me. Is there any one of us who claims Jesus as Lord whose heart does not beat with a passion to hear the voice of God? Who wouldn't sell every possession to be able to walk in a garden alone with Jesus? But the truth is that I can't see God. He leaves no footprints in the sand, no fingerprints on the doorknob, no lingering aroma of aftershave in the breeze."

A few have been granted fleeting glimpses of God. The people of Israel were terrified by a fiery, thunderous manifestation of God on Mount Sinai. Moses asked to see God and was only allowed to see his receding glory as Moses hid in the cleft of a boulder. Isaiah glimpsed a bit of the divine glory and screamed, "Woe is me. I am doomed—utterly destroyed! Every word I speak is sinful."

Yet God has given us himself in human form. We can know him as the sinless one who still hungered, thirsted, perspired, stressed out, and was tempted in all the ways we are. Sure it would be nice to see Jesus physically, to touch him, to converse with him for hours face to face. But God has willed that in this generation, it's better for us to get to know him in a different way. We know him through his written letter of love and through spirit-to-spirit fellowship available every hour.

LIFE FOCUS: Jesus said, "Blessed are those who haven't seen me but believe." Are you committed to intimacy with God, though it be more challenging than getting to know a flesh and blood human?

⚓ JUNE 25 ⚓

JAMES 4:11–12

SELF-APPOINTED JUDGES

Those who slander and judge other believers slander and judge God's teachings (James 4:11).

I grew up in a strict Christian environment, and it became easy for me to feel morally superior to other believers. It may be that some respected my moral discipline during those days, but I wonder if those same people felt genuinely loved by me.

I know a man whose first reaction usually seems to be a fault-finding negative criticism when he reads a book, meets a person, or hears a sermon. It's sad to see one with so much spiritual zeal, knowledge, and ability consumed with such a harsh attitude.

Oswald Chambers believed the average Christian tends to be critical, with a judging spirit that makes us hard and vindictive—finally leaving us with the flattering idea that we're spiritually superior. But every wrong thing we see in others, God locates in us, and every time we judge, we condemn ourselves.

We are not the gatekeepers and judges of who is genuine and godly in Christendom and who is not. We're just fallible brothers and sisters who should be lovingly helping each other through the eternal pilgrimage.

LIFE FOCUS: It's not only easy but somehow gratifying to judge and criticize others. That's one reason it's so insidious. Keep a guard over your attitude.

JAMES 4:13–16
DOES GOD PLAN OUR LIVES?

If the Lord wants us to, we will live and carry out our plans (James 4:15).

Does God have a sovereign life plan for each of his own, or is his will limited to how we should behave morally? Friesen's book *Decision-Making and the Will of God* is considered somewhat of a modern classic on the subject. Friesen's bottom line seems to be that though God has a moral will for each of us, he has no detailed blueprint for the events of our lives. We simply must use wisdom to figure what life choices might be best.

I can understand Friesen's frustration. He's fed up with the many ways we fabricate God's will to fit our own desires or discredit those around us: A preacher claims God's made a death threat unless contributors raise so many millions. A man tells a shocked woman friend that God has told him to marry her. A lazy Christian says God hasn't given her peace about serving anywhere in the church.

However, as I studied Friesen's book, I wondered if he's overreacted to the abuses. James mentions a geographical move—a real life event all too common in our day. Instead of telling Christians to simply use independent decision-making, James challenges us to sort out God's specific will, saying, "'If the Lord wants us to, we will live and carry out our plans.'" Many other Scriptures testify to or imply that God has a specific plan for Christians as they seek it out through wisdom.

LIFE FOCUS: Discovering God's specific will can be confusing at times, but that doesn't mean it doesn't exist.

JAMES 5:1–6

HOLDING MONEY WITH A LOOSE GRIP

The wages you refused to pay the people who harvested your fields shout to God against you (James 5:4).

James definitely didn't cater to the wealthy. He knew they have the same faults, problems, and dissatisfactions as any human in need of redemption. John D. Rockefeller had every possession a person could possibly desire, yet he said, "I have made many millions, but they have brought me no happiness." W.H. Vanderbilt moaned, "The care of two hundred million dollars is too great a load for any brain or back to bear. There is no pleasure in it."

In chapter five, James opens with six blistering verses heaping judgment upon the rich. What was it with James? Did he simply have a giant chip on his shoulder, a bitter urge to damn to eternal judgment the more affluent members of society? James may not have felt as much distaste for the rich as he felt compassion for the poor. He seemed to be feeling a gut-wrenching concern for the disadvantaged which expressed itself in an anguished reproach against the selfishness of some.

Jesus wasn't easy on the wealthy either, but perhaps Jesus and James would not outlaw wealth as much as attack the abuse or misuse of it. There is certainly nothing wrong with inheriting money, or winning money, or earning money. The primary issue, of course, is not whether individuals possess money, but whether it possesses them.

LIFE FOCUS: Remember, money is only a tool. It enables us to survive and, through us, it can also further God's work and bring hope to those who are without.

⚓ JUNE 28 ⚓

JAMES 5:7–11

WHAT'S SO GREAT ABOUT JOB?

The LORD asked Satan, "Have you thought about my servant Job? No one in the world is like him! He is a man of integrity: He is decent, he fears God, and he stays away from evil" (Job 1:8).

We would be hard pressed to find anyone in the Bible whom God praises more highly than Job. But there are also modern-day Jobs. I heard a testimony by a man who lost fourteen million dollars in one fell swoop. Then in the middle of fighting vicious lawsuits, the man's lawyers quit the case. On top of that, his wife got sick and his daughter had a nasty arm fracture. He choked back tears as he quoted victorious Bible verses he was clinging to through the hellish months.

In spite of a life devoted to others, Job faced the same tragic losses as thousands of other humans through the centuries. He learned that the sun and rain fall equally on the evil and the good. James never claimed that doers of the Word will receive special treatment or lead a charmed life. And Jesus said that when servants have obeyed the master, they should simply say, "There is no merit in our service. We have merely done our duty."

Paraphrased, James 5:11 reads, "You've heard of Job's steadfastness and you've seen what the Lord brought out of it and that the Lord is tender and merciful." We must always look to the end result a loving God is working to produce.

LIFE FOCUS: When your goodness seems rewarded with calamity, endure with patience. Your circumstances are not a sign of God's indifference or harshness. He still loves you just as much.

⚓ JUNE 29 ⚓

HEBREWS 13:12–16

PRAISING THROUGH CLENCHED TEETH

If any of you are having trouble, pray. If you are happy, sing psalms (James 5:13).

John Hyde, known by many as Praying Hyde, was a tremendously effective missionary in India. A great secret to his effectiveness was his spirit of prayer. He and his fellow-missionaries used a phrase for it: "Praising God through shut teeth." In other words, though our teeth may be clenched in pain or frustration as we face some hardship, we should continue to thank God anyway. Hyde exhibited the same attitude toward the people around him—always grateful, always encouraging, always bringing out their best side, not their worst.

During the Japanese occupation of China, missionary Darlene Deibler was separated from her husband and interned to a concentration camp. Despite torture and despicable conditions, like Hyde, Deibler learned the importance of a thankful heart. She would pray about some pressing problem or need and peacefully leave the result to God. Facing malnourishment, one day Deibler saw a guard with some bananas, and she longed for just one to satisfy her hunger. After praying about it, she should not have been shocked when a compound authority, impressed with her life, brought ninety-nine bananas and laid them in her cell.

One beautiful evidence of a committed heart is the ability to look up, even during the worst of times, and sing a psalm or thank God for his character. It's an act of the will.

LIFE FOCUS: God can give us a spirit of praise even when everything in our world seems to be going haywire.

⚓ JUNE 30 ⚓

James 5:13–18
Pray about Everything

Never worry about anything. But in every situation let God know what you need (Philippians 4:6).

There are some Christian sects who believe only formal, ritualized prayers should be used. They pray the prayers of famous or devout saints or quote from prayer books. There is nothing wrong with this. Some of these prayers express rich, deep thoughts and feelings which may be beyond our own ability to compose.

However, it's difficult to believe those who claim the Bible doesn't encourage conversational, original prayers. In James 5:13–18, the practical aspect of prayer is repeated over and over: "If you're having trouble, pray. . . . If you're sick, ask church leaders to pray. . . . Prayers in faith save the sick. . . . Prayers offered by God's approved are effective."

James reiterates that Elijah was human and ordinary like us, yet he prayed that it wouldn't rain and his prayer was answered. Three and a half years later, he prayed the drought would end, and it rained. This is very simple and straightforward. God wanted to punish an evil king and his followers, and Elijah prayed for a punishment according to God's will. When we pray in line with what God wants, it's that simple for us, too. God will act. The secret, of course, is to figure out what God wants to do, and with spiritual maturity comes added insight and wisdom into how God does things.

Life Focus: Pray today that God will give you increasing discernment in your prayers so you'll ask for those things he wants you to have.

JULY

Love Never Fails

⚓ July 1 ⚓

1 John 4:8–10

Believing God Loves You

"If your child asks you for bread, would any of you give him a stone? Even though you're evil, you know how to give good gifts to your children. So how much more will your Father in heaven give good things to those who ask him?" (Matthew 7:9,11).

I love my dad. He's certainly imperfect, but he cares. He asks, "How's the world treating you?" or "Is there anything I can do for you?" He sincerely believes in me: "That was quite an accomplishment, Steve;" "You can do it—I know you can;" "I appreciate who you are as a person and as a Christian."

I share my thoughts with God: "I know the Bible says you're the essence of love and you're my Father too, but with you it seems different. I fear you're really not the sort of God who cares about the minute details of one solitary life. I get the feeling that if I don't use the right words, you won't understand or respond—that if I tell you how scared, angry, or disillusioned I am, you will say, "Oh, get a life!" and turn away in anger or disgust.

Then, God, I read in your book that you are love personified, and I'm tempted to imagine that it's a different kind of love. It can't be the type of love that smiles and encourages and gives and protects and sacrifices. Then I read that you sacrificed your life on a hilltop for me. I read that since you gave up your very life for mine, you will also richly provide me with everything to enjoy (1 Tim. 6:17). That is love.

Prayer: Forgive me, Father, for imagining that human love can compete with yours. Give me a true realization of your love.

⚓ July 2 ⚓

Psalm 139:7–10

Living Life with God

Enoch walked with God; then he was gone because God took him (Genesis 5:24).

Brother Lawrence helped popularize the concept of practicing the presence of God. But, of course, living in God's companionship began with the first humans created. In fact, we read specifically of Enoch, a remarkable man, who walked in habitual fellowship with God. It seems as if the transition to heaven was no shocking jolt for Enoch. He was so intimate with Yahweh that he slipped from earth to heaven with barely a passing glance. The two planes of reality merged into one vast experience of knowing God.

Christians know that one becomes acquainted with God through prayer and Bible reading. But it's easy for these habits to become mechanical and tedious. What prevents boredom from setting in? Part of living in the Spirit is involving God in all the ordinary and extraordinary events of life. As we go through a day, events trigger emotions, questions, choices, a sense of need, or simple thankfulness and joy. We discuss these things calmly with God or, at times, we unleash a torrent of frustration and doubt. Daily life should consist of a constant give-and-take conversation with God. It involves a consistent consciousness that God is there and he will never leave us alone.

The "experts" tell us that the most intimate interpersonal level comes when individuals share meaningful experiences together. Enoch could have told them that centuries ago. Enoch lived with God.

Prayer: Father, show me how to involve you in my daily experiences.

⚓ July 3 ⚓

John 15:13–16
Jesus Loves Me, This I Know

Jesus loved his own who were in the world, and he loved them to the end (John 13:1).

It was shortly before Christ's arrest and crucifixion. These last hours were spent with eleven disciples. John 13–17 captures many things Jesus did and said during that time. Jesus washed their feet, and they shared a private Passover dinner. Over and over he mentioned his love for them. "I don't call you servants anymore," Jesus said, "I've called you friends" (John 15:15). He said he was about to lay down his life for them but assured them they wouldn't be alone; he'd send a helper, the Spirit of Truth. He was going to prepare a place for them, that they might be with him forever. Jesus prayed that, even in his absence, their joy would be abundant and fulfilling. He even prayed for us: "I'm not praying only for them. I'm also praying for those who will believe in me through their message" (John 17:20).

Jesus had some challenges for his followers, too. He urged them to remain in him and bear fruit. "Everyone will know that you are my disciples," Jesus said, "because of your love for each other" (John 13:35). The disciples were warned that the world would hate them, persecute them, even kill them, thinking they were doing God a service. With profound sadness, Jesus said, "The time is coming, and is already here, when all of you will be scattered." Yet instead of a sharp rebuke, he tenderly added, "I've told you this so that my peace will be with you. In the world you'll have trouble. But cheer up! I have overcome the world" (John 16:31–33).

Prayer: Jesus, as I glimpse a fresh perspective of your deep warmth for your own, it reassures me that you care about me, every day, every hour.

⚓ JULY 4 ⚓

2 CORINTHIANS 4:11–18
IS GOD SADISTIC?

Our suffering is light and temporary and is producing for us an eternal glory that is greater than anything we can imagine (2 Corinthians 4:17, PH).

"You ask how I can allow suffering," says Yahweh, "if I am truly a loving God. You are too finite to understand all the reasons, but listen to a few.

"Suffering began as a result of that initial choice for sin; and much earthly suffering comes of sinful roots. When souls become evil, they injure one another.

"One of your own has said that pain is my megaphone to rouse a deaf world, and it is true. I may use it to shatter the illusion that all is well and to drive a conceited, self-sufficient person toward me.

"I take great pleasure in seeing my created beings gradually take on the character of my Son. At times I use suffering to prove the godliness of an individual and to aid in the forming of Christlikeness.

"There are my own special trophies—those who trust in me and exhibit a sweet humility in spite of loss, injury, disease, or persecution. These rare jewels will be recompensed a thousand times in eternity. If I were to describe the ways, some may even wish for earthly testings that they might reap the benefits.

"My child, know that I hurt with you. Some day there will be a new order where there will be no more mourning, crying, or pain. Live in anticipation of that new order."

PRAYER: God, teach us to trust your love even through tears.

⚓ July 5 ⚓

Galatians 5:13–15
The New Law of Love

Love never does anything that is harmful to a neighbor. Therefore, love fulfills Moses' Teachings (Romans 13:10).

A lawyer, trying to stump Jesus, asked him which was the greatest commandment in God's Law. Jesus answered that it was wrapped up in loving God with all one's heart and loving one's neighbor as oneself. The whole law depends on this love factor.

Jesus' law of love simplifies following God. The Spirit of God enters a life, shedding his love abroad in the heart. The spiritual Christian becomes an individual whose thoughts, words, and actions are initiated and guided by the perimeters of unconditional love. Therefore, love is not a painstaking, failure-riddled effort to accomplish hundreds of divine dos and don'ts—life becomes an exciting outflow of the kinds of words and actions which love motivates. If Christians are guided by God's love, they will automatically find themselves obeying God's standards.

We can't overestimate the importance of love in God's plan for life. Love is meant to be the great distinguishing trademark of the Christian. Occasionally a believer is asked, "By the way, are you a Christian?" Maybe a smile, a word of encouragement, or a caring act prompts the question. We should be so characterized by love that, simply by observation, we are recognized as followers of Jesus.

Prayer: God, thank you for the new law of love that simplifies my walk with you.

⚓ July 6 ⚓

Psalm 73:21–25

Those Who Love Him

Love the Lord all you godly ones! (Psalm 31:23).

Yahweh is not a sniveling, lovelorn deity, pining away for love and pouting or erupting in a divine temper tantrum if we don't respond. God is entirely self-contained; he needs nothing from us. Yet for a reason we don't understand, he wants our love and it brings him pleasure.

Over and over in Scripture, the one who loves God is singled out. Romans 8:28 reads, "We know that all things work together for the good of those who love God." First Corinthians 2:9 reads, "No eye has seen, no ear has heard, and no mind has imagined the things God has prepared for those who love him." And James assures us that a crown of life is promised for those who love him (James 1:12).

Jesus had recently risen from death. At dawn one morning, he appeared on the seashore and began grilling some fish for several disciples. After breakfast, there was conversation. He asked, "Simon, son of John, do you love me more than the other disciples do?" Peter answered yes, but Jesus posed the question two more times. Then he said, in effect, "Yes, Peter, you love me, but feeding my sheep may cost your very life. Are you willing?"

And, in the end, he was.

Prayer: Jesus, I know you may not require the ultimate sacrifice from me, but give me this love of ultimate willingness, all for your pleasure.

⚓ July 7 ⚓

1 Samuel 15:17–23

Facing Up to Lovelessness

We know that we have passed from death to life, because we love other believers. The person who doesn't grow in love remains in death (1 John 3:14).

Most of us are great rationalizers. Take, for example, our explanation of attitudes that are wrong.

"That wasn't anger—it was righteous indignation."

"Sure, I'm irritable; I had a lousy day at work."

"You say I'm always hurting people—hey, I just tell it like it is."

"I don't care if I'm out of line; she deserved it."

We need to come clean with God—no more rationalizing, no more fooling ourselves, just recognizing those attitudes and words for what they are.

It seems as if the home tends to be the greatest testing ground for our Christianity. There we have no one to impress, so we relax and expose our true selves. The pain family members inflict on one another is incredible. Police officers tell us that, in a physical sense, domestic strife is always the most difficult to handle and the most vicious of violent crimes.

It all starts with a word—a sharp, impatient word. Until we learn to be controlled by love, our anger will eat away at the joy in our homes and beyond. Lack of love should be recognized for what it is: sin. God must be allowed to change our hearts and to heal the wounds we've caused.

Prayer: God, I've learned to be a rather skillful rationalizer. Help me to face up to it when I'm wrong.

⚓ July 8 ⚓

2 Samuel 9:1–10

Love Is Something You Do

Dear children, we must show love through actions that are sincere, not through empty words (1 John 3:18).

Do you remember your first public testimony?: "I love the Lord and I want to go all the way with him!" You were floating on clouds and you wanted everyone to know how you felt.

Then you woke up one morning and felt nothing toward God. You prayed, "God, what's going on? Quick, give me back those waves of emotion I used to feel. I can't go on without those terrific feelings of love."

God sends the overflowing emotions at times, but he may not be as sentimental as we make him out to be. Nowhere in the Bible does he press us to emote toward him. Love is described as an active thing—we prove our love for him by keeping his commands.

It almost seems irreverent to say it, but it's easier to love the visible brother than it is to love the invisible God, and the former will testify to and enhance the latter: "People who don't love other believers, whom they have seen, can't love God, whom they have not seen" (1 John 4:20).

You may say, "I'm in a terrible state. I don't even think I can love my fellow Christians." But "we know that we love God's children when we love God by obeying his commandments" (1 John 5:2). Begin by simply reading God's Word and obeying it as fully as you can. Don't try to work up your emotions to accomplish great works of love. The habit of love will gradually develop out of a lifestyle of obedience.

Prayer: Lord, help me not to live by feelings, to choose to love you by a decision of my will.

⚓ July 9 ⚓

Romans 15:1–3

Love: Not a Dread but a Privilege

Don't be concerned only about your own interests, but also be concerned about the interests of others (Philippians 2:4).

I grew up in a hard-working family with three other brothers. We were each assigned daily jobs plus a long list of chores on Saturday mornings. When it came to chores, I sometimes crawled around looking like a grieving basset hound. I loved myself and my freedom too much and those around me not nearly enough.

However, when our focus is turned outward instead of inward, our efforts toward others change from drudgery to privilege. Jesus said that if we do something for even the least esteemed individual, it's as if we do it for him. So our focus is not only outward but it is directed to Christ himself. To run his errands and exhibit his truth becomes not forced, but willingly volunteered. We are responding to sheer grace.

Under her plate one morning, a mother found a bill made out by her son Bradley, age eight. "Mom owes Brad: for running errands, 25 cents; for being good, 10 cents; for taking piano lessons, 15 cents; for extras, 5 cents. Total: 55 cents."

Brad's mother smiled but made no comment. At dinner he found the bill under his plate with 55 cents and another slip of paper. The paper read, "Bradley owes mom: for nursing him through chicken pox and measles, 0; for meals, 0; for taking care of him, 0. Total: 0."

Is your love more like Bradley's or more like his mother's?

Prayer: God, I recognize my need to think more about helping others than helping myself.

⚓ July 10 ⚓

2 Thessalonians 3:14–15

"Truthing" in Love

Brothers and sisters, if a person gets trapped by wrongdoing, those of you who are spiritual should help that person turn away from doing wrong. Do it in a gentle way (Galatians 6:1).

Praying Stephen was his derogatory nickname, given by fellow students at a Bible school in Germany. Stephen felt it was his duty to confront every sin he saw committed among the students. One way he did this was through public prayer. At school prayer meetings, Stephen prayed long and loudly, raking unnamed students over theological coals. When he finished praying, students felt summarily whipped with words. Stephen never realized that his methods of confrontation were not leading anyone to repentance.

We Christians are generally poor at confrontation, and matters of church discipline are often handled shoddily or not at all. Of course, the secular world doesn't enjoy confrontation any more than we do and probably doesn't handle it any better. But that doesn't take us off the hook.

It seems as if much of confrontation's possible success relates to questions we ask before we confront. T. Whalin suggests questions like: Why am I really confronting? Is God directing me to confront and have I earned the right? Is my own life in order in this area? Do I have my facts right and have I tried to understand why this happened? Have I planned what I'll say and have I considered the consequences?

Prayer: Lord, make me more willing both to confront others and to accept reproof myself. I know humility and compassion are just as important in both roles.

⚓ July 11 ⚓

Acts 2:42–47

Moving Past Small Talk

Finally, everyone must live in harmony, be sympathetic, love each other, have compassion, and be humble (1 Peter 3:8).

Imagine that you enter a new church. A few people grin, ask your name, tell you they're glad you're visiting. In the weeks following, you meet more people who are friendly but never go beyond the "Nice weather," "What do you do for a living?" lines. You attend that church for years—going to services, socials and Sunday school. You talk and laugh with these people yet never feel you know them in a personal sense.

How is Christian fellowship reflected in an authentic, practical way? Much true fellowship goes beyond church meetings and social gatherings. Maybe it's reflected when believers pray for each other over a sink of dirty dishes; when someone spends fifteen minutes on the phone laughing and talking with a lonely person; when one mails an encouraging note to another; when several enjoy a conversation about Jesus or a Scripture passage; when one fixes a brother's car or another cooks a meal for a family in crisis. This unique bond is an experience that, for whatever reason, many starve for and few experience.

Jesus said, "'Everyone will know that you are my disciples because of your love for each other'" (John 13:35). Everyone? Apparently the secular world is longing so much for real love that even the "private" love between Christians will be detected by their searching eyes. The Holy Spirit can use this love to draw them longingly toward Christ.

Prayer: Father, there are caring Christians out there. As I meet them, make me willing for closeness.

⚓ July 12 ⚓

Hebrews 3:12–14
A Non-Isolationist Policy

We should not stop gathering together with other believers, as some of you are doing. Instead, we must continue to encourage each other even more as we see the day of the Lord coming (Hebrews 10:25).

When we feel abandoned or depressed or when we're slipping spiritually, we have a tendency to run away from people. We think, if I can just get alone with God, maybe I'll get back where I ought to be—back where the good feelings are. But our isolation can thrust us into a spiral of self-pity. Feeling sorry for ourselves, we tell all to Jesus, but when we finish pouring out our woes, we may feel worse than when we started.

I love solitude and it's indispensable to nurture aloneness with God, but in certain cases it may be better to find a caring friend. Reuben Welch believes that when we're hassled, lonely, or sad, we need Jesus, but we also need someone to be Jesus to us. In a real sense, Christians are to offer the smile, the comfort, the very embrace of Christ to one another.

It's easy at times to become so self-contained and individualized that we forget how much we need others. We think, humans always let humans down, so now it's just Jesus and me. That's fine, but right now we're in a world swarming with billions of other humans, and the Christian life is about people, compassion, and mission. We can be sure Jesus will be with us through it all.

Prayer: Lord, when I'm down I want to allow others to be Jesus to me instead of wallowing in discouragement.

⚓ July 13 ⚓

Luke 10:38–42

Learning to Listen

Be happy with those who are happy. Be sad with those who are sad (Romans 12:15).

A friend told me about a high schooler who came to him in high anxiety. The highschooler pleaded: "Ken, I've got this giant problem. If I don't get some help right away, I'm gonna go crazy."

Ken said, "Come to my office in half an hour and I'll make time to talk to you."

So the student showed up at the office and poured out his heart nonstop. All Ken did was insert profound things like "Uh-huh" and "Really!"

Finally, the student took a breath and Ken opened his mouth to utter some words of wisdom. But the student blurted out, "Thanks a lot, Ken! You've really helped me. I think I understand what God wants me to do." With that, the student cheerfully bounded out of the office, leaving Ken with his mouth still poised.

This world is crying for listeners. If anyone's ever told you you're a good listener, it was a great compliment. In our day-to-day lives, we need to learn to look directly into that man's eyes and sense what he's feeling, to really listen to that woman, and identify with that hurting kid. We don't need to prepare gems of insight that will solve all problems. Maybe what a lot of people need is simply a sympathetic ear.

Prayer: Jesus, help me listen without feeling the need to always straighten people out or pour forth gems of wisdom.

⚓ July 14 ⚓

Matthew 20:25–28
Unconscious Usefulness

Don't be selfish; don't live to make a good impression on others. Be humble, thinking of others as better than yourself (Philippians 2:3 TLB).

Especially in the Western world, we tend to be very pragmatic. We think in terms of how useful and productive we are; we thrive on praiseworthy achievement. Many of us Christians live as consciously devoted to God's work. Oswald Chambers writes that the mature stage, however, is unconscious caring, like the life of a child: "We should become so abandoned to God that the consciousness of being used never enters in. When we are consciously being used as broken bread and poured out wine, there is another stage to be reached where all consciousness of ourselves and what God is doing through us is eliminated."

Ruth Graham follows up on this idea with a personal observation: "The people who have affected my life most deeply and influenced it for good have seldom, if ever, been aware of the fact. On the other hand, people who think themselves a blessing seldom are. Self-conscious goodness is a contradiction of terms."

Sure there are good feelings associated with doing for others. Enjoy the good feelings and encouragement you may receive, but don't chalk up your good deeds, don't expect praise, and try not to do things in a self-righteous, self-serving way. The more habitual and natural the lifestyle of love becomes, the less self-conscious it will be.

Prayer: God, don't even show me when my life has blessed someone. You take the honor; I can't be trusted with that knowledge.

⚓ July 15 ⚓

John 13:21–26
Tears and Touching

Everyone cried a lot as they put their arms around Paul and kissed him. The thought of not seeing Paul again hurt them most of all (Acts 20:37–38).

We live in a strange secular culture. It's acceptable to go to bed with a new acquaintance, but even patting a child on the back may send up molestation alarms. Women are expected to cry at any emotional occasion but if men shed tears, they're suddenly wimps. Males do not kiss, embrace, or walk arm-in-arm, as is common in some European and Asian countries, but women can kiss almost anyone without raised eyebrows.

Some of our guidelines are legitimate. Still, it is sad that babies and dogs sometimes seem the only creatures safe to hug, and we tend to shed more tears in dark movie theaters than we do for humans in the theater of real life.

Jesus did something unthinkable one day. He reached out his hand and actually touched a leper. A leper was considered one of the most despicable outcasts in society. If one was even glimpsed by another person, the leper was to scream, "Unclean! Unclean!" Rocks would fly. If the leper didn't flee, he'd be killed. But Jesus touched a leper and risked being stoned as a carrier of the disease.

Maybe it's time for us to risk a tear or a touch for someone who really needs it. Are you willing to take that risk?

Prayer: Jesus, you were never too macho or inhibited to shed a tear or hug a human being. Let me be more like you.

⚓ July 16 ⚓

Hebrews 12:1–2
A Unique Race

We wouldn't put ourselves in the same class with or compare ourselves to those. . . . Certainly, when they measure themselves by themselves and compare themselves to themselves, they show how foolish they are (2 Corinthians 10:12).

The speaker was dynamic: "The Christian life is the greatest race! We must all press toward the mark. Christ wasn't a loser; the Apostle Paul wasn't a quitter. They were winners. Are you striving for the prize today? There's a golden crown waiting for you if you're a winner."

For all his enthusiasm, the speaker missed a vital distinctive of the Christian race—our race is not vicious comparison or blind competition; we help one another reach the finish line. Our joy is in assisting as many as possible to win.

Reuben Welch tells about a college class that topped off their course with an outing: a three-mile hike followed by a picnic. But, alas, the slower students got left behind by the faster ones. A few never made it to the picnic. Sadly, this was a class on group and interpersonal relations. The class decided to try again, and this time they made some new rules—it was everybody go or nobody go. This time they all made it to their destination.

Some of us are so busy competing and comparing ourselves to other believers that we've forgotten what words like support, challenge, and encourage mean in this unique race in which everyone can win.

Prayer: Father, thanks that we can all be winners in your race. Help me to help others win.

⚓ July 17 ⚓

John 4:7–29
Taking Time to Talk

If you give some of your own food to feed those who are hungry and to satisfy the needs of those who are humble, then your light will rise in the dark, and your darkness will become as bright as the noonday sun (Isaiah 58:10).

The day had been frantic and exhausting. Already tired, he'd just preached his heart out to hundreds of teens. Now, as the auditorium cleared, he headed thankfully for the exit. Suddenly a raspy voice called out. He turned, intending to put the person off.

A huge figure stood there—long, stringy hair, severe acne, scattered whiskers, and folds of flesh bulging out in all the wrong places. Reaching out a hand, the person said, "Hi, I'm Kathy. Do you have a few minutes?"

He nodded numbly and, for the next half hour, she poured out a tragic story of family turmoil. Finally she said, "You're probably wondering why I look like this. Well, I have this disease and the doctors think that male hormones might help."

Before parting that night, the two cried together and prayed desperately.

A couple years later, at another convention, an attractive young lady greeted the man, "Remember me? I'm Kathy!"

After the initial shock, there were excited hugs. Then she said, "Things are a lot better at home, and my health is improved. Thank you for caring and praying with me that night. You'll never know how much it meant."

He breathed a prayer of thanks. She never knew how close he came to sending her away.

Prayer: Lord, let me not think I'm too busy for those in need.

⚓ July 18 ⚓

Acts 7:54–60
Miracle of Forgiveness

When people verbally abuse us, we bless them. When people persecute us, we endure it (1 Corinthians 4:12).

It's amazing how many movies focus on the theme revenge. The movies sell because, vicariously, we feel a deep sense of satisfaction when the despised villain is dealt his own treatment in kind. In a sense, justice is a legitimate form of avenging evil, but Jesus instructs his own: "Love your enemies. Do good to those who hate you, and pray for those who persecute you."

Corrie Ten Boom tells of the incredible hate she felt as she saw, well after war's end, a guard who had shared some responsibility for her sister's death in a Nazi concentration camp. Ten Boom knew the bitterness would eventually ruin her relationship with God, so with all the determination she possessed, she prayed for love. Then she forced her feet to move in the German's direction. It was not until she reached out her hand to the surprised man that the hate was replaced by a spirit of forgiveness. Ten Boom explained to the man why she could forgive him; and out of what had been mutual animosity, a friendship grew. Eventually this former Nazi gave his life to Christ.

"Don't take revenge," says God the Blameless. "Let God's anger take care of it."

Prayer: Jesus, convince my stubborn heart that since you've forgiven me so freely, I must also forgive.

⚓ July 19 ⚓

1 Corinthians 13:1–7
Romance and Bedrock Love

Love never stops being patient, never stops believing, never stops hoping, never gives up. Love never comes to an end. (1 Corinthians 13:7–8).

The media overload of glorifying romantic love is mind-boggling. The vast majority of pop/rock music deals with romantic topics. Moreover try counting the ads, magazine stories, novels, TV shows, and movies centered around a romantic or sexual theme. Is it possible that our overemphasis on deceptive or unstable indicators of genuine love is at least partly to blame for marriage relationships that are manipulative, fickle, and over-emotionalized?

Romance is like the delicious icing on a cake, but it must not be confused with the foundational stuff that holds a relationship together. Romance alone cannot make marriages permanent. Frederick Buechner decries this overblown sentimental romanticism as a feeling that comes and goes like the pink haze it is. It may overlay a relationship with doubts and unreal expectations, undercutting its potential for spontaneous, unself-conscious growth in the reality of daily life and interaction. It seems as if romanticism should be balanced within the friendship-building experience of mutually shared activities of many kinds. When the infatuation ebbs, it's the solid rock friendship of loyalties and realistic intimacy that will prove unshakable in the long haul.

Prayer: Father, I pray that I wouldn't contribute in any way to the misconceptions of lasting love in our society. Help me balance romance with an intimate, developing friendship.

⚓ JULY 20 ⚓

DEUTERONOMY 15:7–11

ALL IN THE FAMILY

Whenever we have the opportunity, we have to do what is good for everyone, especially for the family of believers (Galatians 6:10).

I left a pastoral position is Texas and flew out to Los Angeles. I'd been hired to serve on program staff at a camp in the San Bernardino mountains, after which I planned to complete my seminary training in Los Angeles. Most of my belongings remained in Houston; there was simply no way to store them at the camp.

If you know about camps, you're aware they can't afford to pay much. At the close of the summer, I didn't even have enough extra money for air fare back to Houston. A friend at the camp became aware of my situation and you'll never guess what he decided to do. He actually paid my air fare to Houston as well as his own. Then he helped pack the moving van and shared the driving time on the hot, grueling trip back to Los Angeles.

I was amazed at my friend's act. Seldom had I known anyone to give so generously—not out of his abundance but in spite of his own need. It reminded me of the impoverished widow Jesus praised for her "reckless" giving. Taylor states that giving is to our great benefit: "It doesn't make you a saint or martyr to give. In giving you are simply reflecting God's image—he who gave everything. Miserliness in all forms, monetary and emotional, diminishes us. The more we keep the less we have. And the less we are."

PRAYER: Lord, make me willing to give what I cannot keep to gain what I cannot lose.

⚓ July 21 ⚓

Proverbs 19:18
Tough Love

Brothers and sisters, in the name of the Lord Jesus Christ we order you not to associate with any believer who doesn't live a disciplined life and doesn't follow the tradition you received from us (2 Thessalonians 3:6).

A friend of mine is a wife and a mother of four. When I asked her for her insights on the subject of love, she thought about it for a few days, then responded, "You know, I think sometimes Christian love has to be tough."

I smiled, because just looking at her, one wouldn't think of toughness. She's petite and cute and soft-spoken, always ready to joke.

"My stepdaughter was an older teen living at home," she explained. "I tried to lay down some rules, but my husband wouldn't back me up. Things finally became unbearable. The girl left the house in a mess, came in at all hours of the night, basically acting as if she were living in a hotel. She'd totally rejected our Christian way of life. At last I had to tell my husband, 'I'm sorry but it's either me or your daughter. Either help me enforce the guidelines with her or I'm going to have to leave. I can't handle this.'"

Though her husband began backing her up, the stepdaughter rebelled and left home. It can't be promised that tough love will always result in reconciliation or reformation, but nonetheless, sometimes it's the only way to go. Don't be afraid to exercise it if a situation demands the firmness tough love entails.

Prayer: Father, when I have to exercise tough love, please give me a Christlike balance between toughness and love.

⚓ July 22 ⚓

Luke 14:12–14
Showing Hospitality

Don't forget to show hospitality to believers you don't know. By doing this some believers have shown hospitality to angels without being aware of it (Hebrews 13:2).

Dave, a former housemate of mine, wouldn't classify himself as a spiritual giant. He's simply a guy who cares about people.

Once, Dave met a man who was down on his luck, roaming our area on a job search, but running short on funds for food and hotel. Dave invited him to spend a few nights with us until the man headed back to his waiting family in Oregon.

Several months later, a friend was laid off from his physician's assistant job. Dave invited him to stay at our place for several weeks until he found another job.

Then Dave met a guy who'd been thrown out of his house. The man stayed with us while he tried to reconcile with his wife.

Being a single man, doesn't stop Dave from having people over to dinner. He's not a bad chef, but his big goal isn't four star food and a spotless place. He just wants his guests to relax and enjoy themselves.

Don't let petty fears keep you from entertaining people. Your hospitality will cheer up and encourage those around you.

Prayer: Lord, teach me how to be hospitable by giving me opportunities to practice it.

⚓ July 23 ⚓

James 3:2–12

Practicing Speech Awareness

Sin is unavoidable when there is much talk, but whoever seals his lips is wise (Proverbs 10:19).

The average person engages in approximately thirty conversations a day, which amounts to about 25,000 words for a male and 30,000 for a female. This represents approximately one-fifth of a person's lifetime. For most of us, there's no activity that's easier to do and can do more good or more damage than our speech.

Personally, I'm not a renowned conversationalist. I love to sit and talk with friends or family, but when it comes to non-stop, spontaneous small talk with strangers or acquaintances at gatherings, I'm not the life of the party. I'm a rather quiet person, and in some circles a quiet person may be viewed as snobbish or boring.

At times I've wished I could impress people by always knowing what to say and exactly how to say it with charm and wit. Lately, though, I've been wondering if I shouldn't be content with my personality. Sure, it would be great to never be at a loss for words, but outgoing people may struggle more than I with letting the wrong words slip out.

It's important for all of us to remember the principle of speech awareness—developing the habit of sifting our words through the Holy Spirit's grid of purity, kindness, and edification. If we're walking in the Spirit, speech awareness will prevent the careless flow of words we sometimes regret.

Prayer: Jesus, help me to think before I spout off words I may regret.

⚓ July 24 ⚓

Romans 15:1–6

Fight Spiritual Wet Blanketism

Knowledge makes people arrogant, but love builds them up (1 Corinthians 8:1).

A bubbly new Christian joins the church. She keeps saying things like, "Jesus has filled my life with happiness. He's taken away all my problems" and, "Isn't our pastor the greatest?"

Older saints nod their heads knowingly and mutter, "We'll see if she's whistling the same merry tune six months down the road. Wait 'til she learns the truth about things."

Then the new Christian testifies at a meeting, "I ran out of gas yesterday and God sent along this guy to help me. Praise the Lord!"

Older saints smile wearily and say, "How simplistic can you get?"

But we are all in the same boat—we were all once lost and were beside ourselves at being found in Christ. "To smugly distance ourselves from this," says John Fischer, "is to lose all sense of compassion for my kind . . . to lose something of myself, for though I am found, much in my experience remains lost and found on a daily basis."

Being realistic, we find that pastors are fallible, that Christians gossip, and that certain church folks cause constant friction. There is no perfect church, and all saints are sinners. Sure, we should be realistic, but it's tragic if we allow our realism to destroy the freshness of the life Christ brings. Our cynicism, and our deadly spirit of judgment can hamper much that the Holy Spirit wants to do.

Prayer: God, keep me from stifling the Spirit's work in others' lives. Keep my Christianity fresh and compassionate.

⚓ July 25 ⚓

James 2:1–9

Labels Are for Products, not People

My brothers and sisters, practice your faith in our glorious Lord Jesus Christ by not favoring one person over another (James 2:1).

We like to smack labels on people; to depersonalize, categorize, slip them into tight little slots: "Oh, those _______ are a bunch of ignorant hicks;" "Those shiftless ______ are always lazy;" "Yeah, you let those _______ in and they'll ruin your neighborhood."

And we like to label one another: "You never give a rip about anyone but yourself" or "You always blow it. Why can't you do things right for once?"

Welch believes that one trouble with that way of thinking is that it locks the object of our labels into fail mode. It's almost impossible not to fail when someone is continually communicating, "You can't do it. You're a failure. You'll never amount to anything."

A second problem with the labeling habit is that it's dishonest. We're not facing up to our own failures and weaknesses; we're too busy pointing the finger at everyone else.

But you ask, "Aren't you being a little over-sentimental? Whatever happened to telling it like it is?" I have news for you. Family, friends, and strangers are all sensitive. Love says, "I won't stick you into my thoughtless labeled slot. I will treat you as a unique and valuable human being. And if at some point I forget, please remind me of who you are."

Prayer: Father, help me be impartial and label-free in relation to people of all backgrounds.

⚓ July 26 ⚓

Philippians 2:3–8

Loving the Unlovely

Don't be arrogant, but be friendly to humble people. Don't think that you are smarter than you really are (Romans 12:16).

Nobody paid much attention to Frankie. He was cross-eyed and somewhat mentally retarded. Frankie helped his father do custodial work at the church. I remember the glow in Frankie's eyes one day when I invited him along for a milkshake. It was nothing really, but years later, his dad told me Frankie still remembered the milkshake.

Sarah is overweight and her mind doesn't work quite right, but I'm glad she's in the young adult Sunday school class I teach. She's the most faithful attender. Occasionally, when I ask her a Bible question, she freezes up and stark fear rises in her eyes. But when she blurts out a comment or correct response, the praise heaped on her brings a momentary gleam to her eyes. The other day she lugged cupcakes and drinks to Sunday school and we all celebrated her birthday.

A woman I know spent years caring for her father-in-law in her home. When she bathed him, he cursed her; and when she cleaned up his bedwetting, he never thanked her. The old man ransacked the refrigerator, wandered away and got lost, caused no end of trouble, yet this woman faithfully cared for him, making light of his antics instead of resigning to bitterness.

Is there a person in your world who some may consider unlovely? God may be calling you to that very person.

Prayer: Jesus, you spent time with ordinary people, and even outcasts felt comfortable with you. I want to be like you.

⚓ July 27 ⚓

Matthew 6:1–4

Loving without Fanfare

David asked, "Is there anyone left in Saul's family to whom I can show kindness for Jonathan's sake?" (2 Samuel 9:1).

Ernest Shackleton is known for exploring the Antarctic. In his book, he describes a crisis moment for an exploring party. They had been isolated for days in a blizzard. The rationed food was almost exhausted and the situation was desperate. In the middle of the night, Shackleton sensed a stealthy movement and opened his eyes. It was a terrible moment as he glimpsed one of his trusted friends reach over and open the biscuit bag of the next man. But instead of stealing, the man added a biscuit to it from his own bag.

A biographer writes that Lincoln was "a man who was always doing merciful things stealthily, as men do crimes." Jesus said that when we do good, we shouldn't let our left hand know what our right hand is doing. Our hearts are simply too deceitful to do good publicly in a humble, disinterested way. There is something in us that wants praise and recognition. But when we garner an ounce of glory, gallons of praise are stolen from God.

There's a Christian in Oregon whom God has blessed financially. He has no degree in theology and he's never filled a pulpit. But God has used him to sponsor over fifty evangelistic crusades all over the world. Because of his heart for God, lay leaders are being trained in Brazil, pastors are being taught in Africa, and plans for a Bible college in mainland China are forming. Few will ever know this man's name—he is one who does merciful things stealthily, as unto the Lord.

Prayer: Jesus, you who are always finding new ways to love, please give me the same creative compassion.

⚓ July 28 ⚓

Isaiah 10:1–3

Freaks or Special Angels?

Defend weak people and orphans. Protect the rights of the oppressed and the poor. Rescue weak and needy people. Help them escape the power of wicked people (Psalm 82:3–4).

The movie *Elephant Man* is a true story about John Merrick, a grossly deformed man who was featured in English circus sideshows. His head was bulbous and twisted. His tumored flesh covered a misshapen skeleton, and defective legs were capped with club feet. Merrick suffered under the ownership of scoundrels until an English surgeon rescued him and eventually gave him permanent residence in a London hospital.

Once, a surly mob chased Merrick and cornered him. Horrified, Merrick screamed, "I am not an animal. I am a human being." Dead silence settled over the crowd and murderous rage dissipated like a vapor.

As it dawned on Merrick that he'd finally found friendship in the surgeon, his amazement was almost palpable. He'd repeat the words "my friend," visibly relishing the rare sound of the words. Shortly before his death, he said to his friend, "You don't know how very wonderful it is to be loved."

Why did God allow such human deformity? Obviously the curse sin initiated resulted in a twisted, groaning planet. But could there also be another reason? Could those whom some call freakish animals be special angels allowed by God to test the human heart? Without any detestable condescension, have you ever loved one from whom most recoil. Jesus would.

Prayer: Lord, teach me how to love.

John 11:32–36
Who Does Jesus Love?

Jesus loved Martha, her sister, and Lazarus (John 11:5).

When he was on earth, Christ loved everyone. He even wept over the masses in Jerusalem who were blind to spiritual realities. But it's interesting to note special references to his personal love. Of course, Jesus often repeated his feelings for his followers. Of those, John is known uniquely as the disciple whom Jesus loved, and it was John who leaned against Christ's chest at the Last Supper. Peter was also special—even after Peter profanely denied ever knowing Jesus, Christ especially sought him out after the resurrection. Several times in John 11 Christ's special love for Lazarus, Mary, and Martha is repeated. Surprisingly, Scripture also reports that Jesus beheld a young rich stranger and loved him (Mark 10:21). But then Jesus challenged him to sell his possessions if he wanted to inherit eternal life.

Did Jesus play favorites? Did he favor certain individuals and stonewall others? It seems as if Christ's love was freely available to those who sought him out. Even the rich young stranger could have become intimately close to Jesus if he was willing. John and Peter practically clung to their master wherever he went. Their closeness was born of months and years in his presence. Apparently, Mary, Martha, and Lazarus had extended an avid open invitation of their hospitality whenever Jesus passed their vicinity. Possibly, Mary was closest to him because she reserved extra time to sit and talk.

Jesus doesn't play favorites—his intimate friendship is available to any willing to take the time and the effort.

Prayer: Lord, free me from the tyranny of the urgent, that you and I may become closer.

1 Peter 3:13–17

Are We Christian Hatemongers?

Keep your conscience clear. Then those who treat the good Christian life you live with contempt will feel ashamed that they have ridiculed you. After all, if it is God's will, it's better to suffer for doing good than for doing wrong (1 Peter 3:16–17).

As this old world gradually chokes itself to death on its own evil, attacks on Christians could worsen. We are already viewed by many as insufferably intolerant. Anti-Christian bias may snowball: "Those Christians spout love but they're the most hateful, bigoted people of all! They shoot abortionists, hate homosexuals, smear politicians, despise liberal thinkers, and condemn teen lovers for doing what comes naturally."

It won't really matter to the world that only one misguided "Christian" out of millions has shot an abortion doctor. And few people will have bothered to distinguish between Christians being against an immoral act and Christians actually hatefully attacking those involved in it.

If we're not careful, we'll find ourselves intimidated by the propaganda. We'll shy away from taking a stand, lest we be misunderstood. Yet, throughout history, true Christians have had the guts to do what is right and condemn what God says is wrong. We must never betray our convictions upon the altar of expediency and public approval.

Through it all, we must be ruthlessly honest with ourselves, and if we sense a seed of hatefulness germinating in our hearts, we must quickly root it out. After all, sin can be so heinous that our hate for it can easily spread to those who commit it. Then we, who are supposed to love even the most vindictive enemy, are suddenly hating with the best of them. Whoever says, "I love God," but hates others is a liar.

Prayer: Lord, please give me courage to stand for what's right without hating those who do wrong.

⚓ July 31 ⚓

Isaiah 49:13–16
God's Infinite Love

With all of God's people you will be able to understand how wide, long, high, and deep his love is. You will know Christ's love, which goes far beyond any knowledge (Ephesians 3:18–19).

You may think it presumptuous that I, a mere human writer, would pretend to understand God's love and explain it. Well, I don't presume to have the last word on it—in fact, I may barely have a first word. God's love is well beyond limit and it successfully defies any description. We, the undeserving recipients of that compassion, can only fall prostrate before him and declare ourselves bondservants, drawn and bound by those cords of mercy and grace. Years ago, F.M. Lehman expressed convictions about God's love that fit my own as a writer:

> The love of God is greater far
>   than tongue or pen could ever tell,
> It goes beyond the highest star,
>   and reaches to the lowest hell . . .
> Could we with ink the oceans fill,
>   and were the skies of parchment made,
> Were every stalk on earth a quill,
>   and every man a scribe by trade;
> To write the love of God above
>   would drain the ocean dry;
> Nor could the scroll contain the whole,
>   though stretched from sky to sky.

Prayer: God, thank you for love so infinite that it boggles my mind and so personal it captivates my heart.

AUGUST

The Infinitely Knowable God

⚓ Aug. 1 ⚓

Philippians 3:7–14

The God Who Can Be Known

"This is eternal life: to know you, the only true God, and Jesus Christ, whom you sent" (John 17:3).

Can you imagine a common Greek citizen saying, "Oh, yeah. Zeus and I are on first name basis"? Or how about a Muslim saying, "Sure, Allah's a personal friend of mine"? Yet we Christians claim that Almighty God is someone we can know personally. Not only that, but the infinite God seeks out a relationship with us infinitesimal, bumbling creatures.

In a real sense, we will always be mere slaves of this Yahweh. However, at one point Jesus told his close followers, "I don't call you servants anymore . . . I've called you friends because I've made known to you everything that I've heard from my Father" (John 15:15). God then went even one step farther. He chose to adopt us as his sons and daughters. He was unashamed to call us members of his own family.

The apostle Paul's greatest passion in life was to know Christ. After that first heartbreaking glimpse of Jesus on the Damascus road, Paul could never get enough glimpses to satisfy himself. He was getting to know a king whose perfect character and limitless facets of greatness invite eternal exploration.

Life Focus: Do you have the unquenchable desire Paul had? Don't you wish it was as easy as walking along a beach with your arm around Christ's shoulders? But in this age, God has ordained that we walk by faith, not by sight. Are you building a relationship with the invisible God these days? He's still there.

⚓ AUG. 2 ⚓

PHILIPPIANS 4:10–19
THE GOD OF PROVISION

My God will richly fill your every need in a glorious way through Christ Jesus (Philippians 4:19).

When I walked into my landlord's office one afternoon, he had some disappointing news. "My son is returning from New Zealand," he began. "He's going to need a place to stay, so you'll have to move out in a few weeks."

I'd spent months painting and repairing the house. It was a quaint old place—beautiful to me—and the rental rate was reasonable. Maybe the fact that the situation threw me for such a loop shows I was trusting more in the gift than the giver.

I couldn't help feeling down about the sudden turn of events, but as the surprise began to wear off, I realized that if I were God, it would give me joy if one of my children expressed praise in the face of loss. I was finally able to thank God, in spite of the fact that I was still stinging with plain, old-fashioned discouragement. It was nothing to my credit—by an act of the will, I was just doing what I thought was right.

F.B. Meyer believed that the education of our faith is incomplete if we haven't learned that there is providence in loss—a ministry through failing and fading things. Thus, emptiness can be a gift and the material insecurities of life can establish us spiritually. "In some way or other," Meyer writes, "we will have to learn the difference between trusting in the gift and trusting in the Giver."

It took several faith-stretching months before God provided a home with not only a large pool but also a beautiful park just over the back fence.

LIFE FOCUS: Are God's options limited? Has he no providential plans beyond your finite thoughts? Remember, when God allows something to be ripped from your grasp, he provides something in its place that is better for you in the end.

⚓ Aug. 3 ⚓

Psalm 96

The God of Majesty

O Lord my God, you are very great. You are clothed with splendor and majesty. You cover yourself with light as though it were a robe (Psalms 104:1–2).

When, through smoky mist, terrified Hebrews experienced God's glory in mind-shattering lightning, thunder, and trumpet blast on the mountain, they begged never to face God again. When Daniel received a visionary message from God, his strength vaporized. Those who were with him began shaking in fear and fled from the area. When three of Christ's disciples merely heard God's thundering voice, they fell on their faces in sheer terror.

However, once as Moses communed with God he asked, "Please let me see your glory" (Exod. 33:18). God answered, "No one may see me and survive. But I will nestle you in the cleft of a boulder and shelter you from my face. You will only see the disappearing trail of my glory" (author's paraphrase).

Yahweh is an invisible God who dwells in light unapproachable. "Fire spreads ahead of him. . . . His flashes of lightning light up the world. The earth sees them and trembles. The mountains melt like wax in the presence of the Lord, in the presence of the Lord of the whole earth" (Ps. 97:3–5).

In a day in which we sometimes overemphasize the warm friendship one may share with God, it seems we need a fresh realization of his magnificence and obliterating presence. God is love, yes; but he is also the majestic King of Glory.

Life Focus: Humble yourself today and lie prostrate before him in worship.

⚓ Aug. 4 ⚓

Numbers 13:1–3, 17–33
The God to Be Respected

We must be thankful that we have a kingdom that cannot be shaken. Because we are thankful, we must serve God with fear and awe in a way that pleases him. After all, our God is a destructive fire (Hebrews 12:28–29).

Most of the Israeli spies returned from the promised land with darkly foreboding reports of men giants and walled cities. Only Caleb and Joshua expressed optimistic faith.

The children of Israel wept when they heard the discouraging report. Their weeping evolved into belligerence against Moses. They picked up rocks to hurl at him. At that point, God declared that of this entire generation, only Joshua and Caleb would enter the land.

Early the next morning, the Israelis sang a different tune: "Here we are! We made a slight mistake but now we're ready to waltz into Canaan."

Moses, however, warned the people not to try to fight the Canaanites because God was no longer on Israel's side. Ignoring this, the people hurried into battle and were soundly trounced.

Has anyone ever treated you terribly and then later passed it off lightly with some sort of lame excuse? We treat God that way when we refuse to do things his way, then act later as if nothing happened. When we reject God, repentance must occur before we can enjoy the former fellowship.

Life Focus: God will never cater to your immature temper tantrums. You'd be wise to learn how to relate to him, not as to a doormat, but as to the Almighty.

⚓ Aug. 5 ⚓

Jeremiah 7:23-26

The God of Patience

Do you have contempt for God, who is very kind to you, puts up with you, and deals patiently with you? Don't you realize that it is God's kindness that is trying to lead you to him and change the way you think and act? (Romans 2:4).

About seven hundred years had passed since an elderly Joshua had announced, "My family and I will still serve the Lord" (Josh. 24:15). The Hebrew people had rejected God numerous times. Over and over God raised up judges to free his people from idolatrous captors. Judges like Samuel warned the people of their corrupt ways, and for a time the people would turn back to God. Then came a long line of kings, most of which encouraged evil practices. For close to five hundred years, God sent prophets to warn his people of judgment for their sin.

Mothers complain wearily of having to yell instructions over and over again before their children finally respond. Yet God warned and pleaded with his people for hundreds of years before his patience finally gave way to judgment. Can you doubt that God is as the Scriptures say—compassionate, gracious, slow to anger, and overflowing with lovingkindness?

He puts up with our idiocy, our sin, our weaknesses, and our mistakes. He doesn't write us off or get even with us when we live as if he doesn't exist, and he will never disown us.

Life Focus: Sometimes we tax God's patience with our foolishness, but he suffers long and is very kind.

Hosea 6:1–7

The God of Forgiveness

You, O Lord, are good and forgiving, full of mercy toward everyone who calls out to you (Psalm 86:5).

"You don't know the life I've lived. God could never forgive the things I've done!" This is a common non-Christian objection to giving one's life to Christ. But John 3:16 says God loved the world this way: He gave . . . That's the way God revealed his forgiving spirit. He sacrificed himself to the awful limit so justice could be satisfied.

After centuries of shameless rebellion and idolatry, Israel finally exhausted God's patience. God allowed Assyria to defeat Israel and drag them into captivity. But the prophet Hosea begged, "Let us return to the Lord. Even though he has torn us to pieces, he will heal us. Even though he has wounded us, he will bandage our wounds" (Hosea 6:1). Hosea knew that God could forgive even the most horrid sins against him, but the people had to humble themselves in genuine repentance. God not only wanted to forgive but to again reveal himself to them. Hosea went on to challenge them, "Let's get to know the Lord" (v. 3) because God delights in loyalty rather than sacrifice, and in the knowledge of himself rather than burnt offerings (v. 6). The God of the Bible forgives in love, and out of that forgiveness he wants a relationship to blossom —a relationship that's closer than any other.

Life Focus: When you confess and reject your sins, God doesn't sullenly place you on probation for ten years. He is approachable—ready to welcome you back into his arms of forgiveness.

Psalm 78:1–54

The God of Integrity

"God is not like people. He tells no lies. He is not like humans. He doesn't change his mind. When he says something, he does it. When he makes a promise, he keeps it" (Numbers 23:19).

Did you ever hear anyone claim to have been ripped off or burned? These are American colloquialisms which mean an individual has been cheated or grossly misled in some way.

Maybe you've been fired from a job unfairly or have been the object of insidious rumors. Maybe you've been forsaken by a friend or cheated by a business associate. God is the only one who will never act unethically or dishonestly toward us. He's the God of absolute integrity. When he makes a claim or states a promise, he always fulfills it. Though we ourselves are unfaithful, God remains faithful.

In Ezekiel 36:24, God states, "I will take you from the nations and gather you from every country. I will bring you back to your own land."

Ezekiel prophesied this promise in the 580s B.C. Hundreds of years crept by, yet the Jews remained a scattered people with no land. It looked for all the world as if this was one promise God simply couldn't keep. Then, more than twenty-five long centuries after God spoke those words, against all odds Israel finally was incorporated as a nation! God had once again proved his integrity.

Life Focus: You, too, can trust God to treat you honorably and honestly. Let down your guard and relax in the firmness of God's promises.

⚓ Aug. 8 ⚓

1 Samuel 1:1–20

The God Who Listens

Before they call, I will answer. While they're still speaking, I will hear (Isaiah 65:24).

Hannah wasn't a holy woman or a spiritual leader. She was a common peasant. Year after heartbreaking year, she made the pilgrimage to Shiloh to pray for a child. The other wife of Hannah's husband mocked and taunted her barrenness. As Hannah knelt in the tabernacle and mumbled incoherently, the high priest was convinced she was more than a little tipsy. Tears coursed down her cheeks as she again begged God for a child. Was God listening to her desperate plea?

Many of us throw in the towel too soon when God doesn't grant our requests. In Hannah's case, she could well have given up after years of seemingly useless prayer. But the all-knowing God heard before she spoke and was withholding a response in light of his own purposes and timing. She was finally promised a son, and sure enough, within a year she bore him.

In the Bible, God actually pleads with us—Call upon me, ask, commune with me, pour out your heart, and don't give up. Few temptations in the life of prayer are more common than the failure to persevere. To stop praying after a day or a month sows disheartenment and doubt in the reality of prayer, and that can be fatal. We should not stop praying until either the need has been granted or we're convinced the request is not in accordance with the promises and purposes of God.

Life Focus: Jesus feels your trembling faith, and he hears your repeated request. In one way or another, he will eventually reward your persistence with a response.

⚓ Aug. 9 ⚓

Psalm 139
The God of Tenacity

Where can I go to get away from your Spirit? . . . If I go up to heaven, you are there. If I make my bed in hell, you are there (Psalm 139:7–8).

"Leave at once for the important city, Nineveh." God commanded Jonah, "Announce to the people that I can no longer overlook the wicked things thy have done" (Jonah 1:2). But Jonah wasn't about to go preach to those perennial heathen foes of Israel. He flipped on his afterburner and zoomed, leaving the Almighty in his wake.

Now suppose the account went on, "Then God declared, 'You have refused to obey my will. Therefore, I will leave you. Though you cry to me, I will not hear you.'"

That, of course, is not how God responded to Jonah's rebellion. God was not willing to give up on his servant that easily. In fact, he worked to bring Jonah to such a point of profound discomfort that Jonah became willing to repent.

Though some may see God's reaction to Jonah's waywardness only as a sign of his disciplining anger, it can also be viewed as a sign of his patient love. It is comforting to know that God will not forsake us in wrath every time we resist his will. He is not a God to be toyed with, yet he waits and challenges and sometimes disciplines us until we realize his way is the only way.

Life Focus: It's important to cultivate an attitude of submission to God, but the Father will never reject you in one of your less cooperative moments nor disown you when you fail him. Thank God he cares enough to straighten you out instead of snuffing you out.

⚓ Aug. 10 ⚓

Ezekiel 18:1–9

The God of Fairness

"Does God distort justice, or does the Almighty distort righteousness?" (Job 8:3).

In Ezekiel 18, God states that a father will not be unfairly judged for his son's sin, nor a son for this father's. In John 15, Jesus says that if people had not heard his Good News, they would not be considered guilty, but there is no excuse for those who know better. In Luke 12, Christ's fairness even appears to reflect itself in varying degrees of punishment for those judged in the last day.

Ours is a God of total and absolute fairness. The God who loved us enough to die for us will never condemn us unless he is forced to on the basis of his holiness.

When we read in the Bible of divine judgments that seem very harsh, we may secretly wonder at times whether we are actually fairer than God. When we react in that way, we fail to understand at least two key facts. First, we lack a true understanding of what the pristine holiness of God requires. Second, we don't understand that our love and concern for people is totally insignificant in comparison to God's limitless, matchless love. Somehow God's love and holiness find perfect balance in his judgment of the human race—he is justice personified.

Life Focus: You can trust in a God who balances his holy justice with merciful love.

⚓ Aug. 11 ⚓

Deuteronomy 6:1–19
The God of Reminders

"The Lord your God will bring you into the land and give it to you. . . . This land will have large, prosperous cities that you didn't build. . . . Be careful that you don't forget the Lord, who brought you out of slavery in Egypt" (Deuteronomy 6:10, 12).

I'm an absent-minded person. So when I was advised to buy a calendar, I obediently went out and bought a fancy one. I faithfully listed all my upcoming appointments and events . . . then promptly forgot to refer to it. God knows we all tend to be forgetful, and in the Bible he's placed multitudes of necessary reminders for us.

God asked the Israelites to offer animal sacrifices on a regular basis as a reminder of their sin and of their need for a redeemer. The various Old Testament feasts instituted by God were intended to be observed periodically in remembrance of God's past dealings and present desires for his followers.

We also find God's gentle reminders in the New Testament. For example, Jesus stated that the Last Supper should be re-enacted regularly in his remembrance and that humble acts equivalent to his washing of dusty feet should become habits in our lives.

God knows that if we read or hear something enough times, we may retain it long enough to put it into practice. So each epistle isn't completely original in content. But nearly identical instructions are repeated many times throughout those letters.

If your love for Jesus has faded into a land of foggy forgetfulness, transport your thoughts back to those early days of faith—your first love. Realize you can go back there again.

Life Focus: God remembers you constantly. Can you set aside the thousand daily distractions long enough to remember him and the things that will make his memory of you a delight?

Isaiah 6:1–8

The God of Holiness

I saw the Lord sitting on a high and lofty throne (Isaiah 6:1).

In Leviticus 20:7–8, God emphasizes a challenge over and over: "'Live holy lives. Be holy because I am the Lord your God. Obey my laws, and live by them. I am the Lord who set you apart as holy.'" Some get the message; some don't. But whatever the case, it is doubtful anyone can aspire toward holiness until they see a glimpse of God in his separated perfection.

Isaiah saw a vision of God's holiness and was never the same again. In the vision, he saw God on a throne, high and lifted up. Traditionally, the longer the train of a monarch's robe, the greater the royalty. God's train literally wound throughout the entire temple. Attending angels used their six wings to cover their eyes and their feet and to fly. They covered their eyes because no one can look on God and live. They covered their feet because where they stood was holy ground. And they cried, "Holy, holy, holy is the Lord of Armies" (Isa. 6:3). The Hebrew repetition of the word holy is similar to our American idiom, "There is holiness, and then there is holiness!"

Through billows of smoke, temple posts wobbled like tops losing their spin. Isaiah was utterly devastated. He screamed, "I'm doomed! Every word that passes through my lips is sinful." Flesh sizzled as an angel touched a white-hot cleansing coal to Isaiah's lips. When God then called for a messenger to plead for holiness in the land, Isaiah was ready to softly whisper, "Here I am. Send me." He had glimpsed God's Holiness.

Life Focus: It is only through God's holiness that we may learn to be holy.

Daniel 3
The God of Protection

"If our God, whom we honor, can save us from a blazing furnace and from your power, he will, Your Majesty. But if he doesn't, you should know, Your Majesty, we'll never honor your gods or worship the gold statue that you set up" (Daniel 3:17–18).

Does God play a sort of divine Russian roulette with Christians—watching some survive with a click of his revolver and blasting others to kingdom come? While the Bible contains many examples of his protection, the converse is also true. Did God spare all Old Testament saints from battle, famine, and disease? Did he guard all New Testament believers from hardship, deprivation, beatings, and imprisonment? In some cases, yes; but in many cases, no.

When Daniel's three friends were threatened with a white-hot fiery inferno, they told the king, "If our God, whom we honor, can save us from a blazing furnace and from your power, he will, Your Majesty. But if he doesn't, you should know, Your Majesty, we'll never honor your gods or worship the gold statues that you set up" (Dan. 3:17–18). The men weren't giving poor God an excuse. They were simply acknowledging that God calls the shots—his sovereignty may require martyrdom, and for that, they were willing.

God doesn't promise to protect us from all negative experiences. However, he'll allow those events in our lives when they serve a vital function in his eternal purposes for us. Some purposes we may understand right away; others may not be known until eternity.

Life Focus: Thank God for the many ways he preserves and protects you each day, and when he allows a hardship to break through his mighty wall of protection, accept it and learn from it all you can.

⚓ Aug. 14 ⚓

Acts 9:1–19

The God of All Comfort

Grant me some proof of your goodness so that those who hate me may see it and be put to shame. You, O Lord, have helped me and comforted me (Psalm 86:17).

Some may feel a slight tinge of resentment that Saul of Tarsus, the brutal Christian-killer, would actually hear the voice of Christ singling him out to a great missionary career. We may forget that at that time, the Lord said of him, "I'll show him how much he must suffer for [my] sake" (Acts 9:116).

During his missionary career, Paul enjoyed a unique intimacy with God. He was entrusted to write many of the New Testament epistles and he experienced unique manifestations of God's love and power. However, he was also imprisoned, stoned, shipwrecked, and beaten repeatedly and unmercifully.

It is true that God allows certain of his children to experience great testing in the form of disaster, illness, or persecution, but it is also true, as Annie Johnson Flint writes, that God gives "more grace as the burdens grow greater." There often seems to be in God's economy the principle of allowing us to sense more of his presence and love during the most trying and heartbreaking periods.

Haralan Popov and Richard Wurmbrand endured years of extreme deprivation and torture in Communist prisons. At times they were close to the limits of their endurance. It was then, however, that God made his presence known in a way they would later describe as being submerged in God's pure, warm love.

Life Focus: God gives more comfort as burdens grow greater. He will also embrace you—just when you need it the most.

⚓ Aug. 15 ⚓

Psalm 8
The God of the Unexpected

"Where were you when I laid the foundation of the earth? . . . Who laid its cornerstone when the morning stars sang together and all the sons of God shouted for joy?" (Job 38:4, 6–7).

Do you think of yourself as one who likes doing the unexpected? You may like to go places on the spur of the moment, or enjoy unusual experiences, or surprise others in creative ways. No matter how unpredictable you think you are, you can't hold a candle to God's unique ways.

Stop and think about the incredible diversity of God's creation —we may imagine that most plants or animals are more or less predictable. Then we glimpse another one in a documentary or nature magazine that wows us with its weirdness.

Jesus walked on water without skis, created the choicest wine at weddings, loved kids and moral rejects, and said things that drove Pharisaic theologians to distraction. He was never a man to be placed in a box.

Think back on God's dealings in your life. Has he always worked things out just when and how you asked? Most likely his hand in your affairs has excited you, surprised you, and tried your faith at times. He's proved in your experience that your plans are inferior to his. He says, "'My thoughts are not your thoughts, and my ways are not your ways'" (Isa. 55:8). God thinks and acts from a fuller perspective and a higher plane than we do. We must get used to it.

Life Focus: When things don't work out according to your hopes, prayers, or dreams, accept the situation, and allow God to be the refreshing, unpredictable Creator who wills only your good.

⚓ Aug. 16 ⚓

2 Samuel 6:1–11

The God of Wrath and Judgment

They said to the mountains and rocks, "Fall on us, and hide us from the face of the one who sits on the throne and from the anger of the lamb" (Revelation 6:16).

With joy and pageantry, King David was bringing the ark of God back to Jerusalem. As the procession passed a threshing floor, the oxen pulling the cart nearly upset the ark. Uzzah reached out to steady it and was immediately struck dead for his irreverence.

Some may be tempted to recoil from God's show of wrath, but God had clearly commanded that the ark was not to be touched or even seen by anyone unless authorized by him. And it was to be transported upon the shoulders of holy Levites.

In our day, the wrath and judgment of God seems to be largely ignored, replaced with an overemphasis on his love and acceptance. But the Bible emphasizes both his love and his holy wrath. There is nothing God hates more than evil (Prov. 6:16), and he has paid the ultimate price to do away with its power (1 John 3:8).

We've been told that fearing God entails only a healthy respect, but more seems to be involved. "To fear the Lord is to hate evil" (Prov. 8:13). God is the very essence of love. The only time we need to fear him is when we're doing what we know he detests. Fear of God is a biblical deterrent to the sin which so easily leads us away from him.

When we persist in wandering, God, as a father, has the right to discipline us. Charles Spurgeon writes, "I sometimes question whether I have ever learned anything except through the rod." God's spankings can be quite painful, yet they yield the fruit of peaceful goodness.

Life Focus: Sometimes God's justice scares us because we realize our own sinfulness. But maybe we should spend more time seeking to understand God's holiness than condemning his severity.

⚓ Aug. 17 ⚓

Acts 13:22–39
The God of Our Ambitions

I am happy to do your will, O my God. Your teachings are deep within me (Psalm 40:8).

Over and over we hear David called a man after God's own heart. The meaning of that phrase confused me a bit until I studied Acts 13:22: "God removed Saul and made David their king. God spoke favorably about David. He said, 'I have found that David, son of Jesse, is a man after my own heart. He will do everything I want him to do.'" Other translations render the latter segment, "a man agreeable to my mind who will carry out all my purposes," "who will do all my pleasure," or "who will carry out my whole program."

Being a person after God's heart appears to entail a desire to accomplish God's purposes for us on earth. At times we think of God's purposes as only the great global movings of his Spirit, but his purposes also involve the rather mundane daily responsibilities he assigns to us.

In Acts 13:36 we read, "After doing God's will by serving the people of his time, David died. He was laid to rest with his ancestors, but his body decayed." David eventually faced death as we all will, but death couldn't touch him until he'd completely fulfilled God's specific purposes for him. We simply cannot die until we've done all that God designed us to do on this earth. That is a comfort.

Life Focus: God has purposes for you in this generation. As he shows them to you, are you willing to faithfully follow through?

⚓ Aug. 18 ⚓

John 1:43–51
The God of Awareness

Nathanael asked Jesus, "How do you know anything about me?" Jesus answered him, "I saw you under the fig tree before Philip called you" (John 1:48).

Did you ever feel that maybe if you accomplished a great spiritual feat, you might attract God's attention? Actually God is aware of even the smallest good deed of his children. Jesus said that if, out of love for him, we give a child a cup of cool water, we will be rewarded (Matt. 10:42). He encouraged his followers to do good deeds without fanfare because God, who knows all secrets, will reward them openly (6:4).

Along with this truth, though, there is another side to his awareness. He also knows our every idle thought and word (Matt. 12:36). Our joy in knowing that God delights in our smallest kindnesses must be balanced with the sobering truth that he's also displeased with our careless misdeeds. The same God who saw Hagar dying in the sweltering desert also viewed David gazing at Bathsheba.

El Roi means the God who sees. He doesn't ever doze; he's never caught off guard; and neither the deepest sea, the mightiest boulder, or the blackest darkness can hide us from those eyes. Isaiah 18:5 reveals God silently, intently observing the earth from his dwelling place. God has his finger on your pulse—his mind on your racing thoughts. He is the God of total awareness. Nothing in this world escapes his notice. He's in control.

Life Focus: When you're living in fellowship with him, God's awareness is a very reassuring, comforting thought; if not, it can make you uncomfortable. The truth of God's omniscience can be a pleasant incentive to live in unashamed transparency before him.

Psalm 13

The God of Encouragement

God our Father loved us and by his kindness gave us everlasting encouragement and good hope (2 Thessalonians 2:16).

Depression looms over me today like a giant specter of darkness. I'm only one of millions who struggle with chronic depression. The stigma that says Christians should be immune from emotional struggles is gradually dissipating. Excellent missionaries and ministers of the past have fought these struggles, and even some of the prominent Scriptural characters face dark despair.

Job cried out, "Scratch out the day I was born" (Job 3:3). Elijah prayed, "Take my life" (1 Kings 19:4). And Jonah groaned bitterly, "I'd rather be dead than alive" (Jonah 4:3).

Note how God responds to these prayers: In Elijah's case God gives him rest and sends an angel to refresh him. Then he asks Elijah what he was doing sulking in the wilderness. For a long time God seemed to ignore Job's pleas, but eventually God humbles Job with questions. Then he restores Job's former blessings. Jonah's despair was actually bitterness toward God, and God patiently uses an object lesson to convince Jonah of his lack of compassion toward the Ninevites.

Life Focus: Much as God responds in different ways to each person in his or her time of deep discouragement, God will respond in a unique way to you when you hit the pit of despondency. He is the great encourager.

⚓ Aug. 20 ⚓

1 Samuel 16:1-13
The God of the Underdog

Our bodies are made of clay, yet we have the treasure of the Good News in them. This shows that the superior power of this treasure belongs to God and doesn't come from us (2 Corinthians 4:7).

The new Miss America flashed a smile, and with tears of excitement, accepted the glimmering crown which represented prestigious acclaim, glamour, and financial benefits. The applause was tumultuous.

But God judges humanity on a different scale.

God doesn't see as we see. "Humans look at outward appearances, but the Lord looks into the heart" (1 Sam. 16:7). There are no age limitations in God's book. He calls a child named Samuel and an eighty-year-old named Moses. Financial status makes no difference. He blesses a man of wealth named Abraham, and he also blesses a poor widow in Zarephath. God places no premium on looks. He uses a beautiful woman named Esther, but he also uses a coarse man of the desert named John.

A paraplegic lay silent and embittered on a hospital bed. She is completely helpless—devoid of feeling from her neck down. Then God calls her name and tells her he has plans for her. Now, many years later, the lady has encouraged millions with her story, her teachings, her musical recordings, her paintings, and her best-selling books. Her name is Joni Eareckson Tada—just a "helpless" paraplegic called by God.

Life Focus: You don't have to be a star—just be receptive to God. Is he calling your name?

⚓ Aug. 21 ⚓

Matthew 14:22–33
The God of Disguises

Then their eyes were opened, and they recognized him. But he vanished from their sight (Luke 24:31).

"Jesus is apt to come," writes Frederick Buechner, "into the very midst of life at its most real and inescapable. Not in a blaze of unearthly light, nor in the midst of a sermon, not in the throes of some kind of religious daydream, but . . . at supper time, or walking along a road."

When a soft voice called to Samuel in the darkness, he didn't realize who it was. When God appeared in human guise to individuals such as Jacob and Joshua, they did not recognize him. When a mysterious figure moved through turbulent waves toward the seasick disciples, they shrieked in terror. And when the Emmaus disciples discussed the Scriptures with Christ, they couldn't identify him until he vanished.

Sometimes when Christ moves in our lives, he does not reveal himself clearly. He challenges or confronts us through another Christian or through circumstances, and we allow fear to creep in. We don't always recognize Christ, nor do we understand his purposes. It's vital that we know Jesus well enough to distinguish his voice and image and know our Bible well enough to recognize his promptings. If we ignore him or shrink back in fear, he won't be able to accomplish his sanctifying will in us.

Life Focus: God can give you more spiritual awareness of his presence in your life. You can rest in him even when he works in an unexpected way.

⚓ Aug. 22 ⚓

John 8:1–8
The God of Tender Mercy

Your mercy is so precious, O God, that Adam's descendants take refuge in the shadow of your wings (Psalm 36:7).

As I lay on the beach reading one afternoon, I saw a little boy with an aluminum walker wallowing his way jerkily across the sand. His spindly legs needed a rest after each awkward step. Ten minutes later, he was only about halfway to the surf. Finally his dad came over, picked the boy up in his arms, and carried him the rest of the way to the beach blanket.

If the father had carried his son all the way, how could the boy's fragile self-respect and perseverance ever grow? However, if the dad didn't help at all, the boy could easily be plowed under by discouragement. This father was constantly, caringly judging how far his son could exert his energy before he needed someone to lean on.

Jesus grasped Peter just as he sank, he put him in his place when Peter waxed dictatorial, he applauded Peter when the fisherman showed character, and he accepted a dejected Peter over a pan of fish after his resurrection. But Jesus never babied him or shielded him from life's realities.

Like Peter, we have problems and weaknesses that sometimes seem too much to conquer. God watches over us at those times, but he knows that if he immediately bails us out of every crisis, our character will never develop indispensable traits such as patience and persistence. God also knows the very moment when we need to be hoisted up in his arms and carried a ways.

Life Focus: Trust that God knows when to watch and when to hoist. He knows how much you can handle.

⚓ AUG. 23 ⚓

LUKE 19:36–47

THE GOD OF FEELING

We have a chief priest who is able to sympathize with our weaknesses. He was tempted in every way that we are, but he didn't sin (Hebrews 4:15).

Few Bible passages reflect the vast contrast of emotions exhibited by God Incarnate as we find in a brief segment of Luke 19.

First, we find Jesus entering Jerusalem amid the acclaim of multitudes (Luke 19:36–47). There was joy as he rode humbly through the waving palm branches and cloak-strewn path. Jesus wouldn't allow the Pharisees to spill bitter bile on the short-lived rejoicing of his friends.

Then as Jesus saw the city, he broke down and cried. His heart ached as he realized the catastrophic consequences that would occur because they rejected him.

Next, as Jesus entered the temple, he was overwhelmed with indignation because of the defilement of his Father's house. He bodily threw the offenders out of the temple.

Finally, the text records that Jesus then taught daily in the temple courts. It took courageous compassion to teach the crowds when he knew he was in mortal danger from his enemies.

We see Christ full of joy, racked by grief, torn with anger, then courageously caring. While on earth, Jesus experienced every one of the emotions we feel.

LIFE FOCUS: Even when you're riding an emotional roller coaster, you can be assured Jesus understands.

⚓ Aug. 24 ⚓

Numbers 25:10–13
The God of Jealousy

"I, the Lord your God, am a God who does not tolerate rivals" (Exodus 20:5).

In writing to Corinthian believers, Paul called them fleshly because there was jealousy and strife among them (1 Cor. 3:3). In another passage, however, we find God actually inciting jealousy in the Jewish people by granting salvation to the Gentiles (Rom. 10:19). In still another place, we read that God himself is a jealous God (Nah. 1:2).

Obviously, jealousy is condemned by God as sin. Yet he not only tempts his people to jealousy but is also characterized as being jealous. What's the explanation for this seeming moral contradiction?

The word jealous is defined as a demand for exclusive devotion and a complete intolerance for rivalry. There is a godly jealousy. The apostle Paul spoke of it when he challenged the church in Corinth to be completely devoted to Christ without the curse of divided loyalty (2 Cor. 11:2).

God is a jealous God, but his jealousy is holy jealousy (Josh. 24:19). He will not tolerate a splintered loyalty; he will accept no rivals to our devotion. Not only that, God has a great blessing for those who are jealous on God's behalf—those who press people toward unrivaled devotion to him (Num. 25:10–13).

Life Focus: Are you jealous today for the honor and commitment due to God? He won't allow worship of two masters.

⚓ Aug. 25 ⚓

James 1:2–8
The God of Testings

"He knows the road I take. When he tests me, I'll come out as pure as gold" (Job 23:10).

Shortness of money, health problems, words which humbled you, disappointing situations—does it seem impossible for you to believe that God allowed those things in your life? God doesn't test us laughingly to watch us squirm, but because the character it can produce is beyond value.

In the Bible, testing is compared to the "trying" of metal, whereby it's heated, melted, and refined until there is only the purest substance remaining (Zech. 13:9; Job 23:10; Ps. 66:10). In a spiritual sense, God wants to burn out the deceit and misdirection from our motives, attitudes, and actions.

There are three basic reasons why God initiates the purifying process in our lives. First, he wants to prove how far we've come. Second, he wants to test our present spiritual condition, and third, his intent is to send us further down the road toward Christlikeness.

At times we may feel that a bitter test contradicts divine love, but when we harden and resist, the trial makes us less like Christ. How have you been responding lately to the daily testings of life? Are you learning from them or spurning God's attempts to increase your faith?

Life Focus: The strain of stretching faith may be agonizing, but it will yield for you an eternal weight of glory beyond comparison.

⚓ Aug. 26 ⚓

2 Corinthians 9:6–11

The God of More Than Enough

"Give, and you will receive. A large quantity, pressed together, shaken down, and running over will be put into your pocket" (Luke 6:38).

The all-encompassing sufficiency of God's grace is emphasized at least five times in 2 Corinthians 9:8: "God has power to shower all kinds of blessings upon you so that, having, under all circumstances and on all occasions all that you can need, you may be able to shower all kinds of benefits on others" (TCNT).

In the context of this verse, Paul urges us to give freely, cheerfully, and generously to help those facing a need. One principle in Scripture is that, even if we're barely squeaking by financially, we should give to others, and we will receive from God. This seems illogical and strange to us, yet in the verse above, we're promised with a five-fold repetition that God will make sure we have enough for ourselves and an overflow for others. Just like the Zarephath widow's bottomless cruse of oil, God's hand will keep pouring out what we need to survive.

God is the God of extra blessings—inwardly to develop character or outwardly to meet tangible needs. Sometimes his grace enables us to endure lean times; at other times, we prosper like kings. His grace takes many forms, but it is always a love focused on the undeserving.

Life Focus: Why does God give you more than you'll ever need? The only answer is grace. Thank him that he's the God of extra blessings.

⚓ Aug. 27 ⚓

Isaiah 55:6–9

The God of Ambiguity

God's riches, wisdom, and knowledge are so deep that it is impossible to explain his decisions or to understand his ways (Romans 11:33).

To paraphrase Frederick Buechner, Christ is our employer, but chances are that we'll never see his face this side of paradise except mirrored in dreams, shadows, and one another's faces. He's our shepherd, but down here we'll never feel his touch except as we are touched by joy, pain, and the holiness of each other's lives. He's our guide, but often when we need him most, he seems farthest away because he's gone on ahead, leaving only the faint print of his feet on the path to follow. He leaves pending questions in our minds that spur fervent quests for truth and clarity.

In his book True Believers Don't Ask Why, Fischer emphasizes the fact that Jesus was never the smug "Answer Man." He told numerous veiled parables, posed tough queries, and sometimes even answered questions with questions. Jesus wanted to find individuals who were sincere—those who genuinely quested for truth and for God himself, instead of those merely seeking an intriguing new teaching or a dogma to attack.

Fischer believes Jesus approaches us in a similar way today. Christ doesn't bombard us with forced truth. He still makes us think, but instead of asking us questions face to face, he allows life to throw questions at us, forcing us to scramble for biblical answers. Life itself draws our faith out of us. Sometimes the answers we uncover offer solid comfort or encouraging reassurance; other times they shake up the superficial system we've subtly substituted for Christ.

Life Focus: God did not create fleshy marionettes. He always welcomes questions asked humbly. And he probes us with his own questions. The secrets of the kingdom are whispered to those who take the time and effort to search and ask and learn.

⚓ Aug. 28 ⚓

Psalm 104:1–24

The God of Creativity

What a large number of things you have made, O Lord! You made them all by wisdom. The earth is filled with your creatures (Psalm 104:24).

The teacher smiled self-confidently and said, "This is a class on creativity. We are all going to learn to be creative." So a student bought a kit and embroidered a wall hanging.

And God smiled and said: "Where were you when I created the stars, comets and planets that make up my celestial playground?"

"Where were you when I created my own botanical hothouse—replete with vivid, colorful displays of exotic plants and flowers?"

"Where were you when I made microscopic amoebas and massive whales, millions of living creatures to roam a planet?"

"Where were you when I fashioned beings in my own image—beings each unique in their own way?"

"Where were you when I visited your planet to save you from yourselves through an act of love never to be matched?"

"And where were you when I sent my Spirit into human hearts in order to bring out of chaos, hate, and sin a race of people whom I can unify in a bond of sacrificial love and worship?"

"My dear human child, I wrote the book on creativity. Read my book and learn what creativity really means."

Life Focus: God doesn't frown on innovation. He invented it. Use it for his kingdom.

⚓ Aug. 29 ⚓

1 Kings 19:9–13

The God of Infinite Character

No god is like you, O Lord. No one can do what you do (Psalm 86:8).

Our minds can only grasp at the outer fringes of God's infinity, eternality, omnipotence, omnipresence, and omniscience. Though these traits boggle our minds, they seem vague, ethereal, impersonal. With mouths agape, we hear accounts of mammoth mountains God has moved. But we tend to segregate attributes like these from those such as love, holiness, and goodness.

First of all, though infinite, God knows how to relate to each of us in every situation. When God approached the depressed, exhausted Elijah, he demonstrated his vast power through lashing winds, raging flames, and a rock-crushing earthquake. But when he finally spoke to the prophet, it was with a whispering voice in the stillness.

Christ confined himself to human limitations in many ways, but occasionally God Incarnate would allow a flash of infinity to surface. He demonstrated his omnipotence in healings, exorcisms, feedings, and storm-calmings. Jesus would never commit himself to the public because his holy omniscience knew the innate deceit and evil in humanity. But he used his complete knowledge to convert a Samaritan woman by showing her that he knew her immoral past yet still cared about her. Christ's bodily presence was voluntarily limited, yet somehow he showed omnipresent compassion by healing several people who were miles away. There are many additional examples in the Bible, but these may suffice to show that Christ's "impersonal" attributes are inextricably linked to the "personal" ones.

Life Focus: Your God is not a splintered impersonal force with some personal qualities tacked on. He is a personal God with infinite personality.

⚓ Aug. 30 ⚓

Genesis 45:1–8
The God of Sovereignty

"The Lord kills, and he gives life. He makes people go down to the grave, and he raises them up again. The Lord causes poverty and grants wealth. He humbles people; he also promotes them" (1 Samuel 2:6–7).

Joseph saw only bleak hopelessness as he jumped from Potiphar's frying pan into prison's fire. Years passed before God released Joseph, placing him as a top Egyptian ruler to save millions from famine. Covered with oozing boils, Job mourned the loss of family and possessions. But at long last God finally replied to Job's endless questions. As Nehemiah's heart broke over the crumbling walls and the disillusioned inhabitants of Jerusalem, God eventually moved the heart of a pagan king to finance Nehemiah's rebuilding of Jerusalem's walls. Esther felt panic paralyze her as she learned that the king had decreed death for her and her fellow Jews. But God worked inexplicably behind the scenes to rescue these people. David was anointed as king of Israel, but he spent years as a homeless fugitive before God made the kingship a reality.

Many years may pass in darkness, and we begin to imagine an indifferent God who is light years away. It is often only as we look back that the intricate workings of his will take on beauty and clarity.

Life Focus:

Some things might be hurtful if alone they stood,
But they work together, and they work for good,
All the thwarted longings, all the stern denials,
All the contradictions, hard to understand,
And the force that guides them,
  speeds them, and retards them,
Stops and starts and guides them—
  is our Father's hand.

—*Annie Johnson Flint*

⚓ Aug. 31 ⚓

Revelation 19:5–8

The God of Celebration

"Let us rejoice, be happy, and give him glory because it's time for the marriage of the Lamb. His bride has made herself ready" (Revelation 19:7).

Most of us like celebrations—holidays, birthdays, anniversary parties—there's one for every occasion. God loves celebrations, too. It was God, not humans, who initiated festivals such as Passover, Firstfruits, Pentecost, Trumpets, and Booths. The Passover was meant to celebrate the exodus from Egypt. Firstfruits symbolized the consecration of the year's harvest to God. Pentecost pointed toward an offering which would someday redeem humanity. Trumpets celebrated the beginning of the civil new year. Booths commemorated God's provision for the Israelites in bringing them through the wilderness.

Then about 1500 years later, Jesus instituted the Last Supper and asked that the bread and wine always be served in remembrance of his death for us. It will not be until Christ's return that we'll enjoy the greatest celebration of all time. It's called the lamb's wedding banquet (Rev. 19:9). The occasion will be the symbolic marriage between Christ and his church, the most sacred and wondrous celebration of all.

Can the Lord throw a great banquet? Well, Isaiah describes one that sounds pretty classy: "The Lord of Armies will prepare for all people a feast with the best foods, a banquet with aged wines, with the best foods and the finest wines. On this mountain he will remove the veil of grief covering all people and the mask covering all nations. He will swallow up death forever" (Isa. 25:6–8).

Life Focus: We've planned many parties for one another; let's prepare for the party which will honor the one who made all this possible.

SEPTEMBER

Hope for the Imperfect

⚓ SEPT. 1 ⚓

1 CORINTHIANS 10:1–12
WRITTEN FOR OUR EXAMPLE

These things happened to make them an example for others. These things were written down as a warning for us who are living in the closing days of history (1 Corinthians 10:11).

I like Bible heroes. And there are plenty of them. However, occasionally our yen for larger-than-life heroes results in exalting individuals who seem to have no warts, no imperfections—none of the moral blemishes all too common among us modern mortals. Buechner writes, "Whatever else they may be, the people in the Bible are real human beings . . . and it is not the world of the Sunday school tract that they move through but a Dostoevskian world of darkness and light commingled, where suffering is sometimes redemptive and sometimes turns the heart to stone." In today's Scripture reading, we find that even in the evil of the unbelieving wilderness Israelites was recorded for our example, as a heavenly caution to us.

This month, we'll learn from some biblical saints and even a few rebels with tilted halos. As you read, we hope that several benefits will occur in your life. First, in the past you may have felt you could never identify with the pristine purity of Scripture's saints. I hope you'll find release from this sense of hopelessness. Second, I trust you'll gain valuable insights as you learn from their various foibles and failures. Third, it's my prayer that you'll become a messenger of God's grace to others who may be bound up in visions of a fierce God who refuses to be patient with our all-too-human struggles. God reaches out in mercy to us forgiven sinners and fallible saints as we stammer and stumble our way ever closer to him.

PRAYER: "Father, help me realize that I can risk living for you, because you know what I'm made of and you love me anyway."

⚓ Sept. 2 ⚓

1 Corinthians 1:20–25

Too Real Not to Be True

God's nonsense is wiser than human wisdom, and God's weakness is stronger than human strength (1 Corinthians 1:25).

If you wanted to found a religion that would take the world by storm, what would you do? You might locate a terrifically attractive, charismatic, squeaky-clean leader, gather a wealthy, talented think tank around him, hire a top public relations firm, and begin spreading a message of sweetness and light.

Ironically, the roots of Christianity reflect the exact opposite. A rather plain-looking Jewish carpenter suddenly appears claiming deity. He rounds up a motley crew of followers made up of uneducated peasants, a few fishermen, and a tax collector. The carpenter's teachings come across as far too radical, thus alienating religious leaders, the very group one would think he'd court. He does miracles, then incessantly warns people not to tell anyone. When countrymen flock to crown him their king, he scrams for the hills.

Between ego-trips about being their master's bodyguards and arguments about who is the greatest, his band of disciples seems quite hopeless. Then the carpenter begins morbidly predicting his own violent death. And, quite tragically, it happens! He's finally executed with a couple of outlaws on a stony hill outside Jerusalem. His followers scatter in terror and disarray. When a few begin claiming they've seen the resurrected carpenter, the others greet the report with unbelief and derision. Then he reputedly appears to them all, claiming that he died for the sins of the world.

The story is too peculiar, too unpersuasive to be concocted. It is too unique and authentic not to be true.

Prayer: Father, thank you for a gospel that seems so simple, yet is so amazingly profound.

⚓ Sept. 3 ⚓

1 Kings 19:1–18

The Prophet and the Pity Party

[Elijah] answered, "Lord God of Armies, I have eagerly served you. The Israelites have abandoned your promises, torn down your altars, and executed your prophets. I'm the only one left, and they're trying to take my life." . . . Then the voice said to him, "What are you doing here, Elijah?" (1 Kings 19:10, 13).

Elijah had bravely stood for God against the priests of Baal. Then suddenly he found himself sprinting for his life from Queen Jezebel. "I've had enough now, Lord," he moaned. "Take away my life." God refreshed him with food and rest, but Elijah continued running. Finally God asked Elijah what in the world he was doing. The prophet said, in effect, "I served you faithfully while my countrymen blew it. Now I'm the only faithful guy left and they're trying to kill me." God replied that if he insisted on leaving the ministry, OK. He mentioned a few final errands and named Elijah's successor. Then almost as if in passing, God said, "By the way, Elijah, you were never the lone ranger. I still have seven thousand people whose knees haven't knelt to Baal."

For years my health has limited me a bit, and I used to pity myself, as if I were alone in my struggles. When people condemned self-pity, I would think, "What stone-cold jerks. If they ever had some tough times, they'd change their tune." But, in reality, I don't think they were saying we can never feel sad or even angry about trials, and they weren't saying that we don't all need regular empathy and encouragement. I think they were saying that if we whine, become bitterly sorry for ourselves, and blame everybody around us including God, then we slowly destroy ourselves. I still give in to self-pity occasionally, but I'm doing better. What about you?

Prayer: Lord, when I'm tempted to feel bitter or sorry for myself, remind me of the destructiveness of the habit.

⚓ Sept. 4 ⚓

Judges 11:1–33

Least Likely to Succeed

The God who is in his holy dwelling place is the father of the fatherless and the defender of widows. God places lonely people in families (Psalm 68:5–6).

He was the illegitimate result of his father's visit to a prostitute. His half-brothers hated him and denied him any inheritance. When the elders of Israel banned him from Gilead, he became a bandit chief over a ragtag group of malcontents. His name was Jephthah; and amazingly, he was eventually appointed a judge in Israel.

This occurred when the region of Gilead was threatened by the Ammonite army and the elders turned desperately to Jephthah for military leadership. He reluctantly agreed to defend them if, upon victory, he'd be appointed chief over them. They agreed, and a God-dependent Jephthah soundly thrashed the Ammonites.

In a high school yearbook, Jephthah would probably have been voted least likely to succeed. Seemingly, the only thing he had going for himself was a lion-hearted toughness that wins human conflicts. Yet in his rough-edged way, Jephthah believed deeply in God, and he gallantly defended God's people. He was even listed alongside biblical heroes like David and Samuel in Faith's Hall of Fame (Heb. 11:32).

You may bear scars, just as Jephthah did. But God loves to build his heroes of faith out of the unlikeliest people. He may just want to build one out of you.

Prayer: Father, if you can use an outcast like Jephthah, I believe you can use me to win victories for your kingdom.

⚓ Sept. 5 ⚓

Daniel 6:1–23
Humble Consistency

The other officials and satraps tried to find something to accuse Daniel of in his duties for the kingdom. But they couldn't find anything wrong because he was trustworthy. No error or fault could be found (Daniel 6:4).

One of the great challenges of the Christian life is maintaining consistency. It seems evident that God is pleased more by the humbly consistent believer than the flamboyant person who vacillates between sensational achievement and spiritual negligence.

Daniel had the reputation of being humble and steady in his walk with God. In contrast, Gideon was inconsistent as a leader. (His story is in Judges 6–8.) He finally agreed to lead Israel into battle but not without repeated supernatural signs from God. He showed humility when selected by God and wouldn't usurp kingship after victory, but he multiplied personal riches and wives, a practice condemned by God. He destroyed the altar of Baal at the risk of his life but later made a gold ephod which the Israelites worshipped. Apparently devoted to God himself, Gideon didn't train others in God's ways and, after his death, the people immediately turned back to idolatry.

Let's go Daniel's way and determine to be humbly consistent before God. Faithfulness is far more important to him than spiritual notoriety or public appeal. Though some may flip-flop between exploits and negligence, let's kneel quietly at our prayer window each day, resolutely being faithful before a watching world.

Prayer: Lord, I want to be more consistent—like Daniel. Make me devoted and determined to be dependable.

2 SAMUEL 21
"I GOT YOU COVERED"

Two people are better than one because together they have a good reward for their hard work. If one falls, the other can help his friend get up. But how tragic it is for the one who is all alone when he falls (Ecclesiastes 4:9–10).

One conscientious rule of military strategy is not to rush into battle without adequate coverage. In other words, there should be enough firepower from the ground or the air so a battalion doesn't get trapped and annihilated.

King David led his army into battle against the Philistines and forgot that cardinal rule himself. David was on the front lines fighting valiantly along with his troops, but he was no longer a young chicken. He began gasping hoarsely and his arms felt like tree trunks. Realizing David's weakness, Benob, a giant Philistine, rushed at him jabbing with a huge bronze spear. In a split second, a soldier named Abishai leaped in, driving back the rabid warrior and saving David's life. After a brief brutal clash, Abishai's sword slid past Benob's defense, and he went down for the last time.

When the battle was over, David's men were very upset. He had placed himself in a precarious situation without adequate support. Abishai's name means "source of wealth," and he certainly proved he was worth his weight in gold that day.

Shortly before Peter denied Christ, Jesus told him that Satan longed to run the apostles through the wringer, but Jesus said he was praying for him. "When you recover," continued Jesus, "strengthen the other disciples." He was saying, "I've got you covered now, Peter, and when you emerge victorious, keep the others covered." We must not make the mistake David made.

PRAYER: God, let me always face the battle with brothers and sisters who can strengthen me and who can keep me conscientious and accountable.

2 SAMUEL 14:23–33

SALVAGING DIFFICULT RELATIONSHIPS

Whoever loves his son disciplines him from early on (Proverbs 13:24).

Absalom belonged on the cover of *Gentleman's Quarterly*. This son of David was rivetingly handsome and deftly charming. Folks even raved about his head of hair, which was magnificent. He got tons of attention—that is, from everyone except his own father.

When David committed adultery and murder, surely his sons heard all about it. Not long afterward, David's eldest son, Amnon, raped his own sister, and David didn't so much as raise a finger in discipline. Maddened by the injustice of it all, Absalom invited all his brothers over for a barbecue and had a couple of hit men knock off Amnon.

Fearful of reprisal, Absalom fled the vicinity and went into exile. For three long years, his father had no contact with him. When he was talked into allowing Absalom to return, two more years crept by during which David avoided him. Finally, Absalom sent someone to beg an audience with his father, and at long last, David relented and saw his son. But evidently the father/son relationship had hit the red zone from which there is rarely a recovery. Bitter and vindictive, Absalom won the hearts of David's subjects and led a revolt against him.

When God gives us relational responsibilities, as difficult as they can be, we must communicate, talk things through, work things out. Otherwise, splintered relationships can snowball into disaster.

PRAYER: Father, help me not to allow relationships to spiral out of control because of my refusal to work things out.

⚓ Sept. 8 ⚓

2 Samuel 6:16–23

Mutual Acceptance

Why do you criticize or despise other Christians? Everyone will stand in front of God to be judged (Romans 14:10).

King David was ecstatic with praise. Wearing only a linen ephod, he danced before the Lord. His wife Michal watched from a window above, despising his uninhibited worship.

That evening, Michal greeted David with dark sarcasm: "'How dignified Israel's king was today! He was exposing himself before the eyes of the slave girls of his palace staff'" (2 Sam. 6:20).

Numbed, he replied, "'I didn't dance in front of the slave girls but in front of the Lord. . . . Even if I am humiliated in your eyes, I will be honored by these slave girls you speak about'" (2 Sam. 6:21–22).

Christians practice many forms of worship. Some bow silently on their knees and some raise their hands in solemn gratitude, while others pour out their hearts in unbridled praise. It's easy to criticize styles of worship that are different from ours.

God hates scornful, judging attitudes. We should try to be accepting of true Christians who scripturally express their faith in ways that differ from ours, remembering that God judges attitudes of the heart, not simply the mode of expression.

Prayer: Lord, govern my attitudes toward brothers and sisters who worship in ways that seem unusual to me.

2 CHRONICLES 26

BELIEVING YOUR OWN HEADLINES

Everyone with a conceited heart is disgusting to the LORD. Certainly, such a person will not go unpunished (Proverbs 16:5).

Uzziah is not a household name. Yet, it seems he should be as well known as David or Solomon. The Bible presents Uzziah as one of the greatest kings of Judea because he did right in God's sight and served him devotedly.

Only sixteen years old when crowned, King Uzziah built many cities, and Judah flourished under his rule. His own plowmen irrigated Judah and made it fertile and productive. Uzziah also developed a vast and powerful military and even invented engines for war. Thus, "[his] fame spread far and wide because he had strong support until he became powerful" (2 Chron. 26:15).

But when his power reached its zenith, Uzziah began to believe his own headlines. One day, he entered the temple to offer incense on the altar. Priests confronted him, insisting that God had decreed that only priests could burn incense before the Lord.

With incense in his hand and rage flashing from his eyes, Uzziah stuck out his chin, rebelliously refusing to leave. Suddenly the white rash of leprosy broke across his forehead, and the king was escorted out of the temple, finally humbled by God. Maybe this is why one of the greatest kings of Judah is not well-known.

Have you met a person who thinks he or she's exempt from God's commands? There is more hope for a fool than for those who resemble Uzziah.

PRAYER: Lord, when life's circumstances lift me to the mountaintops, may I not forget you. May I credit you with every success.

⚓ Sept. 10 ⚓

Acts 8:9–24
Spiritual Simony

[Quarreling] produces jealousy, rivalry, cursing, suspicion, and conflict between people whose corrupt minds have been robbed of the truth. They think that a godly life is a way to make a profit (1 Timothy 6:4–5).

"Just name your price," Simon argued to the apostles. "I want some of that power, too." Simon Magus was a sorcerer in the city of Samaria, and when he saw the Holy Spirit's power in action, he figured he could buy it and add it to his repertoire of tricks.

"May your money be destroyed with you," answered Peter, "because you thought you could buy God's gift. You won't have any share in this because God can see how twisted your thinking is. So change your wicked thoughts, and ask the Lord if he will forgive you for thinking like this" (Acts 8:20–22).

Maybe the most surprising thing about Simon's bribery is that it occurred after he claimed to believe in Christ and was baptized. He then followed Philip the apostle everywhere, listening to the Word of God and seeing divine power at work. Yet, in spite of all this, Simon still missed the point. He watched the miracles of God with envious eyes. "Ah," he dreamed, "if only I could add this power to my sorcery! Surely I'd be the greatest showman in the world."

Even today, Simon's reputation lives on in the term "simony," which means the purchase of church position or any sort of profiteering from sacred things. Is it wrong to grow rich using our spiritual gifts? Is it wrong to give to a church in order to impress or to sway its leaders our way? You must decide for yourself.

Prayer: God, let me never think of using my faith selfishly—as a means of profit or personal advantage over others.

⚓ SEPT. 11 ⚓

LUKE 7:18–23
TEMPORARY DELIVERANCE OR ETERNAL RESOLUTION?

"Whoever doesn't lose his faith in me is indeed blessed" (Luke 7:23).

At the bike shop, Andrea, Max Lucado's three-year-old, begged for a two-wheeler like her sister's. Her dad kept telling her she was too young to ride anything but a tricycle. "Daddy knows best," said Max. Finally, Andrea hollered, "Then I want a new daddy!"

When we doubt the Father or don't understand him, sometimes we momentarily feel that way. After John the Baptist was arrested, Christ continued his public ministry, seemingly oblivious to his cousin's dilemma. Finally, John sent a message which implied doubt as to Jesus' concern and authenticity: "Are you the one? . . . Or should we look for another?" (Luke 7:20). Not exactly something an image-conscious public relations firm would record.

Christ replied, "Tell John what you have seen and heard: Blind people see again . . . deaf people hear again, dead people are brought back to life, and poor people hear the Good News" (Luke 7:22). Jesus was saying in effect, "Everything's going as planned, John. The kingdom is being inaugurated." John was asking for temporary deliverance while Jesus was resolving eternal tragedy. And later, as Lucado writes, "the Father did nothing while a cry a million times bloodier than John's echoed in the black sky, 'My God, my God, why have you forsaken me?'"

In the fires, God knows that every disciple struggles with doubt at some point. God aches for our pain, but he must always do what he knows is finally and eternally best for us and those he wants to touch through us.

PRAYER: Jesus, thank you for understanding my fears and doubts. Thanks also that you enact what's best for me, even when it tries my fragile faith.

⚓ Sept. 12 ⚓

John 11:1–44

No Favorites

"Place my yoke over your shoulders, and learn from me, because I am gentle and humble. . . . My yoke is easy and my burden is light" (Matthew 11:29–30).

Jesus loved Lazarus. That fact is repeated from three sources in our Scripture reading. First, Lazarus' sisters send Jesus a message that "He whom thou lovest is sick" (John 11:3 KJV). Then we read, "Jesus loved Martha, and her sister, and Lazarus" (John 11:5). Finally, when Jesus sheds tears at Lazarus' tomb, bystanders whisper, "Behold how he loved him" (John 11:36).

Apparently Jesus spent much time with Lazarus and his sisters. Their home even served as his headquarters during passion week. Yet, Jesus didn't call Lazarus to be one of his close disciples. And it appears that he didn't make the high demands of this quiet man that he made of the twelve disciples. Of course, this doesn't mean Lazarus never served others. But we wonder why Jesus asked much of some and less of others—why he didn't ask more of this close friend.

Jesus didn't stonewall people who weren't part of his inner circle. He accepted Lazarus at his level of commitment and, in fact, counted Lazarus as a loved and trusted friend.

You may be tempted to think that only the busiest, or most committed, or best-known Christians are close to Christ and greatly loved by him. But you, too, are very important to him. As you walk through life with him, you can also come to know him as an intimate friend.

Prayer: Lord, thank you for taking me where I am and gently leading me toward maturity as far as I can go.

⚓ Sept. 13 ⚓

John 15:18–27
Think It Not Strange

Alexander the metalworker did me a great deal of harm. The Lord will pay him back for what he did (2 Timothy 4:14).

From Whyte's old classic *Bible Characters* come his comments about Alexander: We first come upon Alexander, a coppersmith of Ephesus, when called upon as a clever speaker before a mob of metalsmiths (Acts 19:33). Next he finds it apparently in his interest to be baptized and seen openly with Paul. But Paul's side does not turn out to be as serviceable to him as he expected, so we eventually find him in complete shipwreck of his faith (1 Tim. 1:20). In the end, Alexander is portrayed as a bitter man who so hates Paul that he hunts him down and does him much wrong (2 Tim. 4:14).

Some scholars question if the Bible refers to the same Alexander in each of these passages. If it is the same man, his initial devotion hid a core of soul-rot. In the end, his true colors showed, for he became a blasphemer of God and a formidable enemy of Paul.

If you've ever been hounded by someone whose pure meanness oozes out all over, you recall the sense of shock: "How could a person be so vindictive to a nice Christian like me?" Or we may think, "How can he be so brutal? Doesn't he know I'm a woman?" But Jesus was tormented, his apostles were martyred, and Christians are still baited and despised today. Like Jesus and like Paul, we must take any abuse without revenge and trust the Father for final justice.

Prayer: Father, when I'm suffering harm from bad people, let me remember that you're walking beside me and are shielding me.

⚓ SEPT. 14 ⚓

JOHN 11:49–52
BEYOND COLD MATHEMATICS

Caiaphas, who was high priest that year, told them, "You people don't know anything. You haven't even considered this: It is better for one man to die for the people than for the whole nation to be destroyed" (John 11:49–50).

Caiaphas was the high priest during Christ's lifetime, and this title also made him president of the Sanhedrin, the highest Jewish court. He was to hold this position for eighteen tumultuous years. Caiaphas was a tough, wily old politician.

Buechner also calls him a mathematician and explains why. Especially after the raising of Lazarus, Christ's growing notoriety spooked the religious leaders. They saw visions of a tough Roman crackdown if Jesus' following snowballed. Caiaphas argued that it would be better for one to get it in the neck than for many to get nailed for one man. It is doubtful that the high priest's padlocked mind ever honestly searched out and examined the truth about Jesus. Humanly speaking, though, his grim arithmetic was undeniably convincing.

"The arithmetic of Jesus," writes Buechner, "was atrocious. He said heaven gets a bigger kick out of one sinner who repents than out of ninety-nine who don't need it—that God pays as much for one hour's work as for one day's—that the more you give, the more you have."

But, in a sense, Jesus reached the same conclusion as Caiaphas and took it in the neck for the sake of many. It was not, however, the old laws of mathematics he was following. It was the New Math.

PRAYER: Jesus, thank you that you didn't use the grim math of human greed when you deliberated Calvary.

⚓ Sept. 15 ⚓

Acts 5:27–41

Wisdom without Faith Is Dead

They will appear to have a godly life, but they will not let its power change them . . . always studying but . . . never able to recognize the truth (2 Timothy 3:5, 7).

Shortly after Pentecost, the apostles stood before the Sanhedrin. Most of the council wanted to murder the apostles on the spot. Then Gamaliel stood and declared that political rebels like Jesus had risen up before and each had met his doom. "'I can guarantee,'" said Gamaliel, "'that if the plan they put into action is of human origin, it will fail. However, if it's from God, you won't be able to stop them. You may even discover that you're fighting against God'" (Acts 5:38–39).

Words of wisdom, yes, from a man whose heart was dead toward God. At this supreme crisis in his nation's history, this smooth-tongued opportunist came forward with insightful policy instead of decisive faith. With his great influence, Gamaliel could have had an impact for God on multitudes, but he chose otherwise.

Individuals make Gamaliel's mistake when they espouse an orthodoxy they don't themselves possess—when they're politically correct but miss the life of the gospel; when they worship or pray not out of sincere devotion but merely to impress others with their urbanity or eloquence; when they depend more on human insight than spiritual wisdom.

There is no evidence that Gamaliel ever concluded he was opposing God. We are Christians, yet maybe even we occasionally get so bound up in political correctness that we fight God's intentions for spreading his truth.

Prayer: God, open my eyes lest I be like the blind guide who ever learns but never comprehends the truth.

⚓ Sept. 16 ⚓

Genesis 25:21–34

Bad Choices; Bitter Harvest

Make sure no one commits sexual sin or is as concerned about earthly things as Esau was. He sold his rights as the firstborn son for a single meal (Hebrews 12:16).

Life may be viewed as a collection of choices since the choices we make determine much about both the direction and quality of our lives. Bad choices can lead to a lifetime of regret.

Esau bombed out in the choice department. He is described as a fornicating, profane man. This impetuous hunter chose to sell his birthright to his younger brother for the soup of the day. He chose to marry two pagan Hittite women. He chose to give in to murderous rage when his brother later claimed the birthright and the blessing. In Hebrews we read that Esau bitterly deplored the fruit of his decisions, but the tears couldn't flip back the years or improve his circumstances. It was too late.

Three hints may help you avoid making life choices you'll regret: (1) Take plenty of time to think through the pros and cons of choices before you commit yourself. (2) Pray for discernment and seek the wisdom of others. (3) Consider the far-reaching implications of particular choices for you and for others.

If you've made rash decisions in the past, it isn't too late to begin turning that around. It all starts with one wise choice.

Prayer: Father, give me wisdom far greater than my own as I make decisions, both small and great.

⚓ Sept. 17 ⚓

2 Chronicles 33:1–17

No Grace So Great

They took Manasseh captive . . . and brought him to Babylon. When he experienced this distress, he begged the Lord his God to be kind and humbled himself in front of the God of his ancestors. . . . And the Lord accepted his prayer (2 Chronicles 33:11–13).

Manasseh must have been a child prodigy. At age twelve, when most kids are collecting baseball cards, Manasseh was crowned co-ruler of Judah, joining his righteous father, Hezekiah.

But when his dad died ten years later, Manasseh's true colors emerged and all hell broke loose. The Canaanites were so evil that God had wiped them out, but the Bible says Manasseh embraced their gods in a way that gave new meaning to the word evil. As king, he obliterated the Scriptures, built idolatrous shrines, initiated temple prostitution, cast evil spells, appointed royal mediums and psychics, murdered innocents throughout the land, and even offered his own son as a sacrifice to Molech.

Finally God's anger spilled over, and he allowed Assyria to invade Judah and transport Manasseh in bronze chains to Babylon. Months passed in Assyrian dungeons, and Manasseh recalled a past almost too nauseating to face. When he could no longer stand himself, he cried out to God for forgiveness. In that dark prison, he humbled himself and pledged his last years to righteous living.

Our brand of grace would have consigned him to suffer out his days in a foreign cell, but God thought differently. God moved the Assyrian king to eventually allow Manasseh's return to Judah, where he spent his final years trying to repair the damage he had done.

Never underestimate the grace of God.

Prayer: Lord, I'm tempted to think I'm far more righteous than Manasseh, but I know that without your grace, I'd have been equally doomed.

⚓ Sept. 18 ⚓

1 Samuel 2:12–29

Being a Responsible Nurturer

A priest's lips should preserve knowledge. Then, because he is the messenger for the Lord of Armies, people will seek instruction from his mouth (Malachi 2:7).

The sons of Eli were worthless men who didn't know the Lord (1 Sam. 2:12). The sons of Samuel took bribes and denied people justice (1 Sam. 8:1–3). Aaron's sons were destroyed because they offered unauthorized incense before God (Lev. 10:1–2). Weren't all these the sons of high priests, the most revered holy men among the Jews? Weren't they reared within the very precincts of the sanctuary? Didn't they see their father always beside the altar, offering sacrifices?

In the case of Eli, we don't know exactly how he failed as a father. It seems as if he didn't spend much time with his sons. He only found out about their evil conduct through the grapevine via reports that his sons stole the best of the meat before it was sacrificed and were sleeping with women who served at the tabernacle. Eli asked his sons, "'Why are you doing such things? I hear about your wicked ways from all these people'" (1 Sam. 2:23).

Finally God declared judgment on Eli and his sons. He asked Eli, "Why do you show no respect for my sacrifices? . . . Why do you honor your sons more than me by making yourselves fat on the best of all the sacrifices?" (1 Sam. 2:29). Maybe Eli didn't sin personally, but he didn't stop his sons and may have secretly enjoyed the juicy steaks his sons brought home.

God holds spiritual leaders responsible for those he's placed in their care. The torches that shine brightest have been well lit in the home and the church.

Prayer: Lord, make me someone people can safely follow in the journey toward Christlikeness.

⚓ SEPT. 19 ⚓

2 SAMUEL 9:1–13
A HOLLOW BRAND OF SUCCESS

"You know that the rulers of nations have absolute power over people and their officials have absolute authority over people. But that's not the way it's going to be among you. Whoever wants to become great among you will be your servant" (Matthew 20:25–26).

David had loved King Saul's son, Jonathan. After Saul and Jonathan died, David invited Jonathan's son Mephibosheth to live in the royal palace, and he gave him all the land Saul had owned. David also insisted that he eat at his table along with his own sons.

Years later, David's son Absalom revolted against his father. All those still loyal to David had to evacuate the city. Ziba, Mephibosheth's servant, met David with supplies. When David inquired about Mephibosheth, Ziba replied, "He's staying in Jerusalem. He said, 'Today the house of Israel will give me back my grandfather's kingdom.'" David responded, "In that case everything that belonged to Mephibasheth now belongs to you" (2 Sam. 16:3–4).

After the kingdom was restored to David, Mephibosheth met David outside Jerusalem as the king and his followers returned. As a sign of mourning, the cripple had not trimmed his beard or washed his clothes since the day David had fled. He claimed he'd been intentionally left behind, but evidently David was still suspicious and gave half of the land to Ziba.

A similar sort of ruthless jockeying for position occurs today in the business world. In the heat of competition, we can find ourselves stomping on others to reach a goal. Success gained that way is lonely and hollow in the end.

PRAYER: God, let me not live as one who has forgotten that my greatest privilege is as servant to the Most High.

⚓ Sept. 20 ⚓

Job 16:1–8
Job's "Comforters"

Careless words stab like a sword, but the words of wise people bring healing (Proverbs 12:18).

When the bottom fell out of Job's life, and he plummeted to the pits, who was there to extend a rope of encouragement and lift him? Surely his wife and three closest friends would wrap him in comfort. But his wife said, "Curse God and die!" His friend, Eliphaz, told him he was wicked and that there was no end to his wrongdoing. Bildad said that if Job's dead children were living in sin, God allowed them to suffer the just consequences. Zophar asked accusingly, "Don't you know that the triumph of the wicked is short-lived?"

During college days, I recall a time when a friend was slogging through excruciating spiritual confusion and doubt. Once, as we studied in a corner of the library, he began unloading his anguish. Thinking I knew what he needed, I began lecturing him non-stop about all the technical reasons why he could trust the Bible. He snapped at me so angrily, I was struck speechless. It was the only time he attacked that way, and I think I deserved it. I wasn't perceptive enough to realize he didn't need a seminar on apologetics; he needed quiet support, encouragement, and the knowledge that I accepted him and cared whether he was angrily struggling with his faith or resting in calm trust.

Prayer: Father, make me a wise Christian who knows when to simply listen and love rather than challenge and correct.

⚓ Sept. 21 ⚓

Exodus 32:17–25

Followers with Backbone

Aaron had let the people get out of control, and they became an object of ridicule to their enemies (Exodus 32:25).

As the older brother of Moses, Aaron served as his spokesman and was the revered high priest of the Hebrews. Generally, he appeared to prefer righteousness over wrongdoing. The great weakness that emerged in his life, however, was that the man possessed no backbone.

Aaron did OK as long as his brother was around to set the example. Then Moses trekked up Mt. Sinai to receive God's Law and was gone for weeks. The Hebrews decided that their leader was dead and convinced Aaron to let them fashion a golden bull, which they began to worship. When Moses reappeared, he raged about the idol, and the bewildered Aaron only mumbled lame excuses. Later, when Miriam, Moses' sister, slandered Moses' leadership and his choice of wives, Aaron was again swept along in tides of rebellion.

Surprisingly, God never overtly punished Aaron. Maybe he took into account that, though Aaron found it difficult to say "no," he rarely initiated evil himself.

Some of us tend to be like Aaron—we prefer to follow rather than lead. But we must also be able to stand for what is right. Followers with backbone are the best kind. They know when to say "no."

Prayer: Lord, teach me how to set wise boundaries—how to say no at the right time and in the right way.

⚓ SEPT. 22 ⚓

PSALM 118:4–9

INTIMACY SPAWNS TRUST

"I can guarantee that God's angels are happy about one person who turns to God and changes the way he thinks and acts" (Luke 15:10).

How does Heaven respond to our earthly encounters? Jesus said that there is resounding joy among the angels over one single sinner who repents, and the author of Hebrews speaks of a great cloud of heavenly witnesses (Luke 15:10; Heb. 12:1). We're not sure exactly how much the heavenly watchers know of human activity, and we can only imagine their possible reactions. When the disciples went berserk during the storm with the Creator himself in the boat, did the angels laugh, staring in amazement at the doubt? Did angels shake their heads when the disciples fought about who was the greatest as they walked with the infinite Son of God? And what about the time when Philip hopelessly quoted to God Incarnate the amount it would cost to feed the multitude?

Why is our faith so weak so often? Joseph Caryl, Puritan minister, writes, "We say of some men, 'They are better known than trusted,' and if we knew some men more, we should trust them less. But the truth is, God is always trusted as much as he is known; and if we knew him more, we would trust him more." Caryl goes on to emphasize that with deeper closeness to God, we only discover him more worthy of our faith.

PRAYER: Father, let this old chorus reflect my faith—a faith that knows you very well:

> Faith, mighty faith, the promise sees,
> And looks to God alone;
> Laughs at impossibilities,
> And cries, "It shall be done!"

⚓ SEPT. 23 ⚓

GENESIS 19:1–26

TEARING AWAY THE TENTACLES

The angels urged Lot by saying, "Quick! Take your wife and your two daughters who are here, or you'll be swept away when the city is punished." When he hesitated, the men grabbed him, his wife, and his two daughters by their hands (Genesis 19:15–16).

Lot may have called himself a follower of God, but we are never told one selfless, big-hearted thing about him. He chose the lushest land for himself. His men fought Abraham's servants for grazing land and water. Making his home in Sodom, Lot became quite attached to a city crawling with evil perversions. And he chose a wife whose heart never left the city's seductions behind.

Yet, we read that Lot's soul was daily troubled by the filthy lifestyles around him (2 Pet. 2:7). So why didn't he leave Sodom before having to flee with brimstone smoldering in his robes? It appears that he'd invested too heavily in the profits of the city, whatever they were. Something about Sodom's prosperity and luxuries may have made it a very difficult place to leave. Lot is like those whose souls are vexed with the life they're leading yet will not finally break ties with it and begin again.

Are human associations or habits wrapping tentacles around your heart? As much as it hurts, God is asking you to tear those tentacles loose and sprint out of your personal Sodom. The wages of sin have never been reduced. But God offers a harvest of righteousness and peace for those who submit to his discipline and do not lose heart when he rebukes them (Heb. 12:5,11).

PRAYER: Lord, help me rip free of any associations, habits, or idols that are sapping my spiritual health or productiveness for you.

⚓ Sept. 24 ⚓

1 Kings 11:1–11
Faithful for the Long Haul

Since we are surrounded by so many examples of faith, we must get rid of everything that slows us down, especially sin that distracts us. We must run the race that lies ahead of us and never give up (Hebrews 12:1).

Near the end of his life, Paul wrote, "I have fought the good fight. I have completed the race. I have kept the faith" (2 Tim. 4:7). It's important to finish our spiritual pilgrimage with at least as much commitment as we began it.

King Solomon is rightfully known as one of the wisest individuals who ever lived. In many ways he showed exceptional wisdom during his reign. Yet, somewhere along the way, Solomon began losing spiritual perspective. He married foreign women who introduced him to other gods. At first, he may have thought, "Well, she speaks respectfully of my God—maybe I should treat her beliefs with the same respect." The trouble was, idolatrous beliefs crept gradually into the hearts and minds of Solomon and his subjects. As he reached his twilight years, his great wisdom was fading quickly into the sunset. If written by Solomon, the book of Ecclesiastes appears to be a sort of confession written when he woke up and realized just how stone-hearted and cynical toward God he had become.

Shortly before he died, missionary David Brainerd said, "I do not go to heaven to be advanced but to give honor to God. My heaven is to glorify him." Let's determine that, by God's grace, we'll finish the race in triumph.

Prayer: I pray that I won't simply be a great sprinter, but one with the spiritual endurance of a long-distance runner.

⚓ Sept. 25 ⚓

2 Chronicles 10

The Harsh and the Proud

Arrogance comes, then comes shame, but wisdom remains with humble people (Proverbs 11:2).

With one harsh, conceited word, Rehoboam forever lost the ten tribes of Israel. From his father, Solomon, the young man had inherited leadership over one of the wealthiest and most powerful nations in the world. Solomon had built up Israel mostly through heavy taxation and the backbreaking slave labor of his subjects. When Rehoboam became king, the Israelites begged him to ease the burdens of taxes and hard labor. The older, mature counselors told the young monarch, "'If you are good to these people and try to please them by speaking gently to them, then they will always be your servants'" (2 Chron. 10:7). Rehoboam's rash young peers said, "No way—give them an inch, they'll take a mile. Tell them that if your dad used whips on them, you'll use scorpions."

Rehoboam liked the idea of projecting a hard, macho image of power and bravado, and he made the fatal mistake of following the advice of immature young firebrands. After his tough guy routine, Rehoboam glimpsed only the clouds of dust as the Israelites left him high and dry. Only Judah and the Benjamites stuck with him. The damage had been done.

Like Rehoboam, there is also something that appeals to us about gaining the upper hand, telling people off, refusing to budge or compromise. It makes us feel superior and powerful, but, in the end, it will leave us very lonely. Most people run from the harsh and the proud.

Prayer: Lord, may I learn gentleness and wisdom in all my dealings with people.

NUMBERS 22:21–41
SLIPPERY OPERATORS

Balaam loved what his wrongdoing earned him. But he was convicted for his evil. A donkey, which normally can't talk, spoke with a human voice and wouldn't allow the prophet to continue his insanity (2 Peter 2:15–16).

Balaam lived in northern Mesopotamia and was not an Israelite. He was an odd cross between an Eastern clairvoyant and a prophet. When the wandering Israelites poured into the Jordan Valley, Balak, the Moabite king, tried to hire Balaam to curse them in the name of Yahweh. Balak figured if he could turn their own God against them, he'd have the Israelites licked.

When Balak sent for Balaam with promises of lavish gifts, at first Balaam refused hands down. Later, God allowed Balaam to go with the stipulation that he say only what he was commanded. Apparently, Balaam was still harboring a longing for Balak's rewards if he could squeak out even a few curses against Israel because God used Balaam's stubborn mule to stage a ventriloquial act, warning the old diviner against using any tricks (Num. 22).

Balak took Balaam to several different locations, but all the man could do was bless Israel. Finally, the raging king packed the prophet off with no rewards.

Still hungry for money, Balaam evidently advised Balak that one way to weaken Israel was to seduce the country into evil (Num. 31:14–16; Rev. 2:14). So Balak used Moabite temple prostitutes to lure Israelite men into debauchery. Balaam was finally killed in an Israelite campaign against Midian—a just end for a slippery operator.

We follow in Balaam's footsteps when we pretend a loyalty to God that hides our true desires for power or wealth.

PRAYER: God, I know you see past my thin spiritual veneer, when my real motive is lust or greed. Make me sincerely pure in motive.

⚓ Sept. 27 ⚓

2 Chronicles 24:19–22

Admitting We're Wrong

A reprimand impresses a person who has understanding more than a hundred lashes impress a fool (Proverbs 17:10).

King Ahab hated Micaiah because he never prophesied anything good about him. King Joash ordered Zechariah stoned to death because he spoke against disobedient Judah. Uriah prophesied destruction on Jerusalem and was murdered by King Jehoiakim's soldiers. Jeremiah was heaved into a muddy well by permission of idolatrous King Zedekiah because he predicted Babylonian victory over the king.

Of course, we're a little more sophisticated when we're told something we don't want to hear. We ignore it, or slander the messenger, or rant and rave about how righteous we are.

King David allowed his sin to fester for awhile. However, when Nathan the prophet confronted David with adultery and murder, he humbled himself and admitted, "I have sinned against the Lord" (2 Sam. 12:13).

If we are ever confronted with the truth about a sin we've committed, we also need to humble ourselves before God. It does matter to some extent how we're confronted. If it's done falsely, arrogantly, or hatefully, we may need to honestly discuss this with the individual. But nothing should prevent us from examining ourselves to see if there's any truth to charges.

Prayer: Lord, I pray I'll rarely need reproof, but when I do, let me humbly receive it and respond.

⚓ Sept. 28 ⚓

2 Chronicles 16:1–10
When Trust Crumbles

The Lord's eyes are on those who fear him, on those who wait with hope for his mercy to rescue their souls from death and keep them alive during a famine (Psalm 33:18).

Asa was a great king. He tore down all the idol shrines in Judah. He nurtured a prosperous kingdom. When attacked, he placed his hope in God, who led him to impressive military victories.

Then, for some unexplained reason, Asa's trust in God began to crumble. When King Baasha of the northern kingdom captured a portion of his territory, Asa stripped the Temple's gold and silver and sent it to King Benhadad of Syria to enlist his help against Baasha. Benhadad attacked Baasha's outposts and successfully made him retreat.

However, the prophet Hanani condemned Asa because he'd depended on Benhadad instead of on God. "The Lord's eyes scan the whole world," said Hanani, "to find those whose hearts are committed to him and to strengthen them. From now on, you will have to fight wars" (2 Chron. 16:9).

Instead of being receptive, Asa became furious and locked the prophet away in prison. It appears that Asa's bitter spirit never died. In old age, when the king contracted a foot disease, he refused to ask God for healing but depended solely on doctors.

Are you looking everywhere for help except to God? God doesn't resent our calls for help. In fact, he even gets angry at times that we refuse to trust him. You can depend on him.

Prayer: Father, when my independent spirit charges into situations instead of consulting you, stop me, remind me, and help me turn to you in trust.

⚓ Sept. 29 ⚓

3 John 9–10
Rot Among the Winesaps

Many people declare themselves loyal, but who can find someone who is really trustworthy? (Proverbs 20:6).

Diotrophes enjoyed playing the big shot. He slandered the Apostle John to church members. He seems to have rejected one of John's letters to the church. He refused to show hospitality to guests the apostles sent and urged others to do the same. In brief, Diotrophes was a grandstander.

Early on, Demas appeared to be a true Christian and a friend of Paul (Col. 4:14). But shortly before the old apostle's death, Demas ran out on Paul as he languished in prison. The apostle reports tersely, "Demas has abandoned me. He fell in love with this present world and went to the city of Thessalonica" (2 Tim. 4:10). Demas was a traitor.

Alexander the coppersmith not only became an apostate, but he was a dangerous man. He'd attacked Paul mercilessly, and Paul warned Timothy of Alexander's venom. Alexander was a destroyer.

Most spiritual service involves people—caring for them, working with them, relating to them. Many fellow saints are a pleasure to be with and work with. However, mixed in with the gleaming winesaps will be one or two rotten apples. It may be one who loves the spotlight and does anything to grab it. It may be one who seems a growing member of your group until he disappears into the drug culture. It may be one who tries to destroy any good work you're doing.

Don't give up in discouragement. If you do, Satan's the only one who'll be applauding.

Prayer: Lord, when I face betrayal or disappointment in others, give me the grace and the guts to not give up.

⚓ Sept. 30 ⚓

Luke 19:1–10
Jesus Meets a Tax Man

Later, at dinner, Zacchaeus stood up and said to the Lord, "Lord, I'll give half of my property to the poor. I'll pay four times as much as I owe to those I have cheated in any way" (Luke 19:8).

Zacchaeus was a dumpy little guy, and most people hated his guts. After all, he was a Jewish tax collector for the Roman IRS. Besides taking what was owed, Zacchaeus raked in a little extra from each citizen, which eventually made him a very rich man. In Jesus' day, Jewish tax gatherers were about as popular as our crooked politicians.

At one point, reports about a holy man named Jesus had piqued Zacchaeus' curiosity. He heard this Jesus was passing through Jericho. Realizing his height would make it impossible to see over the crowds, Zacchaeus huffed and puffed his way up a tree.

As Jesus approached the tree, he spotted the little man, and surely all Jericho thrilled in anticipation of the fire and damnation he would call down on this sinner. Instead, Jesus said, "Zacchaeus, come down! I must stay at your house today" (Luke 19:5).

This was outrageous! How did Jesus even know Zacchaeus? How could he speak civilly with him? And how could he want to spend time with such a scummy shyster?

Zacchaeus was amazed, too. He was so moved that he decided to clean up his act. When he declared his commitment to restitution, Jesus said, "You and your family have been saved today" (Luke 19:9).

Another sinner had come home.

Prayer: Lord, help me to see the shady and the desperate through your eyes.

OCTOBER

Heaven's Perspective of Success

⚓ Oct. 1 ⚓

Romans 8:14–17

Getting God's Autograph

His servants will worship him and see his face. His name will be on their foreheads (Revelation 22:3–4).

During the Civil War, the army took a rather dim view of desertion. Some deserters were hanged. Others stood publicly as a white-hot *D* was branded into their foreheads, and they were drummed out of the corps. After Cain murdered Abel, God placed a mark on him, but it was hardly a mark of warm ownership or one in which Cain could take pride.

The Bible also mentions positive marks for those God claims as his own. Our names are inscribed in the lamb's Book of Life and are engraved on his palms. Saints in Revelation have God's seal on their foreheads and each saint is given a white stone with his or her new name on it. In addition, the Spirit of God living within us seals us forever as God's possessions.

Life on this earth is a bittersweet mixture. For some, the troubles far outweigh the outward blessings, yet we can take great encouragement if God's autograph is written across our hearts. John Bale, an English reformer, writes, "If adversity, loss of goods, detriment of fame, sickness, or any other troublous cross happeneth, it is evermore for the best to them that are faithful. Perfectly shall all these be taken away in the regeneration, when to their glory both heaven and earth shall be blessed."

Life Focus: Success begins with God's autograph written across a human heart—an indelible mark of ownership. Take restful security in this mark that God will never erase.

HEBREWS 6:9–12

NEVER, EVER GIVE UP

He will give everlasting life to those who search for glory, honor, and immortality by persisting in doing what is good (Romans 2:7).

Perseverance can be defined as steady persistence in a course of action; to maintain a purpose in spite of difficulty or obstacles. Lord Tammarlane saw perseverance embodied as he hid dejectedly from military enemies in an abandoned building. An ant was attempting to lug a kernel of corn larger than itself up a high wall. Again and again the kernel fell. Sixty-nine times Tammarlane watched the dogged ant retrieve the corn and start over. Finally on the seventieth try, the ant reached the top. The insect's persistence gave Tammarlane courage to go on.

What are you about to give up on in discouragement? Your marriage, your occupational calling, the salvation of friends or family, a personal project, an important ministry? Is it something God wants you to give up, or is throwing in the towel just the easy way out?

Coolidge said, "Nothing in the world can take the place of persistence. Talent will not; nothing is more common than unsuccessful men with talent. Genius will not; unrewarded genius is almost a proverb. Education will not; the world is full of educated derelicts." The Christ who persevered through Gethsemanæ to what was beyond can give us power to persevere in his will and accomplish his purposes for us.

LIFE FOCUS: Success means hanging in there when every particle of your being shouts, "Give up."

⚓ Oct. 3 ⚓

2 Corinthians 9:6–13
Give Generously and Cheerfully

"Give, and you will receive. A large quantity, pressed together, shaken down, and running over will be put into your pocket. The standards you use for others will be applied to you" (Luke 6:38).

As a boy, my pastor, Truman, took two nickels to church every Sunday—one for the offering, the other for an ice cream cone on the way home. One Sunday on the walk to church, he dropped one nickel and it fell into a storm drain. A great theological dilemma loomed in the young boy's mind as he gazed sadly into that drain. He was quite certain it was God's nickel that was lost. However, when the plate was passed, he slipped his nickel in, and on the way home his mom bought him a cone anyway.

Many years later, God spoke to Truman as he and his wife moved to a new pastorate. God said to give their new clothes dryer to a Christian family in need. After an inner struggle, Truman finally obeyed. When they located seemingly the only available cottage in a new town, it just happened to be equipped with a washer and dryer ready for their use.

Though the specific ten percent tithe isn't commanded in the New Testament, regular giving is instructed and the tithe is a good starting point. In fact, throughout the Bible, cheerful giving is often linked to receiving. God seems to test our generosity and, as we pass the test, he may pour on more than we had before.

Life Focus: Get-rich-quick schemes don't yield true success. Give the little you have faithfully and generously, and God will make it up to you in his own way.

John 16:20–24

Happiness at Any Cost?

We ask him to strengthen you by his glorious might with all the power you need to patiently endure everything with joy (Colossians 1:11).

"Are you struggling with looming problems and discouragement?" the excited Christian oozes. "Just turn to Jesus and he'll solve your problems and give you happiness forever." Oh, really? Is this God's great purpose—to make us eternally, cozily happy?

C.S. Lewis reminds us that for those about whom we care deeply, we'd rather see them suffer much than be happy in contemptible and estranging ways. And, "If God is love," writes Lewis, "he is, by definition, something more than mere kindness. It appears from all the records that though he has often rebuked and condemned us, he has never regarded us with contempt. He has paid us the intolerable compliment of loving us in the deepest, most tragic, most inexorable sense."

Shallow happiness comes and goes, sometimes from one moment to the next. The happiness that lasts is an inner joy which only God can give. And he doesn't do it with magic wands or sickly sweet potions. Following salvation, God's love must work to make us more lovable. If he was content with us as we are, he would cease to be God. Lewis continues, "What we would here and now call our 'happiness' is not the end God chiefly has in view, but when we are such as he can love without hindrance, we shall in fact be happy."

Life Focus: Joy can fill your spirit because God is making you into someone he can love without hindrance.

⚓ Oct. 5 ⚓

Malachi 1:11–14
Apathy Breeds Whiners

You have tried the patience of the Lord with your words. But you ask, "How have we tried his patience?" When you say, "Everyone who does evil is considered good by the Lord. He is pleased with them" (Malachi 2:17).

King Cyrus had allowed exiled Jews to return to Jerusalem, and Nehemiah and Ezra inspired the paltry group to rebuild shattered walls and initiate temple worship. Eventually Ezra died, and Nehemiah was stuck in Persia. The Jews remained a tiny pocket of life in a backwater corner of the Persian empire. Solomon's glorious temple was only a stripped shell of pillars and walls. Dreams of the past collided with their sparse present existence, and bitter apathy crept into hearts. The priests muddled through ceremonies and burnt offerings continued. The people prayed and wept about the poverty and supposed injustice. They looked simply like a heartbroken people, but God saw something troubling beneath the surface.

A prophet named Malachi appeared and spoke for God in a series of pointed reminders and reproofs. But instead of responding receptively, the people threw back whiny, impudent questions, much like children with an attitude.

God said things like, "I have loved you, but you've despised my name," "You have tried my patience," "You have cheated me." To each assertion the people whined rudely, "How have we done that?" God answered, "Through offering lame, sick animals on my altar, through breaking marriage vows, through corrupted teachings, through refusing to tithe. Turn to me now and become my own special possession, and I will rise with healing in my wings."

Life Focus: You will never be successful if you insist on giving God your leftovers.

⚓ Oct. 6 ⚓

1 Peter 3:13–16

Not Superior, Just Forgiven

But dedicate your lives to Christ as Lord. Always be ready to defend your confidence in God when anyone asks you to explain it. However, make your defense with gentleness and respect (1 Peter 3:15).

A friend has been struggling recently with the pressure to appear perfect to non-Christians. I agreed that we should try to live purely through Christ, but I also encouraged him with the fact that often non-Christians respond more openly to us when we are transparent about our humanness.

Here is the gist of what one observer writes about his perception of born again Christians: They are apt to have the relentless cheerfulness of car salesmen. They tend to be a little too friendly a little too soon and the women to wear more make-up than they need. You can't imagine any of them having a bad moment, a lascivious thought, or saying nasty words when they bump their heads. They speak a great deal about the "Lord" as if they have him in their hip pocket. They seem to feel it's no harder to figure out his desires in any given situation than to look up a recipe in Fanny Farmer. The whole shadow side of human existence—the suffering, the doubt, the frustration, the ambiguity—appears as absent from their view of things as litter from the streets of Disneyland.

Sometimes we let spiritual arrogance seep in, and we become quite self-satisfied with our self-righteous superiority. We should always remember that we have quirks and faults and more than our own share of failures. We are not better than anyone else—only forgiven.

Life Focus: Successful Christians don't swagger. In fact, the most holy often reflect the most humble humanness.

Jeremiah 17:5–8

Those Who Know Him, Trust Him

Turn your burdens over to the Lord, and he will take care of you. He will never let the righteous person stumble (Psalm 55:22).

We never seem fully free from the crashing tides of anxiety about our troubles and the future—about our lack of necessities, finances, or friends. "Do not worry about your life," Jesus says. "Worry about one thing only: your relationship to me." Oswald Chambers acknowledges that this grates absurdly against our common sense. But we must beware of thinking that Christ's statement is made by one who doesn't fully understand our particular circumstances. Jesus knows our circumstances better than we do.

Chambers states that this attitude of trusting keeps us in perpetual wonder until we are not shocked and are adamant about anything he does in our lives. "What an impertinence worry is," writes Chambers. "Let the attitude be a continual going out in dependence upon God and your life will have an ineffable charm about it which is a satisfaction to Jesus."

Abraham went out, not knowing exactly where he was going. Step by agonizing step, God revealed his will to Abraham, but it was always within the context of revealing who he was to the patriarch. And that is how God works. It matters far less to him whether you should move to Utah or Uganda than it matters whether you are getting to know who he is. The relationship is the bottom line.

Life Focus: Walk closely with God and you will find your anxieties fading into his all-sufficience.

⚓ Oct. 8 ⚓

John 12:23–26
Dying to Live

"A single grain of wheat doesn't produce anything unless it is planted in the ground and dies. If it dies, it will produce a lot of grain" (John 12:24).

Once the Apostle Paul became convinced on a Damascus road that this Jesus who called him was really the Son of God, his life did a complete flip flop. Paul became consumed with love for this Jewish carpenter. This is all the more amazing when we remember that Paul had been a haughty Pharisee—insufferably proud of his religious prestige and superior knowledge. He had learned to impress others, condemn those who differed, and fight theological battles with sharp-edged rocks.

Saul was actually put to death on that cobbled road. Once it broke upon him that Jesus was Christ and had died for him, Saul nailed himself to the cross with Christ, and Saul became Paul, that seed which dies in the soil in order to live again as a fruit-bearing plant.

Buechner describes it this way: "If another man dies so that I can live, it imposes a terrible burden on my life. From that point on, I cannot live any longer just for myself. I have got to live for him, as though in some sense he lives through me. I can only live my life for what it truly is: not a life that is mine by natural right, to live any way I choose, but a life that is mine only because he gave it to me, and I have got to live it in a way he also would have chosen."

Life Focus: Some Christians don't live successfully because they have never died.

⚓ Oct. 9 ⚓

Joshua 1:1–9
Saturated in God's Words

"Only be strong and very courageous, faithfully doing everything in the teachings that my servant Moses commanded you. . . . Then you will succeed wherever you go" (Joshua 1:7).

A young Joshua suddenly inherited the intimidating leadership of several million people. The Lord met him for an initial powwow. In the brief conversation, the Lord challenged Joshua three times: "Be strong and courageous!" God reassured him three times: "I will always be with you; I will never abandon you." There was only one condition for success, which was repeated in three ways: Faithfully do the teachings Moses commanded, never stop reciting these teachings, and think about them night and day.

"Do this," God said, "and you will prosper and succeed wherever you go."

We might have expected God to lecture Joshua about how to beat the wayward into shape or how to strategize battles that would scare Canaanite armies. Instead, he challenged Joshua to eat, drink, and sleep God's Law until doing it became second nature.

Similarly, the Hebrews were challenged to repeat the divine laws to their children, to talk about them at home and away and when they rested and roused. They were to write them down, tie them around their wrists, wear them as headbands, and record them on their doorframes and gates.

The reason for such fanaticism may be found in a quote by Bernard of Clairvaux: "My heart is a vain heart—a vagabond and unstable heart. It agrees not with itself, it alters its purposes, changes its judgments, frames new thoughts, pulls down the old, it wills and wills not, never remaining the same." With such fickle, wandering hearts, nothing but a consistent saturation in God's life instructions can keep us on the right track.

Life Focus: Any success will be consumed in fickle waywardness unless the Word of God is central in our everyday lives.

⚓ Oct. 10 ⚓

Philippians 3:1–11

Process, Not Just Product

These things that I once considered valuable, I now consider worthless for Christ. It's far more than that! I consider everything else worthless because I'm much better off knowing Christ Jesus my Lord (Philippians 3:7–8).

In Western societies, we tend to be product-oriented, while many other cultures focus more on the process. Oswald Chambers warns against those who make productiveness the preeminent ground of appeal. If sheer, long-term usefulness is the only test, then Jesus was one of the greatest failures who ever lived.

We also tend to think that if we obey Christ, he'll lead us to overwhelming visible success. "We must never place our dreams of success," writes Chambers, "as God's purpose for us. The process itself is of most concern to God, and if I can stay calm and unperplexed in the middle of the turmoil, that is the end of the purpose of God."

Lazarus was not one of the twelve disciples. The quiet man had one great God-honoring moment when he stumbled out of that tomb wrapped in graveclothes. Onesimus helped care for Paul while the old apostle was in prison, and Paul raved about his Christian companionship. Tabitha wasn't a deacon, and she never prophesied; she simply sat at home and knitted clothing for the poor. Each was doing God's will.

When the seventy disciples returned to Jesus rejoicing because of authority over demonic forces, Jesus said that the actual focus of their rejoicing should be that their names are written in heaven. It is the relationship that is most important to God, not just phenomenal spiritual success. Process, not product.

Life Focus: Don't be puffed up in all that you accomplish for God. Success will emerge through the process of getting to know him.

⚓ OCT. 11 ⚓

1 CORINTHIANS 1:26–31
CRAZY AS LOONS

God chose what the world considers nonsense to put wise people to shame (1 Corinthians 1:27).

"We are fools for Christ's sake," says Paul. We give hard-earned money away, waste valuable time studying a holy book, pray to an invisible deity, reject the enjoyment of immoral fun, and spread the Christian Good News in mosquito-infested jungles where it takes years just to learn a tiny tribe's dialect.

Jesus also seemed to teeter a bit off-center. Buechner reminds us that the world says to follow the wisest course and be a success, but Jesus says, "Follow me and be crucified." The world says, "Always look out for number one." And Jesus says, "Whoever would save his life will lose it, and whoever loses his life for my sake will find it." The world says, "Law and order," and Jesus says, "Love." The world says, "Get," and Jesus says, "Give." The world says, "Further your own business at all costs," and Jesus says, "Be about the Father's business for all time."

It is no wonder that outsiders have reason to laugh at true Christians. The things we value and set as priorities make us seem crazy. If the world is sane, then Jesus is a lunatic. And that simply proves that the "foolishness" of God is far wiser than men, and the "lunacy" of Christ is infinitely wiser than the proud sanity of the world.

LIFE FOCUS: If you're ashamed to acknowledge that you're one of those "crazy Christians," maybe Jesus would sense shame in claiming you as a loyal disciple.

⚓ Oct. 12 ⚓

1 Timothy 6:6–12
Contented Tenants in Clay Mansions

A godly life brings huge profits to people who are content with what they have (1 Timothy 6:6).

We humans are a discontented bunch. We will always be that way if we think of this world simply as a place intended for our happiness. C.S. Lewis suggested imagining a set of people living in the same building. Half of them think it's a hotel, the other half a prison. Those who think it's a hotel might regard it as quite intolerable, while those who think it's a prison see it as surprisingly comfortable. If we think of this world as a place of training, of correction, and of building eternal treasures, it changes the whole face of things.

The Apostle Paul writes that godliness paired with contentment brings great gain. In other words, life yields huge dividends, but only to the Christian who has learned to be content in all conditions. We enter life naked, gasping, empty-handed; we leave it the same way. During our brief stay, we manage some temporal possessions, but we never truly own them. It is only our spiritual possessions that will continue on and hold their value.

Moreover, Petrarch urges bodily contentment, even in discomfort or illness: "Allow him who made your body to determine all things concerning it. Only the use of it, not lordship over it, have you received; and that only for a short time. Think you that you are the lord of your clay mansion? You are but a tenant. He who made all things, he is its Lord."

Life Focus: Contentment doesn't come through self-centered success goals but through a spiritual perspective on life that results in godliness.

⚓ Oct. 13 ⚓

1 Corinthians 12:4–11

Gifted and Called

There are different ways of serving, and yet the same Lord is served. There are different types of work to do, but the same God produces every gift in every person (1 Corinthians 12:5–6).

I've worked a hundred jobs—most of them to make ends meet during long years of schooling. But I've only known a few vocations. The word vocation comes from the Latin *vocare*, to call, and means the work a person is called to by God.

Maybe I should be more careful about what I claim are vocations. I was a youth pastor for six years, and though I still feel I was called to church ministry during those years, some may wonder since I didn't fit the typical youth worker image. Gradually, my motivation also shifted more toward adult ministries and, eventually, university teaching and writing.

Recently, I met a man who hates his job. There are thousands who share his sentiments. Many work chiefly for the purpose of making enough cash to enjoy their moments of freedom. Does God intend for us to find joy and fulfillment in vocation? That's a tough one. People like Moses and Jeremiah didn't necessarily seem to enjoy their calling, but David and Solomon did.

According to Buechner, a good rule of thumb is that the work God calls us to is usually something we are gifted and committed to do and something that the world needs to have done. For the past few years, I have been doing the things I love: teaching, writing, and painting God's creation. So far, there isn't great money in it, but I believe I'm using my true gifts to honor Christ. That's not a bad goal to shoot for.

Life Focus: Try to do what you're gifted and burdened to do, and what needs to be done.

⚓ Oct. 14 ⚓

Galatians 6:7–10

Faithful with Limited Resources

Always excel in the work you do for the Lord. You know that the hard work you do for the Lord is not pointless (1 Corinthians 15:58).

Dr. Stokke and his wife left the U.S. to serve short-term in a Kenyan mission hospital. He began treating patients suffering from a wide variety of tropical diseases, infections, and injuries.

On one occasion, a beautiful African girl was brought in to the hospital. Though she had a severe kidney disorder, there was a good chance of recovery. Through an interpreter, Dr. Stokke instructed the family to follow directions and to restrict oral fluid intake. Then he left for the evening.

Late that night, he was summoned by a nurse, but when he reached the ward, he was too late. The beautiful girl was dead. Stokke learned that the family had kept giving her liquids, as was a native habit. She'd literally drowned internally. He was furious.

The next morning, he sent word to the supervising physician that they'd probably be leaving Kenya early. Bitterly, he told him about the late-night death. Dr. Johnson gave him a piercing look: "Every day is a heartbreak here. I've lost patients that might have been saved in America. We do our best with God's help, and these people are far better off than they ever were before."

As Dr. Johnson turned and strode away, Dr. Stokke suddenly felt humbled—he knew Johnson was right. God used that tragic incident and some tough love to help Stokke focus on what a privilege it was to serve in missions, not in his own endurance but in Christ's. He and his wife stayed the entire tour.

Life Focus: Even when circumstances don't allow you to do all you could do, you can persistently make the best of each situation.

⚓ Oct. 15 ⚓

Philippians 1:20–21
Time Is of the Essence

You know the times in which we are living. It's time for you to wake up. Our salvation is nearer now than when we first became believers (Romans 13:11).

The great day had finally arrived. Denise was going to the prom with Chris. Even during her hurried morning time with God, Denise couldn't help but think about her prom date.

That evening as Denise put on her formal, she allowed herself to dream. She saw herself in a wedding dress with Chris standing by her side, smiling at her. . . . Suddenly the doorbell rang. Minutes later, the couple was headed toward the Grand Rapids Marriott, where the prom was to be held.

It happened in a tragic instant. An intersection, a hurtling car, the screeching of brakes, an ear-splitting scream, the horrible crunch of metal and splintering glass, then a deadly silence. In a brief moment, a drunk driver had snatched away the life of a beautiful young girl.

Her mother found Denise's *Daily Bread* devotional lying open on her bed. The day's reading was entitled "Your Last Few Hours." Part of it read, "If you knew you had only a few hours to live, how would you spend the time? Since you don't know when the Lord Jesus may come or when you may die, now is the time to confess your sin. . . . If you do all the things now that you might wish you'd done differently, there'll be no regrets in your last few hours."

Life Focus: Success means assuming God will give you a rich, long life, but living as if your life could end tomorrow.

⚓ Oct. 16 ⚓

Psalm 127:1–3

God's Will Equals Success

Many plans are in the human heart, but the advice of the Lord will endure (Proverbs 19:21).

God lays out his will for us morally, but he doesn't show his specific will in the practical matters of life. That's a current mentality among Christians. Of course, obeying God's moral will is paramount. And, in a sense, it does seem as if the infinite God has little interest in or desire to reveal things like where we should live, who we should marry, or how we should serve the church.

Yet, if one leafs through the book of Acts, one finds example after example of detailed guidance by the Holy Spirit. For instance, during a prayer time, the Holy Spirit specifically singles out Barnabas and Paul to do mission work. Later, Paul and Silas also team up and preach through Phrygia and Galatia because the Holy Spirit keeps them from preaching in Asia. They try to enter Bithynia but the Spirit of Jesus doesn't allow it. So, instead, they travel to Troas. Then after a vision of the need in Macedonia, they know the Spirit is calling them there (Acts 16:6–10).

Do we too often depend on our own brilliant ideas and well-planned strategies? God's plans may be different—at times, they may seem as if they're weak, yet they succeed while ours, seemingly so perfect, fail. We should pray, think, discuss, and plan and then wait on God. It must grieve him when we write all the music and arrogantly invite him to play the tune.

Life Focus: Don't depend on your own strategies for success, no matter how brilliant they seem. Commit every idea and plan to God and wait on him.

⚓ Oct. 17 ⚓

Romans 12:9–16

No Room for Self-Seeking

Love sincerely. Hate evil. Hold on to what is good. Be devoted to each other like a loving family. Excel in showing respect for each other (Romans 12:9–10).

The name Dale Carnegie is synonymous with achieving a brand of success through interpersonal skills. The motivations for his principles seem an odd mixture of self-serving and self-giving. He writes that since people usually do what they want to, we must somehow make them want to do what we want. On the flip side, Carnegie also states that the world is "full of grabbing, self-seeking people, so the rare individual who unselfishly tries to serve others has an enormous advantage."

Maybe Carnegie is reflecting the losing battle many fight between doing selflessly and desiring some praise or personal profit. When we do good as Christians, we should try to reach the point where carefully weighing the rewards doesn't even enter our minds. John Wesley writes, "Do all the good you can, in all the ways you can, to all the souls you can, in every place you can, at all the times you can, with all the zeal you can, as long as ever you can."

Many principles Carnegie claims—listening, showing appreciation, avoiding criticism and bitter arguments, seeing things from another's viewpoint—really find their source in the Bible. We would do well to apply them; they comprise ways to do good and care deeply.

Life Focus: No Christian who ever genuinely cares about people will be the loser. God will see to it.

⚓ Oct. 18 ⚓

Matthew 12:38–42
A Generation Seeking Signs

The Almighty Lord will teach me what to say, so I will know how to encourage weary people. Morning after morning he will wake me to listen like a student (Isaiah 50:4).

As young college students, my older brother and I reached out for a special closeness to the Almighty. We decided to begin praying for a special, supernatural revealing of God. We spent hours in meditation and prayer. We begged and pleaded that he would show us his glory—communicate with us somehow face to face. The summer melted away and it never happened. Though we were disappointed at the time, later I realized we were wrong.

When Jesus was on earth, onlookers kept asking him for a miraculous sign, and his disciples said things like, "Show us the Father and that will satisfy us." That's the way we humans are. Chambers explained that we look for God to show himself sensationally but, in our day, he manifests himself in his Word and in his children. We face crisis and Christ may speak to us through a friend, or others may actually see Christ reflecting from us.

When Jesus said, "Lo, I am with you always," he meant he is always there on our journeys. "Life itself," writes Buechner, "can be thought of as an alphabet by which God graciously makes known his presence and purpose and power among us." He goes on to imply that we must then be careful in interpreting exactly what God is saying to us. So listen up and watch wide-eyed for him—sometimes the ways he makes himself known are indeed mysterious and wonderful.

Life Focus: Listen for God in his Word and through his children. It's presumptuous to demand sensational signs.

⚓ Oct. 19 ⚓

Colossians 1:24–29
The Church: God's Focus

Christ loved the church and gave his life for it. He did this to make the church holy by cleansing it. . . . Then he could present it to himself as a glorious church, without any kind of stain or wrinkle (Ephesians 5:25–27).

Have you ever heard people claim to be Christians yet admit they don't attend church? Other Christians become consumed with moral causes that have absolutely no connection with the local church.

According to the New Testament, the church is the one organism God has designed to evangelize to the world and nurture converts to maturity. God has never changed or rescinded that plan, and we shouldn't try to either. His great goal is that one day the church would be presented as a perfect, untainted bride for Christ.

John Owen, the great English theologian, describes the supernatural ongoing beautification of the bride: "On some God bestows much grace, that he may render them useful in the strength of it; on others, less, that he may keep them humble in the sense of their wants. Some he makes rich in light, others in love; some in faith, and others in patience—that they all may peculiarly praise him. And he renders his subjects useful to one another, in that they have opportunities, upon the defects and fulness of each other, to exercise their graces."

In a sincere prayer, Buechner offers local churches to Christ as a sacrifice: "King Jesus, make yourself known in them. Make your will done in them. Make our stones cry out thy kingship. Make us holy and human at last that we may do the work of thy love."

Life Focus: Try not to be a lone ranger and don't get caught up in rabbit-trail social causes. The center of God's program is the church.

⚓ Oct. 20 ⚓

Luke 19:11–26

Faithful in the Small and the Great

"The king said to him, 'Good job! You're a good servant. You proved that you could be trusted with a little money. Take charge of ten cities'" (Luke 19:17).

St. Francis was hoeing his garden when someone asked what he'd do if he were suddenly to learn that he'd die before sunset. "I would finish hoeing my garden," he replied. Jesus emphasized that a person should learn to be trustworthy in the little things, and evidently that was a goal of St. Francis.

Amy Carmichael adds a new insight. She acknowledges that we must be faithful in the small duties of life but warns that we not allow the small to forever dominate us. In other words, it's very possible to work ourselves into a deep spiritual rut, so that if God calls us to larger tasks, we're so stuck that we're not ready or willing to face the new challenges.

We should be flexible in God's hands, treating the small and great callings with equal commitment. Pascal writes that we should do the little things as if they were great because of the majesty of Christ dwelling in us, and we should be ready to do the great things as if they were easy because of Christ's omnipotence.

Stephen was appointed by the apostles as a deacon, one who merely distributed food to the poor and served tables. So Stephen did the grunt work, but as time went on, he gradually felt himself drawn to preach the gospel, and he willingly responded to that call. He preached his heart out until rocks whizzed through the air and silenced him once and for all. It didn't matter to Stephen whether he was serving a table or preaching to a multitude—he was faithful in both.

Life Focus: Be content with the small duties, but prepare for the great. Success comes through showing equal commitment to both.

⚓ Oct. 21 ⚓

1 John 1:7–10
Confessing Sin Quickly

Whoever covers over his sins does not prosper. Whoever confesses and abandons them receives compassion (Proverbs 28:13).

The Apostle Paul claimed that he always did his best to maintain a clear conscience both in the sight of God and before all people. Some Christians call this "keeping short accounts," meaning that we don't need to fall into habitual sin, become overrun with guilt, drift aimlessly for a few weeks, and finally crawl back to God doing penance. It also means keeping the conscience clear by forgiving and seeking forgiveness humbly and promptly. It is often not easy to do either.

Most of life involves relationships, and our sinful nature results in both sinning relationally and being sinned against. The old Pharisaic tradition said that if someone sinned against another, the victim must forgive three times only. So Peter must have thought he sounded pretty reasonable when he asked Christ, "How often do I have to forgive a brother who wrongs me? Seven times?" When Jesus answered seventy times seven, it must have blown Peter out of the water.

Jesus also said that before we offer gifts to God, we should seek forgiveness from those who have something against us. Asking forgiveness is sometimes even harder than forgiving. I was impressed when a friend apologized to me even though the conflict was partly my fault.

You, too, can stay in close relationship with God and others by forgiving and asking forgiveness as promptly as possible.

Life Focus: Keep short accounts with God and people—down quickly, back up quickly.

⚓ Oct. 22 ⚓

2 Corinthians 4:13–18
Magnifying God to the World

You were bought with a price. So bring glory to God in the way you use your body (1 Corinthians 6:20).

"I just want my life to glorify God," we exclaim. We may be sincere enough, but sometimes such declarations seem to be catch phrases we don't fully understand. The meaning of glorify, both in the Old Testament and the New, appears somewhat nebulous. In Hebrew it means to be heavy and in Greek it means to give an opinion or estimate. The Hebrew concept is to ascribe heavy importance or greatness to God, and the idea in Greek is to credit God with our highest estimate, thus honoring and magnifying him.

We glorify God for both his acts and his attributes. Of course, it's important to honor God for things he's done, but over and over again, missionary David Brainerd challenges Christians to glorify God for who he is in himself. It's a great thing to rejoice and honor God for eternal life, but, as we know, words can be cheap. To paraphrase Brainerd: If I rejoice only because of self-interest in Christ and because I'll be finally saved, that is a sorry business indeed.

We glorify God through our words and our lives. Again, it is easy enough to praise him when things are going well but what about when trials come? Owen writes, "In all ages, men coming out of great trials have been most useful to others; for God doth not exercise any of his own but with some special view to his own glory."

Life Focus: Are you willing to be an instrument that does nothing but magnify God to the world?

⚓ Oct. 23 ⚓

James 3:2–5

Gentle Words Show Strength

Whoever guards his mouth and his tongue keeps himself out of trouble (Proverbs 21:23).

I recently made dinner for a couple I hadn't seen in many years. During dinner, the husband said something offensive about me. His wife immediately realized it and drew his attention to it. He acted surprised, and it was obvious he didn't even see his remark as rude. We all have blind spots—we're insensitive and sometimes aren't even aware of it. But, if we allow him, God can give us greater sensitivity to those around us.

It's amazing how many proverbs relate to controlling our mouths: "When words are many, sin is not absent, but he who holds his tongue is wise" (Prov. 10:19 NIV); "He who answers before listening—that is his folly and his shame" (Prov. 18:13 NIV); "Pleasant words are like honey from a honeycomb—sweet to the spirit and healthy for the body" (Prov. 16:24). On and on the proverbs go, stating and restating the importance of weighing our words and speaking as wisely and caringly as possible.

It is a sort of tragedy when people display an obnoxious disposition that veils their assets from view. These may be people loaded with potential and intelligence—yet they practically dare people to like them. Remember, there is nothing wimpy about being gently courteous. "Nothing is so strong as gentleness," writes Ralph Stockman, "and nothing so gentle as real strength."

Life Focus: Pray that God will reveal your interpersonal blind spots. Gentle sensitivity always pays off a hundred-fold in relationships.

⚓ Oct. 24 ⚓

Psalm 126
God's Fullness for Emptiness

Those who cry while they plant will joyfully sing while they harvest (Psalm 126:5).

During a famine, Naomi moved to Moab with her husband and two sons. Her husband died prematurely. Then her sons married, but before they could even conceive children, both sons died, too. Naomi was devastated. Finally, she left Moab to return to Judah. Not wanting her daughters-in-law to feel obligated, Naomi tried to talk them into remaining in Moab. Orpah turned back, but Ruth clung to Naomi.

When the two women arrived in Bethlehem, Naomi announced, "Don't call me Naomi [Sweet]. Call me Mara [Bitter] because the Almighty has made my life very bitter. I went away full, but the Lord has brought me back empty."

In Israel, foreigners were often ignored or even despised. Ruth, the Moabitess, could easily have slunk around, returning hard stares with harsh words. Instead, she humbled herself to retrieve bits of grain the harvesters left behind. Thus, she and her mother-in-law survived. Eventually, God also brought a husband for Ruth and a beautiful grandchild for Naomi's empty arms.

Has life left you feeling empty and bitter? Maybe the very foundation and joy of your life has been ripped out from under you. At times like this, sometimes God places a "Ruth" in our lives and we don't even see it. Friends reminded Naomi: "Your daughter-in-law who loves you is better to you than seven sons" (Ruth 4:15). Has God placed such a person in your life?

Life Focus: Don't allow heartwrenching loss to produce bitterness. Look for the encourager God may bring into your life to restore the joy.

⚓ Oct. 25 ⚓

Psalm 107:21–30
Humble Thankfulness

Praise the Lord, my soul, and never forget all the good he has done. . . . As high as the heavens are above the earth—that is how vast his mercy is toward those who fear him (Psalm 103:2, 11).

A friend was furious when she saw a wheelchair-bound acquaintance in a drive-in with a date. Why was she angry? Because she knew the man in the wheelchair was married. For years his wife had lovingly bathed him, transported him, and cared for his peculiar needs. Many times she'd sacrificed her own happiness and comfort for him. Yet he chose to thank her by carrying on an affair with another woman. What a monumental example of ungratefulness.

In contrast, when God moved King David to show kindness to Mephibosheth, the crippled son of Jonathan, Mephibosheth bowed his face to the ground. In profound gratefulness, he whispered, "Who am I that you would look at a dead dog like me?"

What about us? God is constantly there for us. He brings those who care for us in illness, encourage us in disappointment, and love us through our shortcomings. But sometimes we take it all for granted. We ignore, blame, or demand more than can be given. Thankfulness is the only response we should have to God and his kind messengers for the good they have done.

Life Focus: You, who deserve nothing, are daily given gifts of grace for which you should be forever grateful. It is God who grants you success.

⚓ Oct. 26 ⚓

1 Corinthians 9:24–27

Know Yourself to Control Yourself

When you find honey, eat only as much as you need. Otherwise, you will have too much and vomit (Proverbs 25:16).

Ralph Waldo Emerson is known for, among other things, a simple challenge: Know thyself. Why is that phrase considered profound? Because self-knowledge enables us to know the strengths we can use to serve God and humanity and the weaknesses that could lead us to disaster if left unchecked.

But self-knowledge can become vain self-worship unless it takes place in the context of an awareness of God. John Calvin writes, "Man never achieves a clear knowledge of himself unless he has first looked upon God's face, and then descends from contemplating him to scrutinize himself."

Based upon knowing ourselves, the next step is to learn how to harness or discipline ourselves to reach maximum potential. Today's society is notorious for a lack of self-control. A professional basketball player comes to mind. He dyes his hair strange colors, sports numerous tattoos, poses nude and in women's clothing, cracks heads with a referee, and brutally abuses sideline photographers. Self-control is not his strong suit.

"I count him braver who overcomes his desires," says Aristotle, "than him who conquers his enemies; for the hardest victory is the victory over self."

Life Focus: It takes time to develop self-control, and it's a daily struggle. But until you become courageous enough to do battle with drifting passions, you don't have a fighting chance.

⚓ Oct. 27 ⚓

Isaiah 50:10–11

Reverence God; Respect Others

The fear of the Lord is the beginning of knowledge (Proverbs 1:7).

Why is the fear of the Lord the beginning of knowledge? Solomon begins his proverbs with this verse and then goes on for over five chapters proclaiming the surpassing importance of wisdom. Perhaps Solomon was saying that reverence or deep respect for God is foundational to relationships. In other words, if we take God or his words lightly or with disdain, there is no hope of initiating a solid, trusting relationship with him. However, if we begin by reverencing God, we open the way to knowing him and, by that knowledge, gaining wisdom for all of life.

It follows, then, that if we reverence God, we will also respect and care about those he created. Respect for fellow-humans is a commodity in very short supply these days. People would rather gossip, argue, accuse, use, and denigrate those around them. Those who are considered aloof or who don't fit our profile of normalcy or quality are avoided or relegated to an outer fringe of our lives. But maybe perceived coldness simply reflects a reserved personality. Maybe eccentricity may hide genius. Tough ways may be an outgrowth of childhood abuse and soberness may come of great trials. Thus, what we disrespect may be a reflection of the very qualities that make a person worth knowing.

Life Focus: In a day when God is treated with selfish familiarity and people are used or discounted as unworthy, maybe there's a need to relearn a lesson in respect.

⚓ Oct. 28 ⚓

2 Samuel 24:18–24

Honor God with Your Possessions

Honor the Lord with your wealth and with the first and best part of all your income. Then your barns will be full, and your vats will overflow with fresh wine (Proverbs 3:9).

Our financial dealings reflect our attitude toward God. Maybe that's obvious regarding issues like greediness, cheating, envy, tithing, or caring for the poor, but what about issues that are a bit more obscure?

God promised to bless Abraham tangibly and Abraham was soon to become a very wealthy man. In Genesis 14, Abraham joined a posse and rescued his nephew, Lot, from some who held him captive. When Abraham was offered victor's spoils, he adamantly refused it, saying, "I won't take a thread or a sandal strap lest you ever be able to claim, 'I made Abram rich.'" Abraham was determined that God would receive all the glory for anything he accumulated. He was jealous for God's honor.

In another case, King David asked to purchase a threshing floor and oxen in order to offer a sacrifice to God. When the owner offered the items as a gift, David refused with the words, "I won't offer the Lord my God burnt sacrifices that cost me nothing." David realized that a sacrifice to God should be what the word implies—an act of love that costs us something.

In both of these cases, Abraham and David were committed to using earthly resources in a way that honors and pleases the one who made possible any success they'd ever experience in life.

Life Focus: Are you honoring God in your financial dealings? If not, you're treading a very unstable path.

⚓ Oct. 29 ⚓

Mark 14:32–42

Honor, with Courage

"Father, you can do anything. Take this cup of suffering away from me. But let your will be done rather than mine" (Mark 14:36).

Which comes first—courage or a sense of honor? Courage is the quality of spirit that enables one to face difficulty, danger, or pain with firmness and bravery. Honor is personal uprightness resulting in high public esteem. Maybe it's not a question of which comes first. Courage to do right reflects a strong sense of honor, and it takes a person of honor to show courage in constructive, admirable ways.

Lippman writes that a person has honor who holds himself to an ideal of conduct though it is inconvenient, unprofitable, or dangerous to do so. To uphold one's honor often entails risk. "The paradox of courage," writes Chesterton, "is that a man must be a little careless of his life even in order to keep it." True success in life sometimes involves edging out on limbs, and fear threatens to paralyze us at such times. I disagree slightly with Webster's dictionary about one segment of the definition of courage: "courage permits one to face extreme dangers and difficulties without fear." I believe fear often co-exists with courage, and the greatest courage occurs in the midst of the most mind-numbing fear.

Jesus' face reflected incredible strain. "My anguish is so great," he said, "that I feel as if I'm dying" (Mark 14:34). He stepped away from his disciples and knelt. As he prayed, he shook, and perspiration soaked his robe. He begged to be spared the awful sentence. But when the mob came, Jesus stepped forward. It was his great sense of honor before his Father that initiated such unspeakable bravery.

Life Focus: Success is showing even a thousandth of Christ's courage because of our sense of honor before God.

⚓ Oct. 30 ⚓

Jeremiah 9:4–9
Honesty, with Love

As we lovingly speak the truth, we will grow up completely in our relationship to Christ (Ephesians 4:15).

What did George Washington most want to be known for? He stated, "I hope I shall possess firmness and virtue enough to maintain what I consider the most enviable of all titles, the character of an honest man."

I believe it was shortly after the Revolutionary War that Washington stood before his highest officers for one last time. In that day, tremendous stock was placed in the outer strength and force of a man, and any sign of weakness was pounced upon. As Washington looked down to read his farewell, he slowly put on his spectacles. Realizing the shock of his men at this sign of weakness, Washington said, "Gentleman, I'm afraid I have lost my eyesight in the service of my country." Washington's honest, humble admitting of weakness brought tears and a groundswell of respect for a beloved leader.

Few of us would say that our aim is dishonesty, but often a person who self-protectingly lets dishonesty creep into small matters may not be fully trustworthy in the large ones. Integrity is a quality built upon both moral principle and compassion. Ephesians 4:15 emphasizes the importance of lovingly speaking the truth. It is not enough to speak the truth, because blunt truth can devastate. And it is not enough to love if that love prevents us from speaking difficult truth.

Life Focus: For the Christian, honesty and love must always walk hand in hand.

⚓ Oct. 31 ⚓

1 Samuel 17:26–51

In God's Hands, Any Talent Is Significant

David replied to Saul, "I am a shepherd for my father's sheep. . . . The Lord, who saved me from the lion and the bear, will save me from this Philistine" (1 Samuel 17:34, 37).

When David slung that stone at the nine-foot giant, he was doing what came naturally. Young David was a shepherd, not a swordsman. He had an ability and he'd honed it for countless hours in fields alone with his flocks. Some would say stone-slinging isn't much of a talent, but it sure saved the day when all Israel trembled before Goliath. And when the boy volunteered to face the brute, maybe it didn't reflect rash arrogance as much as trust in an almighty God to use his paltry talent so "the whole world will know that Israel has a God."

The Philistines were a dominant culture, partly because they were among the first to fashion effective iron weaponry. When young David was older and King Saul was jealously pursuing him, he holed up for a while in Philistine territory. Possibly during this time he learned their secrets of weapon-making, because in decades following, Israel and nearby cultures appeared with iron weapons and Philistine domination gradually ebbed.

Whether with simple abilities like David's stone-slinging or more complex abilities like Philistine weapon-fashioning, God expects us to use abilities for his honor as he gives opportunity. In the new covenant, could this be partly what Paul meant when he said that he'd become everything to men of every sort in the hope that by all possible means he might win some to Christ?

Life Focus: God can give you success through an amazing ability or through a very simple gift. Dedicate them all to God.

NOVEMBER

Fighting Battles; Braving Trials

⚓ Nov. 1 ⚓

2 Timothy 2:1–4

No Tin Soldiers

Join me in suffering like a good soldier of Christ Jesus (2 Timothy 2:3).

God doesn't call us into a convalescent center but into an army to serve him on spiritual battlefields. Tin soldiers cannot face battles like these. These battles require warriors who volunteer to serve him without counting the cost.

Some of us want to wave flags and march in dress parades. We hide in snug fortresses where we talk strategy, study maps, and deal with nonessentials far from any battles. We sing "Onward Christian Soldiers" but only fence with windmills.

It's no fun fighting evil. One can't simply push a button and annihilate spiritual forces with nuclear warheads. It's a strange sort of conflict. The enemy is so powerful that the only weapons and military force that will work must be borrowed from One far greater than us. Victory is promised but only to the faithful.

There was a Sunday school teacher who volunteered to teach a group of wild junior highers who'd run off two other teachers. This lady knew what she was up against; but she also knew how to pray, persevere, and caringly discipline her students. She doggedly hung in there until one by one, many were won over to Christ. Most of us will not be called to face demon-possessed occultists in Satanic hotbeds, but spiritual battlefields in everyday circumstances and church ministries. Maybe we face less sensational situations, but they are just as vital.

Prayer: Father, teach me to fight the good fight of faith armed with wisdom to use your full armor.

⚓ Nov. 2 ⚓

2 Corinthians 10:2–5

Where's the War?

We take every thought captive so that it is obedient to Christ (2 Corinthians 10:5).

Where is the spiritual war actually fought and won for Christians? It is not in the picketing lines at abortion clinics or porno shops. It is not even in our crushing of physical passions with ascetic disciplines. The war is fought and won in the mind. Jesus said that evil thoughts, murders, adulteries, cursings, and other sins come from deep within the mind (Matt. 15:19).

Second Corinthians 10:2–5 focuses on the wars of the mind. Acknowledging our fallibility, Paul reiterates that it's not in human strength that we fight our battles. The weapons we brandish are divinely potent to demolish strongholds. "Our battle," translates J.B. Phillips, "is to bring down every deceptive fantasy and every imposing defense that men erect against the true knowledge of God" (v. 5). We must try to compel, captivate, and surrender each thought to the authority and use of Christ.

In 1 Corinthians 2:15, Paul states that through the Holy Spirit within, we have the actual mind of Christ. He goes on to share this mindset in Philippians 2, where he describes one who emptied himself of glory, took the nature of a slave, humbled himself, and gave up his body to death. This entire description reverberates with willingness to give all one is to gain eternal glory. Sure, the constant battle for our minds wears on us and we fall too often into immoral or self-defeating thoughts, but we must never give up. God gains glory from each small victory.

Prayer: God, please capture my thoughts so that increasingly I may have the mind of Christ.

⚓ Nov. 3 ⚓

Isaiah 30:19–21
No Pain; No Gain

"The reason I can still find hope is that I keep this one thing in mind: the Lord's mercy" (Lamentations 3:21).

Isaiah 30 is full of bright promises from God to the Judeans: You will live in Zion. You won't cry anymore. I will have pity on you and answer your prayers. I will be your private teacher, guiding you when you get off track.

However, couched between all the comfort is one brief caution: "The Lord may give you troubles and hardships" (v. 20). Ouch! Our human desire is that, along with all the other promises, God will also provide a failsafe wall of protection from hard times. Yet there is a powerful, priceless value in pain.

"Pain humbles the proud," writes Charles Swindoll. "It softens the stubborn. It melts the hard. The heart alone knows its own sorrow, and not another person can fully share in it. Silently and relentlessly, it wins battles deep within the lonely soul" (p. 231).

Etched in the words of Lamentations, Jeremiah's suffering is almost palpable. He claims God is the source of his pain. But then, in chapter three, Jeremiah finally seems to realize that only in silent acceptance of testings will he ever come to know God. He says that it's good to hope and wait silently for the Lord. The burdened should sit alone and remain silent because the Lord has purposely allowed the burdens. And, in the end, Jeremiah becomes ready to admit that only the Lord's mercy keeps us alive. His unlimited compassion is new every single morning.

Prayer: Lord, remind me again that it is often through the tough times that I come to know you better and become more like you.

⚓ Nov. 4 ⚓

Colossians 1:21–23
Hating Evil

"To fear the Lord is to hate evil" (Proverbs 8:13).

One of the realities of our day is the retreat from a healthy, vigorous hatred of sin. The development of a growing indiscriminate tolerance of wrong things may seem rather harmless. But Spurgeon writes, "He who is not angry at transgression becomes a partaker in it. Sin is a loathsome and hateful thing, and no renewed heart can patiently endure it. God himself is angry with the wicked every day, and it is written in his Word, 'Ye that love the Lord, hate evil.'"

Satan has won a great victory by leading so many in the church to accept what God condemns—to actually embrace what Christ died to destroy. We've lost sight of the holiness of God, and because of this, we've lost the beauty of holiness from our own lives.

Someone said, "There is no power in the world so irrepressible as the power of personal holiness." We need to relearn God's perspective of evil and cleanse our minds and hearts of the evil that so easily entangles us. We can become sensitive to his inner voice of warning and caution. Ask him to teach you, like Joseph, to sprint quickly from temptation.

Prayer: Father, forgive my growing tolerance of that which you hate. Draw me ever back into holy living. Teach me in my weakness to draw on your power and to put no confidence in my flesh.

⚓ Nov. 5 ⚓

Psalm 24
The Fad of Sacrilegion

Who may go up the Lord's mountain? Who may stand in his holy place? The one who has clean hands and a pure heart (Psalm 24:3–4).

I watched a stand-up comedian painting a silly picture of Jesus, making him out to be a self-deceived idiot. A sadness passed over me as I switched channels. One of the commentaries on our age is the stylishness of sacrilegious joking. To make fun of things sacred and solemn gives some people a sense of reckless freedom.

Even without evil intent, sometimes God is treated with a condescending over-familiarity. Some say, "Oh, God'll weigh my good deeds against my mistakes and I'll get by OK. After all, isn't he a God of love?" Forgiveness is considered cheap. It's seen as clever to give the impression that we can manipulate God, slap him on the back, and send him on his way.

The Bible warns against trying to use God for our own purposes. It warns that it's a fearful thing to fall into the hands of the living God. Those who know God best come into his presence with awe and profound humility.

The blood-sprinkled holy of holies give us access to God's throne room. There's no place for the cheap insulting approach by which anyone can saunter carelessly into God's presence. Though access to God is open to us, accepting that blood-bought honor must not be taken lightly.

"I live in a high and holy place," God thunders. "But I am with those who are crushed and humble. I will renew the spirit of those who are humble and the courage of those who are crushed" (Isa. 57:15).

Prayer: Father, I want to live reverently in your presence. Keep me aware that my access to you comes at incredible cost.

⚓ Nov. 6 ⚓

2 Corinthians 4:8–10
The Whiny Killer

In every way we're troubled, but we aren't crushed by our troubles (2 Corinthians 4:8).

Everyone faces difficulties, but the magnitude of those trials may differ enormously.

While on a mission trip to Tobago, Pastor Jack Hinton received one of the greatest shocks of his life. He was leading a worship time one Sunday in a leper colony, and church members were requesting their favorite hymns. Suddenly, a woman whose face had been averted turned toward Hinton. Her nose was missing, as were her ears. Most of her lips had rotted away, and when she raised her hand, it had no fingers.

"Can we please sing 'Count Your Many Blessings?'" she lisped.

Overcome with emotion, Hinton had to immediately exit. A team member followed him and sat by him as Jack wept. "Jack," he said, "I guess you'll never be able to sing that song again, will you?"

"Yes, I will," said Hinton. "But I'll never sing it the same way again."

Of course, we all get the blues and need encouragement, but we should flee self pity as we would a serial killer. Like leprosy, incessant whining can eventually eat away at the joy and fulfillment of life. Force yourself, if necessary, to concentrate more on the good things about your life, and there will be less time to commiserate about the bad.

Prayer: Father, never let me forget that life's blessings will always outnumber life's tragedies.

⚓ Nov. 7 ⚓

2 Corinthians 2:5–11

Dealing with the Adversary

I don't want Satan to outwit us. After all, we are not ignorant about Satan's scheming (2 Corinthians 2:11).

Christ had promised to accompany Paul throughout his life mission, but it was no joyride. The apostle carried it out under constant peril. He was stoned, beaten with rods, and shipwrecked. He was maligned by both Jews and Gentiles, ridiculed by the Athenian philosophers, jailed unjustly, and under threat of death by Caesar. Behind the formidable human opposition was the devil and his forces.

It's a fatal mistake to underestimate one's adversary. Sound military strategy involves knowing the enemy's capability and being aware of its movements. Sure, Christ is more powerful than Satan, but that doesn't mean we can lackadaisically ignore the devil's tricks.

Our God is the great I AM, while the devil is the great I AM NOT. He wants us to think of him as non-existent or even as a Halloween character with red tights and a forked tail. He's pleased that many picture him as a comic fictional creature and joke at the idea of a personal devil.

But we must never take Satan and his forces lightly. While we don't need to cower in terror of him, we do need to be alert and on guard. We can fully trust Christ to keep us safe from his schemes. God loves us and will never prove unfaithful to our trust. His unlimited power is available to protect us.

Prayer: Father, deliver me hour by hour from traps laid by the enemy. Help me to depend on your love and power.

⚓ Nov. 8 ⚓

Lamentations 3:17–25

Forging of a Work of Art

God has driven me away and made me walk in darkness instead of light (Lamentations 3:2).

"Our Lord is constantly taking us into the dark, that he may tell us things," writes F.B. Meyer. It may be the darkness of bereavement, illness, loneliness, or some crushing sorrow or disappointment. "But God has a purpose in it all," adds Meyer. "He has withdrawn his child to the higher altitudes of fellowship, that he may hear God speaking face to face and bear the message to his fellows at the mountain foot."

As we've heard, Christian character does not grow best in leisure and pleasant surroundings. Great literature and music were not produced in soft circumstances. John Bunyan wrote Pilgrim's Progress while in prison, Isobel Kuhn wrote her gripping missionary accounts while she was suffering from cancer, and Havergal wrote an immortal collection of songs with insights gained in a nine-year confinement to bed.

We do not become saints in our sleep. Great souls are born in the flames of hardship. Paul does not use the metaphors of soldiering, running, and boxing for no reason. If one wants to excel in these fields, wounds, bruises, and callouses are inevitable.

There may be periods when you feel beaten down and useless to God—when you see and feel no spiritual progress in your life. Yet unknown to you, God is forging in your life a work of art. One day you will see the end product.

Prayer: Father, let me fear no darkness where you lead me, knowing you are there.

⚓ Nov. 9 ⚓

Acts 16:22–25
Songs in the Night

I, a prisoner in the Lord, encourage you to live the kind of life which proves that God has called you (Ephesians 4:1).

Paul and Silas were chained in place in a dank Roman dungeon, purple welts striping their tortured backs. The easiest thing in the world would have been to curse their luck or complain bitterly to God. Instead, the two prisoners calmly prayed and sang hymns in the night. Other prisoners must have been astounded at the peaceful joy emanating from that one lone cell.

Paul didn't consider himself a prisoner of Rome so much as a prisoner of Jesus Christ. He had been so totally captivated by Christ's love that no tragedy, no setback ever darkened his loyalty. Like Paul, we can be so captivated that in spite of all, our restful trust in him doesn't sour or dissolve in panic.

Hudson Taylor received some very discouraging news at mission headquarters one day. A little while later, someone heard him humming a tune and questioned how he could respond in such a way. Taylor replied that he could rest in Christ because all was his responsibility and all was in his control. This was Taylor's "spiritual secret" and this was why his favorite hymn was "Jesus, I am Resting." He had learned to trust.

Prayer: Lord, help me to be at rest when all around me is going haywire.

⚓ Nov. 10 ⚓

Acts 16:16–18
When the Devil Loses Clients

Paul became annoyed, turned to the evil spirit, and said, "I command you in the name of Jesus Christ to come out of her!" As Paul said this, the evil spirit left her (Acts 16:18).

The Prince of Darkness is bold and arrogant in his forays against both Christians and non-Christians. He's a liar, a raging lion, a subtle angel of light, a blinder, a grinder, a source of all evil. He hates Jesus and he despises us, Christ's followers. Every convert won to Christ is snatched from the grip of the enemy. Every time a child of darkness turns to the Redeemer, Satan loses a client.

Paul was instrumental in releasing a demonized girl from Satan's grasp. Only God's power can accomplish that. Following the deliverance, Satan counterattacked. Paul and Silas were arrested and thrown into prison. God had the last word, however. Not only did he send an earthquake to free Paul and Silas, but he also won the allegiance of the jailor and his family, who promptly placed their faith in Jesus.

J.R. Miller states that battles are inevitable but victory is possible: "We say we can never be victorious—that we can never conquer these enemies. But, as we enter the conflict, One comes and fights by our side, and through Him we are more than conquerors." Though at times it appears that Satan's forces are winning, God is sovereign and he holds those forces on a leash. Don't panic or give up. We can withstand the enemy and pray clients away from his possession and influence.

Prayer: Father, lead me today to pray for someone in the enemy's grip. I know you're sovereign in the destinies of all.

⚓ Nov. 11 ⚓

2 Chronicles 20:1–30
The Battle Is the Lord's

"Don't be frightened or terrified by this large crowd. The battle isn't yours. It's God's" (2 Chronicles 20:15).

We live in critical times. A vast army of hostile agents is arrayed against God's people—agents like drug trafficking, alcoholism, pornography, abortion, false teaching, violence, and illicit sex spurred on by the media.

Centuries ago, Jehoshaphat, king of Judah, faced hostile agents, too, in the form of flesh and blood armies. Several different armies had joined forces against the Israelites. The odds against victory were staggering. The king turned his face upward in public prayer, concluding his anguished prayer with the words, "Lord . . . we don't know what to do, so we're looking to you."

Through a prophet, God replied, "Don't be frightened or terrified by this large crowd. The battle isn't yours. It's God's battle . . . take your position, stand still, and see the victory of the Lord for you" (2 Chron. 20:17).

In one of the weirdest military offensives in history, Jehoshaphat's troops approached for battle singing praise songs of God's holiness. Suddenly the shaky alliance between the opposing armies broke down and they began fighting each other. God's people watched as their enemies defeated themselves.

Eastern Europe and the Soviet Union seemed invincibly Communist and opposed to Christianity. Then God made it his battle, and these countries now actually ask for help in planting churches and establishing Christian schools. Let's stand still, praise God, and watch him do the impossible. Let's go singing into battle.

Prayer: Father, teach me to sing in the face of seemingly impossible odds.

⚓ Nov. 12 ⚓

Philippians 4:6–7
Peace in the Madness

Never worry about anything. But in every situation let God know what you need. . . . Then God's peace . . . will guard your thoughts and emotions (Philippians 4:6–7).

Writing from prison, Paul instructed the Philippians to have no anxiety about anything. "He does not deny," Buechner writes, "that the worst things will happen finally to all of us, as indeed he must have had a strong suspicion they were soon to happen to him." Paul simply says that even in the thick of them, the church was to "keep in constant touch with the One who unimaginably transcends the worst things as he also unimaginably transcends the best."

God doesn't promise to build a wall around us which will keep us sterile and without a scratch throughout life. He simply says that in the middle of the madness, his peace, which is well beyond human understanding, will guard our hearts and minds in Christ. It is the fact that we are nestled in union with Christ that makes it impossible for anything to occur unless he allows it. No matter what, we are not to slip into giving Jesus the silent treatment. We must keep on approaching him—asking, thanking, communing, loving—because the moment we turn bitter, we cut ourselves off from our only living lifeline. And that will, in the end, breed frustration and ultimate despair.

Prayer: Lord, let me keep that line to you always open, even when I feel like clamming up and crawling into a dark corner.

⚓ Nov. 13 ⚓

Matthew 16:24–26
A No-Lose Situation

Having nothing, and yet possessing all things (2 Corinthians 6:10 KJV).

Satan once approached a Christian and, with silky smoothness, he hissed, "I have some gifts to give you that will boggle your imagination."

"You can't give me anything," the Christian answered, "because I have everything—life, love, forgiveness, things present, things to come."

Flashing with sudden anger, Satan said, "Fine! Then I'll take away all you have."

"You can't deprive me of anything, because I don't own anything. It's all on generous loan from Jesus."

Livid, the devil shouted, "You fool! I'll tear you limb from limb and feed you to the vultures."

"I'm not afraid, old enemy. For me to live is Christ and to die means gain."

This wondrous combination of poverty yet plenty, having nothing yet possessing all things lifts us above the temptations and anxieties of this life. We escape both the miser's misery and the beggar's need. God is our sufficiency for all things.

Christ lived out this paradox on earth and, as his chosen heirs, we can do no less than follow him in the path he's set before us.

Prayer: Father, thank you that Satan has no leverage in my life because he can give or take nothing from me—I am completed in you.

⚓ Nov. 14 ⚓

Hebrews 10:32–36
Things That Can't Be Stolen

"If someone takes what is yours, don't insist on getting it back" (Luke 6:30).

During graduate school, I roomed for a while in a home where the son of the owner also stayed. While there, I stored some valuable things in the garage. Then a youth pastor whom I was assisting offered to let me stay rent-free in his home for a few months. However, he had no space for my stored possessions, so I got permission from the homeowner to leave them in his garage for a while. The landlord's son didn't like the idea, so he pawned off all my things and used the money to bolt to Alaska with a girlfriend.

In the book of Hebrews, we read of a situation where the possessions of Hebrew Christians were plundered. Few details are offered, but the text does mention that they accepted cheerfully the seizure of their property. Not only that, but these believers were made a public spectacle through taunts and violent sufferings, yet they didn't become bitter or hostile (Heb. 10:32–34).

I have to admit, I didn't respond that way to my loss. I was discouraged, angry, and frustrated. But why should I have been cheerful? The author of Hebrews states that these Christians were joyful because they knew they had a better and more permanent possession in heaven. "Don't lose your confidence because it will bring you a great reward." Build possessions no one can touch.

Prayer: Father, next time I lose something important to me, remind me that the eternal things I possess are still intact and will always remain so.

⚓ Nov. 15 ⚓

Luke 9:57–62
No Looking Back

"Whoever starts to plow and looks back is not fit for the kingdom of God" (Luke 9:62).

History records that when the Spanish explorer Cortez and his army landed in the New World, they burned their ships, thus cutting off all means of giving up and returning to their homeland.

Years ago, a pioneer missionary expressed a similar conviction while en route to a difficult and dangerous mission field. Aboard ship someone warned him he might die in the area he was headed. "I died before I left my country's shores," the missionary replied. He had counted the cost and there could be no looking back.

Citizens of Ephesus had been steeped in occult magical arts for decades. But as some placed their faith in Christ, they held a public book burning when they recognized the danger of keeping things that could lure them back to their old ways (Acts 19:19).

We, too, need to clear the shelves of an old life and put a decisive end to things that keep us from pursuing God's purposes for us. Periodically there must be a renouncing of our incessant collection of selfish comforts, rights, or agendas. We must put a torch to our boats and our bridges—retreat to the old life is no longer possible.

Prayer: Father, teach me to keep the forward look, always keeping you in clear focus.

⚓ Nov. 16 ⚓

Philippians 1:15–16

Joy vs. Happiness

Always be joyful in the Lord! I'll say it again: Be joyful! (Philippians 4:4).

Happiness is often related to pleasant circumstances when all is going quite well. We can understand happiness, for the American dream is involved with the undying pursuit of it. Happiness is good—there's nothing wrong with it. It's just a rather precarious emotion on which to base our lives.

Paul wrote his letter to the Philippian church from a gloomy Roman prison, yet he used the words joy and rejoice fourteen times. Paul's circumstances offered absolutely no reason for inner well-being. The setting was miserable. He was under threat of death. He couldn't count on a good lawyer. His friends were far away. Yet we find Paul rejoicing. Joy is found in one's orientation to Jesus Christ. Its source, its encouragement, its future is based in Christ. So it is significant that in his letter, Paul refers to Jesus Christ forty times.

I learned about joy at my first wife's funeral. After nineteen years of a wonderful marriage, she left me for the angels after suffering for three long years. Our pastor, who had married us, reminded me that the same loving Jesus who had given me my wife had called her back to his companionship. She was with him who she had always loved the most. At that moment, I felt his joy in my heart and I knew peace.

Prayer: Lord, please give me the joy I don't possess even when things go wrong.

—Tony Fortosis

⚓ Nov. 17 ⚓

2 Timothy 2:1–7

Tender Heart; Tough Skin

"I'm sending you out like sheep among wolves. So be as cunning as snakes but as innocent as doves" (Matthew 10:16).

You've probably heard someone say, "I'm a lover, not a fighter." In a spiritual sense, we must be both. We must be tender enough to love and tough enough to fight.

A tender heart without a tough skin may easily be swallowed up in disappointment and disillusionment when everything turns dark and desperate. Perhaps you've seen fellow-Christians give up because they lacked the toughness to keep on going when they were stretched beyond their natural resources.

We must develop wiry endurance for the conflict without evolving into cynicism, harshness, or paranoia. In our world, pressures are steadily mounting. The world can be a rough place, rampant with hostility and relational power struggles. Christians are likened to sheep among wolves. Opposition can come from many directions—even our own friends or family.

Maintaining close contact with our master can enable us to draw from him both the courage for conflicts and the tender compassion for human need. With the wisdom of a serpent must also come the harmlessness of the dove.

Prayer: Lord, please make me tough enough to endure, yet tender enough to care.

⚓ Nov. 18 ⚓

Isaiah 9:2–6

God Isn't Dead

A child will be born for us. A son will be given to us. The government will rest on his shoulders. He will be named: Wonderful Counselor, Mighty God, Everlasting Father, Prince of Peace (Isaiah 9:6).

For nearly twenty years it was my privilege to be the headmaster of a Christian boarding high school. A day school represents great responsibility, a boarding school even more. About half of our students were missionary kids from around the world. We were in *loco parentis,* and trying to function both as parents and teachers was challenging.

Some days the pressures of the school took a heavy toll on me. One morning as I headed out the door, my face reflected the stress. My wife, sensing my defeated spirit, stopped me at the door with upraised arms in mock panic, "How long has God been dead?"

I looked at her quizzically.

"From the look on your face, God is dead and gone." She looked me straight in the eye. "Is the school your responsibility or his?"

We both stared at each other for a moment, then we had to laugh. She sat me down and we prayed, placing the government of the school onto God's expansive shoulders. Peace entered my mind as I acknowledged his sovereignty and took my place as an obedient son. He wasn't asking me to fight overwhelming battles alone but simply to follow his directions for each day.

Prayer: God, help me to transfer regularly my anxieties onto your broad shoulders.

—Tony Fortosis

⚓ Nov. 19 ⚓

Nehemiah 2:1–6
Prayer: Our First Resort

If the Lord does not build the house, it is useless for the builders to work on it (Psalm 127:1).

"Sure, some Jews are again living in Jerusalem," Nehemiah's brother told him, "but the city's in terrible shape. The walls are broken down and the gates are history."

Nehemiah didn't panic, throw a temper tantrum, or give up in discouragement. He knelt down and prayed to the God of heaven. His prayer was humble and penitent, and he also implied willingness to be God's instrument to confront the tragic situation. When he asked his master, the king of Persia, if he could go rebuild Jerusalem's walls, the king agreed.

The mission was beset with formidable opposition from every side. When enemies tried to lure Nehemiah away from his work with smooth coaxings, he said, "I'm working on an important project and can't get away. Why should the work stop while I leave to meet with you?" (Neh. 6:3). Nehemiah stood focused and resolute, with his trust fixed on God.

In any mission for God, there always seem to be at least a few whose basic compulsion is criticism, ridicule, or outright sabotage. Co-workers may grumble and complain. Outsiders may set booby traps with loud threats or the seduction of compromise. God assigns us works of varying magnitude in the building of his kingdom, but every mission is important to him. We must face every challenge first and last with prayer. We must look above the battle to our God who directs us. He will make sure we complete our portion of the wall to his glory.

Prayer: Lord, let me concentrate fully on the portion of the wall you've given me to complete.

⚓ Nov. 20 ⚓

Habakkuk 3:17–19
Praise God Anyway

Even if the fig tree does not bloom and the vines have no grapes . . . even then, I will be happy with the Lord. I will truly find joy in God, who saves me (Habbakkuk 3:17–18).

The prophet Habakkuk is confronted by the seeming silence of God amid the hard circumstances that faced Israel. But he doesn't complain to God with a hint of accusation. He is no sighing martyr bemoaning inevitable defeat, nor is he a self-made optimist whistling in the dark to psyche himself up and onward. Habakkuk faces grim, difficult facts, but since he cannot change them, he transcends them. He takes comfort in the fact that he can trust God's heart when he cannot see God's hand.

Our attitude is important when we face such times. The theories, the arguments, the platitudes, and the clichés just don't fit. Things don't make human sense. Nothing is working out according to the book. Divine promises of success seem to mock us.

What has happened to us may even appear contradictory to God's character. Reality seems to sneer at faith in these times, and we can almost hear our enemies chuckling behind their sleeves at our confusion.

We find in Habakkuk's testimony sufficient encouragement for us. We may rest in a God whose sovereign compassion takes many forms. When we trust and praise him even while groping in dark tunnels, God's eyes light up with joy. He knows courage when he sees it.

Prayer: Father, please let me trust your heart when I cannot see your hand.

⚓ Nov. 21 ⚓

Luke 9:57–62
A Man Under Authority

"Whoever starts to plow and looks back is not fit for the kingdom of God" (Luke 9:62).

Early in my ministry as a school administrator, my wife made an offhanded comment to a faculty member's wife that was taken out of context and became a serious bit of gossip. The distortion spread to other wives, and in a short time we had an ominous situation.

I called a meeting of the faculty and asked that the wives also attend. The atmosphere was tense and charged. Accusations flew at my wife fast and hard. I tried to rebut them but to no avail. My blood was heating to a slow boil. Thoughts flooded my mind. We don't need this! Who do they think they are? I have a good mind to take my wife and leave this place forever.

I was almost at the exploding point when a faculty wife, shocked by the inquisition and praying quietly, began to sob. God used it to awaken the hearts of the faculty. One by one, they came up, took our hands, and we reconciled.

I had come close to forgetting that I was a man under Christ's authority. When the battle gets hot or opposition mounts, we must not run. Jesus must be our advocate. There should be no escape hatch, no return to old hidden shelters once we've embraced the new under his authority.

Prayer: Lord, when battles rage or things seem to be falling apart all around me, keep me at my station with my face like a flint.

—Tony Fortosis

⚓ Nov. 22 ⚓

Hebrews 11:32–38
Of Whom the World Isn't Worthy

We consider those who endure to be blessed (James 5:11).

Joni Eareckson tells of a seventeen year old named Deniece who was struck with multiple sclerosis which blinded and paralyzed her. She couldn't read books or watch TV. In fact, she was too weak to do anything much except lie silently in bed. Yet Joni said Deniece's intimacy with God made Deniece a magnificent witness, though she could do nothing the world would consider great.

I know a guy named Johnny Farese who has muscular atrophy. All his life he's been bedridden, his body dwarfed and twisted. This morning I called him, and Johnny said he had a sore throat and cold. I asked if this ever degenerated into pneumonia, and he said yes and acknowledged it can be life threatening. "We can only pray," he said, "that God will spare me the pneumonia. But whatever happens, it does have a sanctifying effect."

That seemed like a great attitude—not seeking after illness or trial, but realizing its sanctifying value when it does come. Like Deniece, Johnny faces reality head on and he deals with it. Certainly he's not overjoyed, but still, he exudes a quiet peace and acceptance when I see him.

It seems as if these should be inserted in that Hebrews 11 list of beautiful, broken saints of whom the world was not worthy. May God sanctify us too as we follow their path.

Prayer: Father, thank you for Christians who suffer willingly. When called upon to go through the fire, may I be like them.

⚓ Nov. 23 ⚓

1 Corinthians 4:10–13

Unashamed Fools

We are fools for Christ's sake (1 Corinthians 4:10 kjv).

Thomas Smith, secretary of state to Queen Elizabeth, said on his deathbed, "It is a matter of lamentation that men know not for what end they've come into life until they're ready to exit it." Mohammed I of Spain whispered, "Is not the prince to leave the world as naked as a peasant?" Shortly before death, atheist Thomas Paine reputedly cried, "My God, my God, why have you forsaken me?"

In contrast, a young pastor from Zimbabwe on his deathbed declared, "I'm part of the fellowship of the unashamed. I have the Holy Spirit power. The die has been cast—I'm a disciple of his. I won't look back, let up, slow down, back away, or be still. I'm finished and done with low living, sight walking, smooth knees, colorless dreams, tamed visions, worldly talking, cheap giving, and dwarfed goals." This man was later martyred for his faith.

Some would consider the young pastor a fool, but God says the one who loses his life in Christ actually saves it. To greedily clutch and hoard life is to end up with a useless life. "God shows us a man [Christ]," Buechner writes, "who gave his life away to the extent of dying a national disgrace without a penny in the bank or a friend to his name . . . and anybody who thinks he can follow him without making . . . the same kind of fool of himself is laboring under not a cross but a delusion."

Prayer: Father, make me foolish enough to give my life away in order to gain what no one can take.

⚓ Nov. 24 ⚓

Romans 1:18–27
Costly Exchanges

Because they thought it was worthless to acknowledge God, God allowed their immoral minds to control them (Romans 1:28).

To pervert means to exchange a true end for a corrupt purpose. In Romans 1, Paul outlines three costly exchanges that occur in this downhill slide. Verse twenty-two describes the exchange of a desire for God's glory with a loyalty to tangible gods. This is the worship of idols which can take many forms. Verse twenty-five mentions the exchange of God's truth for a lie. With a loss of allegiance comes a growing acceptance of lies that soothe guilt and encourage a spiritual spiral downward. Finally, in verse twenty-six, natural relationships may be exchanged for unnatural, and the door may be opened for sexual perversion.

One day I received a video tape from an old high school classmate. First, Bob reported he would miss our high school reunion. "I have tested positive for AIDS," Bob said, "and unless God intervenes, the doctors give me six to eighteen months to live."

Decades earlier, Bob had begun that Romans 1 nose dive, and on the video he compared this period to a deeper and deeper descent into a dark pit. He'd turned to a homosexual lifestyle and had actually lived it for twelve long years.

On the video Bob told how when he finally, desperately, placed his minute faith in the infinite God, his dark pit became a flood-lit cave. His distorted mentality began a transformation.

Not long after he sent out the video, Bob died from AIDS-related illnesses. His body just gave out, but his soul had found deliverance. He is free at last.

Prayer: Father, keep me close to you always. Make me aware of my own potential for waywardness.

⚓ Nov. 25 ⚓

Romans 8:14–17
Level at the Cross

You haven't received the spirit of slaves that leads you into fear again. Instead, you have received the spirit of God's adopted children by which we call out, "Abba! Father!" (Romans 8:15).

I used to think that God had favorites,
although I knew this was not true;
and every lie insidiously whispered
in the recesses of my mind slowly grew
creating a thicket of despair filled with
brambles and thorns strategically placed
to catch my flesh and make it bleed—
to overlook God's abundant grace.

I was the stepchild, grafted in
but not yet growing in the Vine,
watching others gather accolades,
blinded to Christ's touch divine.

He came quietly, steadily, and blew
His holy breath upon the shadows
dispersing them forever. Then came
the light, the morning of his pleasure,
leaving me at the foot of his cross, not looking
to my left or right, but gazing wondrous
into his pure eyes, looking upon me with
love and joy—my heart opening to trust.

—Pat Baxter

Prayer: Father, let me also sense the loving and encouraging eyes of Jesus letting me know I'm his child and far from ignored.

⚓ Nov. 26 ⚓

John 1:1–5
Off Course

Your word is a lamp for my feet and a light for my path (Psalm 119:105).

We easily lose our way in this world of confusing labyrinths. There are strong pulls and errant voices calling out that can seduce us off course and into the threatening darkness.

Ted was a former student of mine who owned a small Cessna. He took off one weekend to see a friend in a city several hundred miles away. Shortly into the flight, the weather began turning ugly. Ted quickly discovered his radio and navigation equipment weren't working properly. He'd neglected to check them before taking off. Lashing winds buffeted the plane. Murky fog obscured the earth below. Panic grabbed Ted in a vise grip. Suddenly a mountain loomed up just ahead and Ted couldn't pull up in time. In the wreckage, Ted's log showed one terse statement: "Off course."

All of us face danger. As God's children we head into a dark and treacherous world that can threaten disaster. We need to be aware of the potential pitfalls and stay ever close to God. He's given us light and direction in his Word to steer us through darkness and ominous cloud banks. He's granted us access to radio him at any time to be sure we're still on course.

Prayer: God, don't let me stray out of the flight pattern you've set for me. May I be piloted by your Spirit to safe landings in the center of your will.

—Tony Fortosis

⚓ Nov. 27 ⚓

Psalm 119:71–75
Deeper Purposes

"He removes every one of my branches that doesn't produce fruit. He also prunes every branch that does produce fruit to make it produce more fruit" (John 15:2).

The brick collided full force against Brengle's head, slamming it against a doorpost. He was unconscious before he hit the ground, incapacitated by a drunk on a Boston street.

Samuel Brengle had served selflessly for many years as the Salvation Army Commissioner, trying to help street people like the one who attacked him. Now, for weeks he lay teetering on the verge of death. It took over eighteen months before Brengle was finally able to resume some daily duties.

While slowed down by convalescence, Brengle wrote articles which were later compiled into a brief but power-packed book entitled Helps to Holiness. Demand for the little book grew. Eventually it was translated into dozens of languages around the world. Christians continue to read and benefit from it even today.

Whenever people thanked Brengle for writing such a helpful book, he'd grin and say, "Well, if there had been no little brick, there would have been no little book."

Arthur Bacon shared this deep faith in the intricate plannings of a sovereign God. He writes, "I can still believe that a day comes for all of us . . . when these tragedies that now blacken and darken the very air of heaven for us, will sink into their places in a scheme so august, so magnificent, so joyful, that we shall laugh for wonder and delight."

Prayer: Father, remind me to look for your sanctifying design behind the hard times.

⚓ Nov. 28 ⚓

1 Chronicles 4:9–10
A Man Named Painful

"Please bless me and give me more territory" (1 Chronicles 4:10).

Tucked away in a long, rather tedious genealogy is an interesting excerpt about a man named Jabez. The name means painful and is appropriate because his mother bore him in pain and much sorrow. Giving a child a name like that suggests sadness and even possible resentment by the parent, yet Jabez ended up more honorable than his brothers. He didn't allow anything to turn his heart hard against God. In fact, he asked God to bless him and give him more territory or enlarge his sphere of life. "May your power be with me," he added, "and free me from evil so I will not be in pain." And God granted it all.

Andrew Murray writes, "Beware in your prayer, above everything, of limiting God, not only by unbelief, but by fancying that you know what he can do. Expect unexpected things, above all you ask or think." Caleb asked for a great mountain. Paul asked for the countless souls of his countrymen. Jabez asked for an enlarged sphere of life.

We often cling to a spiritual foothold when God wants to give us a mountain. We need to push out our spiritual borders in light of God's promises. To be blessed, to expand life's borders, to rest inside God's palm, to be kept from evil—this is a wise and worthy prayer and God grants such prayers.

Prayer: Father, show me what great things to ask of you. Give me faith to believe you for them.

⚓ Nov. 29 ⚓

2 Chronicles 18:30–32

Help!

When Jehoshaphat cried out, the Lord helped him (2 Chronicles 18:31).

After Daniel received a sobering prophecy from God, he mourned and fasted for three weeks. Throughout this period, we're told of no supplication or prayers offered by the devout man. Yet certainly God communed with his heart.

Prayer can be a spiritual prostration before God or a wordless cry for help—silent, yet more eloquent than words. In moments of tragedy or emergency, prayer may be a groan or an anguished gurgle, but God hears our heartbeat.

Years ago I was involved in a water show at a Christian summer camp. Dressed as Mother Hubbard, my stunt was to jump off a diving board into the pool. When I hit the water, the three billowing skirts I was wearing swept up over me like a shroud. I was trapped! My frantic thrashing only wrapped the cloth tighter around my head. Thinking it was all part of the act, onlookers laughed hilariously. As my lungs filled, my mind screamed out to God. Suddenly the last skirt loosened and I broke the surface just as I was passing out. God graciously heard that silent cry for help and rescued me.

Even when you're too hurt, heartbroken, or desperate to tailor a prayer, God knows your heart-need and he will answer.

Prayer: Father, hear my heart when I'm too frantic or heartbroken to utter a word.

—Tony Fortosis

⚓ Nov. 30 ⚓

Hebrews 10:38–39
Learning Tenacity

We don't belong with those who turn back (Hebrews 10:39).

When we were kids, my dad and us boys sometimes played football in our front yard. My younger brother, Bob, was the only one who had shoulder pads and a football helmet, so we were a bit rougher on him. After getting rough-housed a few times, Bob would yell, "I quit!" and trudge off the field. He's learned since to hang on tenaciously when things get tough.

In Psalm 78, Asaph writes, "The men of Ephraim, well-equipped with bows and arrows, turned and ran on the day of battle." We're not sure when Ephraim hightailed it, but, as Chuck Swindoll puts it, "The sound of battle made them as nervous as a long-tailed cat in a room full of rocking chairs." On the surface they seemed as polished and smooth as a well-oiled engine, but behind the brave veneer was a slippery brand of cowardice.

Swindoll continues, "Ephraimites live on, you know. They ape the lifestyle of heroic saints to perfection. Their words and prayers, verses and vows shine like Ephraim's arrows at dawn. But let the hot rays of hardship beat upon their backs and they melt like butter on the back burner. However, there is not an achievement worth remembering that isn't stained with the blood of diligence and etched with the scars of disappointment."

If you're wading through hardship up to your armpits, don't submerge in despair. Borrow God's perspective and claim his power to survive the battle.

Prayer: Father, develop in me a perseverance that hangs tough through the storms.

DECEMBER

The God of Might & Mystery

ISAIAH 55:6–11

GOD'S MYSTERIOUS WAYS

"My thoughts are not your thoughts, and my ways are not your ways," declares the LORD (Isaiah 55:8).

God's ways are different from ours. We judge by outward appearances; God does not. We pretend to know everything and resist paradox; God, in fact, knows everything and creates paradox. We tend to think bigger is better and might makes right; God may use smallness to accomplish greatness and his might is always right. To us, some of his instructions defy human logic, but he's proven again and again that they work.

We often find God's ways and decrees perplexingly complex. We would like him to spell out why innocent children died in Bosnia, why all don't hear the Good News, why his plan for our lives seems so obscure, and why some of his commands appear irrational.

Yet, in the face of our questions, God seems strangely silent. To Vinet, a Swiss theologian, the silence was untroubling. "The truth of a true religion," says Vinet, "is related to the infinite and thus borders on mystery." But periodically the clouds part and God sheds a glimmer of light on the questions. Then we scan the heavens for more.

This month, we are going to search the Scriptures for some of the mysterious ways of God. We're going to trust that he will allow a few of those shafts of divine light to break in upon our minds. Hopefully, we will know God a little better a month from now.

PRAYER: Father, please help me understand your ways that I might know you as you are and worship the reality of you.

Romans 11:33–36

Trying to Grasp Infinity

God's riches, wisdom, and knowledge are so deep that it is impossible to explain his decisions or to understand his ways (Romans 11:33).

In Anne Tyler's novel *Saint Maybe* an agnostic teenager leers, "Noah's ark: how about that? God kills off all the sinners in a mammoth rainstorm. 'Gotcha!' God says." The teen pictures God as enjoying the flood and questions why God didn't send a few sample rains in advance so the people could mend their ways.

Obviously, some of God's ways seem maddeningly unreasonable to pre-Christians. Some are even difficult for us to understand. It can help to take a closer look at the whole of Scripture. For example, in the account of the flood, God reports horrible wickedness—almost everyone on earth thought about evil continually (Gen. 6:5). In 2 Peter 2:5, we also find that, as Noah built the ark, he preached repentance for at least one hundred years.

Many of us still wonder at times why God behaves the way he does. Yet he demands that we risk everything we hold by common sense. The moment we do, we'll realize that what he asks can only make sense from his divine perspective. Oswald Chambers writes, "Only one out of a crowd is daring enough to bank his faith in the character of God."

Prayer: Father, I praise you for your complexity, for if you were simple, you would cease to be God.

⚓ Dec. 3 ⚓

2 Corinthians 6:3–10
Divine Paradox

"The person who tries to preserve his life will lose it, but the person who loses his life for me will preserve it" (Matthew 10:39).

This message is as grating as fingernails screeching across a chalkboard: "You must die before you can live. You must lose to win. The more freely you give, the more you will receive. Though sorrowful, you can always rejoice." The words of someone who's lost his grip on reality? No, the words of God himself.

These are paradoxes voiced by a wonderfully complex God. He says that we must die to our immoral, self-centered lives before we can rise to new life in Christ. We must lose ourselves in him before he can truly find us. It is in giving generously that we receive from him more than we ever dreamed. And though we may have constant sorrow because of human tragedy, there is also a joy no grief can completely snuff out.

Two examples of contrasting responses to paradoxes presented by Jesus come to mind. Late one night, Jesus told Nicodemus he had to be born all over again. How could a grown man even conceive of doing something so preposterous? Yet later in Nicodemus' behavior, we see evidence of faith. On the other hand, when Jesus announced to a crowd of disciples that they must eat his flesh and drink his blood to have eternal life, many turned away from him, never to return (John 6:53–60).

Will you accept paradox from our all-wise God?

Prayer: Father, even in confusion, let me step out in faith—I know I'll find the paradoxes fading away in the comforting wisdom of your presence.

⚓ Dec. 4 ⚓

Ephesians 1:7–10

In on a Secret

Some things are hidden. They belong to the Lord our God. But the things that have been revealed in these teachings belong to us and to our children forever (Deuteronomy 29:29).

Do you remember how privileged you felt as a kid to have a secret whispered in your ear? God also whispers secrets to his children. Once when the disciples asked Jesus why he always spoke in parables, he said softly, "'Knowledge about the mysteries of the kingdom of heaven has been given to you. But it has not been given to the crowd'" (Matt. 13:11).

What secrets does God explain to us, his church? First, he says that Gentiles have been specially chosen to reach the world with his Good News. When the full number of Gentiles are in the kingdom, God will return to a repentant Israel (Rom. 11:25).

This mystery is wrapped up in God's kingdom plan: Jesus died in our place to redeem us. Then he sent his Spirit to actually live inside us. Thus, sinners though we are, we represent Christ to the world. Jesus is now being revealed to the world through millions of Christians, as reflected in our words and actions. What a plan!

But that's not all. The rest of the plan involves Christians being caught up someday in a rapture to join countless believers throughout history (1 Cor. 15:51). The church will be spiritually married to Christ (Eph. 5:32–33). All creation will then be placed under His sovereign leadership (Eph. 1:9–10).

Now that we know the secret, let's let it shine in our eyes and gleam from our lives.

Prayer: God, thank you for revealing to us the mystery of your kingdom plan. Let me be its living epistle to others.

⚓ Dec. 5 ⚓

Judges 7

When Less Is More

"The Lord can win a victory with a few men as well as with many" (1 Samuel 14:6).

During the Allied-Iraqi conflict of 1991, what if the general had ordered, "Send the heavy armor and the big guns home. Also, send most of the troops packing. We're going to face the Iraqis with three hundred soldiers!" The president would have summarily discharged him from his command, and Schwartzkoff would probably live in infamy as the general who blew a mental gasket in combat.

In the Bible, God doesn't always operate according to accepted military practices. In fact, in the book of Judges, God whittled down General Gideon's army from thirty-two thousand men to a mere three hundred. Then the soldiers were sent into battle—not with mighty weapons and engines of war, but with trumpets, pitchers, and lamps.

Was there a method to this seemingly suicidal mission? In Judges 7:2, God tells Gideon, "'You have too many men for me to deliver you, [lest Israel boast] . . . that her own strength has saved her'" (NIV). It's hard to imagine a commander ever telling a general, "You have too many men to possibly win." Only God can arrange it so that one soldier chases a thousand.

Do you tend to have all sorts of contingency plans just in case God doesn't come through when you need him? Is it easy for you to take the credit for battles won? Try to allow God to do things his way. Then give him the rightful praise when he triumphs.

Prayer: God, rid me of my many contingency plans. Let me trust you more completely to triumph in your way.

⚓ Dec. 6 ⚓

John 11:1–44
His Glory—Not Our Timing

[Jesus] said, "His sickness won't result in death. Instead, this sickness will bring glory to God so that the Son of God will receive glory through it" (John 11:4).

What's the first thing you want to do when someone you love becomes terribly sick? Most people want to be with the person, helping out, giving encouragement, or just offering silent support. And if it's in their power to help the person get better, most would do it without question.

With their brother Lazarus on his deathbed, Mary and Martha sent word to Jesus, "Lord, your close friend is sick" (John 11:3). The disciples knew Jesus was especially close to Lazarus. Yet, when Jesus heard his friend was suffering, he lingered where he was for two more days. Lazarus probably died very soon after Jesus got the message.

Lazarus' sisters were crushed. When Jesus finally arrived at their home, they both told him Lazarus wouldn't have died if he'd been there. Why would someone who had the power to heal a friend show up after the friend's funeral?

Wait. Maybe Jesus wasn't being uncaring. Tears gleamed on his face at the gravesite. He told Martha he's the resurrection and the life. Whoever believes in him won't ever die. Then he told onlookers, "You are going to see the glory of God today." Next Lazarus emerged from the tomb—whole and undecayed. Many believed in Jesus that day as a result of the miracle.

Will you allow Jesus to reveal God and bring glory to him in ways that don't always appear compassionate at the moment?

Prayer: Jesus, when you don't respond when and how I want, make me aware of ways you can be glorified through my waiting.

⚓ Dec. 7 ⚓

Ezekiel 4

The Creator of Creativity

"Son of man, I am sending you to the people of Israel. . . . Whether these rebellious people listen or not, they will realize that a prophet has been among them" (Ezekiel 2:3, 5).

When I was a boy, I used to love to play war with toy soldiers. Now I find it interesting that God told the prophet Ezekiel to play war.

God also told him to cut off his hair, divide it into three sections, and destroy it. In the months following, God instructed him to tell a riddle, dig a hole in a wall, and howl like a wounded animal. Why would God ask someone to participate in such weirdness?

Well, the God who created creativity wanted to communicate messages to his people in vivid and forceful ways. They had not paid attention to his warnings. However, when Ezekiel did these unusual acts, it caught people's attention to a much greater degree than if he'd just spoken forth more of God's judgments.

By cutting off his hair and destroying it in different ways, Ezekiel illustrated ways Israel would be judged by God. Playing war portrayed an enemy siege against Jerusalem if she wouldn't turn from evil.

God sometimes uses refreshingly innovative ways to communicate to us in ways we'll understand and remember. Maybe those of us who communicate God's messages should do the same.

Prayer: Father, teach me to refresh your people with eternal truths that they'll understand and remember.

⚓ Dec. 8 ⚓

2 Samuel 12:7–12
Saving a Ton of Trouble

Nathan told David . . . "The Lord says . . . Why did you despise my word by doing what I considered evil?" (2 Samuel 12:7,9).

One of God's commands is, "You shall not commit adultery." But why? God created marital intimacy to be enjoyable, but why does he say it can only be enjoyed with one person—in a lifetime commitment? Who says the family unit is somehow sacred? Why can't we procreate with anyone of the opposite sex and then all rear the children as one big happy family? Perhaps we could if it wasn't for a horrible thing called our sin nature.

As humans, we tend to distort sex in every way imaginable. Sexuality is sometimes marred by jealousy, covetousness, unfaithfulness, or greed. It is evident in King David's life how destructive it can be to rebel against God in this area.

I experienced an unforgettable example of the wrongness of adultery when I lived in Los Angeles. At 2:00 A.M. one night, we woke to someone pounding at our door. When we answered it, a man dressed only in his underwear rushed inside. He was in such terror, he hyperventilated as he gasped out his story. Apparently, an estranged husband had caught his wife with the man and had fired shots at him as he fled. Now the husband was combing the neighborhood, intent on killing our nighttime guest. A while later, a police cruiser pulled up in our driveway and our guest sprinted out to the car and out of our lives.

But this encounter portrayed to me again why God has commanded faithfulness between one man and one woman for life. It can save a lot of trouble.

Prayer: Lord, help me realize each day that your design for our lives is the best. It can spare us grief.

⚓ Dec. 9 ⚓

2 Kings 5:1–14

No One to Impress

Naaman became angry and left. He said, " . . . the Abana and Pharpar Rivers in Damascus have better water than any of the rivers in Israel. Couldn't I wash in them and be clean?" (2 Kings 5:11–12).

Naaman was the quintessential macho man—tough, fearless, and powerful. He was the captain of the entire Syrian military. When Naaman heard there was a prophet in Samaria who could heal his leprosy, he gathered his entourage and took off for Samaria.

Now, let's do a little advance planning for God. When Naaman arrives, Elisha must burst out of his house dressed in his newest robe, wearing a warm grin on his face. Then he will dynamically call on the power of God and touch the Syrian's leprous skin. Presto! The disease will disappear. Naaman will excitedly place his faith in God, and Naaman's entourage will bow to the ground murmuring praise to the God of Israel.

Apparently, that's somewhat the way Naaman expected it to happen, too. But Elisha didn't even come outside to greet the prestigious guest. He sent a messenger to command the commander to go wash seven times in the dirty Jordan river. What an outrage!

In the end, Naaman humbled himself enough to dip in the Jordan and be healed. Like Naaman, we must remember that God has no one to impress. If you need God's help, don't ever let your inflated ego get in the way. God's help must be received on his terms, not yours.

Prayer: God, shove my ego out of the way. When I pray for help, may I receive it on your terms, not mine.

⚓ Dec. 10 ⚓

Exodus 35:10–19

God of Intricacy

"Have all the skilled craftsmen among you come and make everything the Lord has commanded: the inner tent, the outer tent, and cover, along with the fasteners, frames, crossbars, posts, and sockets" (Exodus 35:10–11).

Can you imagine God sounding for all the world like an interior decorator? Yet in Exodus, we find page after page of God's very detailed tabernacle instructions. Is this the God before whom the nations are like a drop in a bucket?

We sometimes joke about somehow wading through chapters containing genealogies and building instructions. Why are these intricate listings even in the Bible?

Jesus gave one reason when he said, "Aren't five sparrows sold for two cents? Yet God doesn't forget any of them. Even every hair on your head has been counted. Don't be afraid! You are worth more than many sparrows." The same God who claimed awareness of every sparrow that falls wants us to know that, despite his infinity, he cares about the most intricate, intimate details of our mundane earthly lives.

God also knows why you're alive at this particular time in history. Sure he's interested in moving nations by his Spirit, but he's also concerned with your anxiety about moving or changing careers. He cares about all the ups and downs of your relationships. The God who cared about the loops and curtain couplets of the tent cares about the day-by-day details of your life.

Prayer: Father, it's reassuring to remind myself that you care about all the intricacies of my daily routine. Please be involved in each detail.

⚓ Dec. 11 ⚓

Isaiah 58:6–11

Superfluous Generosity

"He defended the cause of the poor and needy. Everything went well for him. Isn't this what it means to know me?" asks the Lord (Jeremiah 22:16).

Recently, I was struck again with God's concern for the disadvantaged—a concern reflected in ways we may typically consider overblown.

For example, in Deuteronomy 15 God commanded his people to open their hands wide to the poor. Once every seven years, they were to release the poor from all debts. If a countryman lived as a servant for six years, on the seventh the master was to release him. Not only that, but the ex-servant was to be sent away loaded down with the master's food and flocks.

Later in Deuteronomy, farmers are instructed not to glean all the grain from harvested fields or all the fruit from picked trees. These were for the poor. Also, the poor were permitted to eat fruit or wheat from the fields as long as they didn't carry it away in containers.

To us these measures may seem too generous. Yet, over and over again in the Bible we become aware of God's tenderness toward the underdog. One way to greatly endear yourself to God is to show mercy to the poor and stepped-on in our world. If you do, you will reap a reward of the Spirit: "He who is kind to the poor lends to the Lord, and he will reward him for what he has done" (Prov. 19:17 NIV).

Prayer: God, I get so caught up in the middle-class rat race. Please show me opportunities for the poor and disadvantaged.

⚓ Dec. 12 ⚓

2 Corinthians 12:1–10
Beacons of Humility

"The greatest among you must be like the youngest, and your leader must be like a servant" (Luke 22:26).

The Apostle Peter was a leader. He was especially close to Jesus—one of the inner circle. It was he who blurted out staunch faith in Jesus' deity. When storm clouds threatened, Peter attempted to rally the troops. On occasion he even tried to tell Jesus what to do (Matt. 16:22–23).

Then, near the end of Christ's time on earth, Peter declared fearless loyalty to Jesus no matter what. One would think Peter's loyalty would be met with effusive gratefulness, but instead Jesus responded with a bombshell: "I can guarantee this truth: Before a rooster crows tonight, you will say three times that you don't know me'" (Matt. 26:34).

If this was, indeed, to be Peter's Waterloo, why burst his balloon at this crisis hour? We are not sure. But we do know that, after his resurrection, Christ went out of his way to re-cement his close bond with Peter.

Could it be that Peter's tremendous potential for either arrogant domination or humble leadership required that his great failure always stand as a beacon to remind him of who he was and to whom he owed everything? Your failures, also, can stand as reminding beacons—beacons calling you to honest humility.

Prayer: Father, instead of leaving me groveling in self-pity, let my failures produce in me an attitude of humble dependence.

⚓ Dec. 13 ⚓

Romans 9:18–25

One Glimpse at the Cross

God loved the world this way: He gave his only Son so that everyone who believes in him will not die but will have eternal life (John 3:16).

When told about some Galileans who'd been murdered by Pilate, Jesus responded matter-of-factly, "Do you think that this happened to them because they were more sinful than other people from Galilee? No! I can guarantee that they weren't. But if you don't turn to God and change the way you think and act, then you, too, will all die" (Luke 13:2–3). If that doesn't seem cold enough, in Romans 9:18 we read that God has mercy on some individuals and somehow hardens the hearts of others.

It's easy for us to question the love of God in dark moments of doubt or disillusionment. We don't think twice about the colossal nerve it takes to accuse the one who created us—the one who originated compassion.

At the same time, I must admit there are times when, from my pigeon-holed vantage point, it appears that God is being less than fair to people. On the other hand, I can think of many times when I thought my viewpoint was the only logical one possible—until in one deft blow, someone destroyed it with an idea that hadn't occurred to me. There is so much we don't know. God's mind is well beyond human comparison.

The bottom line for me is this: Whenever I'm tempted to wonder about God's love, I look up and take one glimpse at the cross. That's all it takes.

Prayer: Lord, there's so much I don't understand about your ways. Whenever I question your love, turn my eyes to the cross.

⚓ Dec. 14 ⚓

1 Peter 4:12–19

No Pain, No Gain

Dear friends, don't be surprised by the fiery troubles that are coming in order to test you. Don't feel as though something strange is happening to you (1 Peter 4:12).

Down through the centuries, humans have struggled with the question of why a loving God permits suffering. Obviously, we don't know all the reasons, but as we try to understand, God gives us some insights.

Paul Brand, a missionary surgeon, sees suffering as something God can use positively. He calls himself the lobbyist for pain. When doing his medical internship in London, Brand read that sixty percent of Londoners who lived through the German blitz consider it the happiest period of their lives. How can this be? Yet, as Brand mulled it over, he realized that nearly all of his memories of acute happiness involved some element of pain or struggle.

A runner's legs ache as he or she triumphantly wins a marathon. Hikers swoon over a barbecued meal after walking all day. Small blessings are greatly appreciated when we know deprivation.

After her missionary husband died in middle age, Brand's mother came home from India broken and beaten down. When, against all advice, she later returned to serve her beloved mountain people, her soul was restored. Deeply content, she wouldn't leave in spite of serious injury and disease. At age ninety-five, the bent, shrunken woman was reverently buried by tearful villagers. Her pain was transformed into blessing as she gave her life for those around her.

Prayer: God, if suffering comes my way, please help me trust you while I reap the benefits of the hardship.

⚓ Dec. 15 ⚓

Jeremiah 1:4–19
The Hound of Heaven

The Lord said to me, "Don't say you're only a boy. You will go wherever I send you. . . . Don't be afraid of people. I am with you, and I will rescue you" (Jeremiah 1:7–8).

What would you do if God appeared to you in a vision and called you to be his spokesperson? "Well," you say excitedly, "if God singled me out as a spokesperson, I mean, I'd be honored. I'd say yes in a heartbeat!" I'm not so sure.

When God called Jeremiah, he answered, "But God, I'm just a child." Moses whined, "If I go, your people will reject me." And Jonah just scrammed like a jackrabbit—in the opposite direction. God could have impatiently declared, "Fine! There are plenty of others where you came from," or he could have simply snuffed out these resistant upstarts.

Instead, God cajoled Jeremiah, he capitulated to Moses by sending Aaron along too, and he played the hound of heaven with Jonah until the prophet finally cooperated. Maybe this persistence is part of what the Bible means when it says, "His mercy endures forever" (Ps. 136).

In spite of our excuses, whining, and reluctance, God nudges, shoves, and leads us along, knowing we can often accomplish things we never thought we could. Aren't you thankful for a God who doesn't write you off when you greet him with a truckload of excuses? His mercy never ends.

Prayer: Father, thanks for not zapping me when I whine about what I can't do. Strengthen me to do what you ask of me.

⚓ DEC. 16 ⚓

HOSEA 2:1–9

HOW TO WAKE THE DEAD

"Did you see what unfaithful Israel did? She went up every high mountain and under every large tree, and she acted like a prostitute there" (Jeremiah 3:6).

God told godly Hosea, "Marry a prostitute, and have children with that prostitute. The people in this land have acted like prostitutes and abandoned the LORD" (Hos. 1:2). Are we hearing God right? Is he commanding a prophet to marry a prostitute? The answer is yes.

Hundreds of years earlier, God had committed himself to Israel. He was like the groom and Israel, the bride. What a happy relationship! Gradually, though, the bride began flirting with other gods. Then she became more and more unfaithful to her divine husband. Finally, she hit the skids—she became a spiritual prostitute!

What act could provide a more hard-hitting illustration of what Israel had done against God than a prophet actually marrying a prostitute? Hosea enacted in real life the heartbreaking devastation a spouse feels when the other partner commits adultery over and over. In so doing, he showed Israel how God felt about their crass unfaithfulness.

Don't be offended that Hosea married a woman of this sort. God took the risk of commanding Hosea to do this in order to bring a nation back to her senses. He will go to great lengths to wake the dead. Sometimes we need awakening too.

PRAYER: God, I want to be faithful to you. Help me stay awake spiritually so I won't need any shocking wake-up calls.

⚓ Dec. 17 ⚓

Lamentations 3:25–33

God: Intentionally Slow

One day with the Lord is like a thousand years, and a thousand years are like one day. The Lord isn't slow to do what he promised, as some people think (2 Peter 3:8–9).

As a young man, I went through a period of excruciating doubt. I questioned my salvation, God's love, the truth of the Good News. . . . Nothing biblical seemed exempt from my doubting mind. It was all very depressing.

In the midst of our doubts, we may wonder why God doesn't rush to our aid with calming assurance or supernatural signs of his reality and the truth of the Scriptures. But most of the time, he doesn't respond that way. In my case, the doubts continued for several years, and when God did begin renewing my faith, it took months for the doubts to ebb.

Why does God at times appear so slow to come to our aid? He hasn't spelled out the reasons why, but I think he implies a few in the Bible. First, he may want to remind us (again) of what wrecks we can be without him. Second, he may want to break us of the tendency to treat him like a magic genie who owes us immediate satisfaction. Third, he may be teaching us priceless lessons in patience, endurance, humility, and dependence on him. Or he may be training us to show empathy for others who are experiencing doubts.

When God is slow as we count slowness, don't panic or hurl accusations—hunker down and wait.

Prayer: Father, you know my exact needs. Make me patient when you don't move as quickly as I want you to.

⚓ Dec. 18 ⚓

Deuteronomy 20:10–18
He Who Abhors Sin

"I will punish the world for its evil and the wicked for their wrongdoing. I will put an end to arrogant people and humble the pride of tyrants" (Isaiah 13:11).

God's command to the Israelites was clear: "You must not spare anyone's life in the cities of these nations that the Lord your God is giving you' (Deut. 20:16). These instructions from God to the Israelites seem very cruel to us. How can we claim to believe in a loving, merciful God if he consigned even women and children to be destroyed by Israelite armies?

In most cases, God instructed mercy. The Israelite army was supposed to proclaim peace. If a city was determined to make war, Israel could fight, but all non-military citizens were to be spared. It was only the Canaanite peoples who were to be wiped out.

The Canaanites worshipped idols, even sacrificing their children to Molech. They practiced witchcraft and dark sorcery. Their young sons and daughters served as temple prostitutes. Totally perverted and abominable ceremonies were a part of their worship. God was fed up with all the wickedness.

God warned that if some Canaanites were left alive, they'd not only lead the people into idolatry but would also seek to obliterate Israel. God knew that many more thousands of people would die in the long run if these enemies weren't removed. God is merciful, but he hates sin with a white-hot wrath. It mocks his character and required the lifeblood of his Son to redeem us from its death grip.

Prayer: God, even when I don't completely understand your vengeful wrath against sin, help me to trust you and to run from sin myself.

⚓ Dec. 19 ⚓

1 Corinthians 7:29–31
Going the Extra Mile

"If someone forces you to go one mile, go two miles with him" (Matthew 5:41).

Why would someone force another to walk a mile? The idea is repulsive to our independent minds today. However, within the Empire a Roman soldier could ask any passerby to carry his pack one mile and, by law, the person had to comply. Jesus said to go two miles. He meant that his followers should then volunteer to walk an extra mile with the load.

Helping people takes time, and free time is a commodity most of us have in scant supply. It is probably, at least partly, for that reason that the time we give to others is such a treasure to God. He realizes volunteering time is something that is truly costing us. Money is cherished dearly by North Americans, yet often we would rather donate a check to a cause than donate precious hours.

I know a woman who goes home after a tough day's work and helps a friend take care of her invalid mother evening after evening. I believe this is a treasure far more valuable than handing her friend a twenty dollar check every day to hire additional help. It costs her far more to read to the elderly woman, or change her sheets, or empty her bedpan.

Are you willing to go the extra mile as opportunities come your way?

Prayer: Jesus, you who walked that hardest mile to the cross, make me willing to go an extra mile for someone who has a need.

⚓ Dec. 20 ⚓

Psalm 145

Glory Becomes Him

"Whoever offers thanks as a sacrifice honors me. I will let everyone who continues in my way see the salvation that comes from God" (Psalm 50:23).

Throughout the pages of the Bible, God encourages us to worship him unceasingly. Then in 2 Corinthians 12, Paul describes a terrible trial that God sent his way in order to prevent him from being overly exalted.

How can it be that God will go to great lengths to keep us from being exalted, yet commands that we exalt him continually? How is it that he requires humble self-effacement for us, yet he exults in the worship of all creatures?

First, he is the essence of perfection, purity, and otherness—nothing and no one in the universe can even begin to compare to him. As his created beings, we should worship God even for our existence (Lam. 3:22). Second, among the persons of the trinity, there is never the slightest iota of envy or malice. In Scriptures like John 17:4–5, we even find the Godhead glorifying one another. Third, we are innately flawed—our evil tendency makes it impossible for us to accept worship without eventually giving way to conceit and self-centeredness. Fourth, when God encourages us to glorify him, he knows that nothing will gain for us a greater reward throughout eternity than glorifying him. In fact, praise is the only thing we can offer to God that he hasn't first given to us.

Prayer: Father, instead of envying your glory, let me offer you a pleasing sacrifice of praise.

⚓ Dec. 21 ⚓

Hebrews 11
Your Faith Is Showing

He didn't work many miracles there because of their lack of faith (Matthew 13:58).

"March around Jericho for seven days," God commanded the Israelis, "and the walls will fall." "Let me put this mud on your eyes," said Jesus, to a blind man. "Pick up your bed and walk," he told the lame. Then, speaking to veteran fishermen, Jesus instructed, "Throw your net on the other side of the boat."

None of this made any sense. When it comes to waging a battle, no strategist in history would say to simply march around and around the enemy. No doctor I know uses mud packs to cure blindness, and it's a cruel mockery to ask a cripple to pick up his bed and walk. Above all, unless one wants to be made a complete laughingstock, one never tells old fishermen how to fish.

Why did God ask these people in need to stick their neck out in such ways? Built into God's plan for us is a powerful emphasis on faith. It delights him to no end when we trust him implicitly. It delights him even more when we trust him against all odds. To the blind man, Jesus could simply have said, "Receive your sight." But in the examples above, it appears that God wanted a sign of faith before he would act. Are you willing to show God you believe in his ability to act?

Prayer: Lord, please give me the faith I need, and teach me how to activate your power through displaying that faith.

⚓ Dec. 22 ⚓

Psalm 139
Is God Approachable?

How precious are your thoughts concerning me, O God! How vast in number they are! If I try to count them, there would be more of them than there are grains of sand. When I wake up, I am still with you (Psalm 139:17–18).

God presents himself in the Bible as very approachable and responsive to us. "God is our refuge and strength," writes the psalmist, "one ever-present help in these times of trouble" (Ps. 46:1). And in Hebrews we're encouraged to boldly approach God's throne of grace and receive mercy and help.

Yet this approachable God is also described as dwelling in unapproachable light (1 Tim. 6:16). And David laments, "Why are you so distant, Lord? Why do you hide yourself in times of trouble?" (Ps. 10:1).

Which is it? Is God approachable or unapproachable, caring or indifferent? God is only unapproachable in the blinding expanse of his glory. If we were exposed to even a fraction of this glory, we'd be scorched to so many cinders. However, when the psalmist complains of God's aloofness, he is speaking figuratively. God does not furtively hide from us. It may seem to us as though he does when he does not respond as quickly as we would like or in the way we'd prefer. But the Scriptures assure us that God is both listening attentively and acting in our best interest (e.g. Heb. 4:14–16). God is not only approachable but lovingly personable. Reach out and touch his throne today.

Prayer: Father, thank you for removing the dividing wall so I can now enter the holy of holies and commune with you.

ROMANS 8:18–39

GOD'S WILL—HAPPILY EVER AFTER?

We know that all things work together for the good of those who love God—those whom he has called according to his plan (Romans 8:28).

Bob is unemployed. Hearing about some job a thousand miles away, he and his wife begin to pray. They pray for wisdom and ask God to close the opportunity if it wouldn't be prudent to move. The company affirms excellent job openings and benefits, so Bob and his family make the move. Everything goes smoothly in the transition. Then three months after Bob's move, the company he joined goes bankrupt.

The Bible seems to teach that God is specifically sovereign in Christian's lives. On the other hand, it is sometimes confusing when ventures that seem approved by wisdom and God's direction don't appear to work out.

It's interesting to look at Paul's track record. Reading through Acts, one sees that, at times, God reveals to Paul that he should go here or there—at others, the Spirit says no. On occasion, Paul goes into a city and is beaten up or jailed. Yet he doesn't whine, and he doesn't lose faith in God's sovereignty in his life and ministry.

We may wonder at the verse, "Don't be foolish, but understand what the Lord wants" (Eph. 5:17). But if we believe in our hair-counting God, we must also believe that, behind the scenes, he is weaving a life tapestry for each of us. It may appear uneven and indistinct on one side, but on the other side it is a magnificent collage of his purposes.

PRAYER: God, now and then when I'm down, please give me a glimpse of my life's tapestry from your perspective.

⚓ Dec. 24 ⚓

Job 38:1–13

God Is Still on the Job

"We accept the good that God gives us. Shouldn't we also accept the bad? Through all this Job's lips did not utter one sinful word" (Job 2:10).

If a Christian gets sick then gets better without the care of a doctor, we claim God's supernatural healing. If not, we surmise God wants to use a doctor's wisdom. If there's money to pay medical bills, we say God provided it. If no money comes in, we figure we lack faith. If the sickness proves chronic, we claim God is teaching patience. If the person dies, we say God provided merciful deliverance from pain.

Do we Christians tend to fabricate reasons for things? Does God need us to make excuses for what seem to be occasional oversights? No, we don't need to come to his rescue when things don't happen the way we want. We must "permit" God his whole range of creative options, even when they seem strange or uncaring.

If God always did what we asked, chaos would result. Who does God heed when one person asks abundant rain for his crops while another asks for no rain during outdoor evangelistic meetings? If he always said yes, we'd boss him around like a heavenly genie. If God blessed us the way we asked, non-Christians might turn to Christ only because "good things always happen to those Christians."

When it seems that nothing is working out right and God is on his lunch break, don't give way to dark speculations. God is still on the job.

Prayer: Father, show me that you don't need a rescuer. Help me trust that you're always sovereign in all situations.

⚓ Dec. 25 ⚓

Matthew 1:18–25

When God Crossed the Chasm

"The virgin will become pregnant and give birth to a son, and they will name him Immanuel," which means "God is with us" (Matthew 1:23).

Ferocious winds whipped the gorge,
And freezing rains iced the landscape,
When God crossed the chasm—
He came crying as an infant.
Intellectuals said it could not be done.
Philosophers still scoff saying,
    Impossible!
    The eternal and the absolute cannot exist on earth.
    Time and change block the way.
But in human flesh, God grew up and stood in a small boat.
He spoke, "Peace, be still!"
And screaming winds instantly obeyed.
Drenching torrents and raging waves were dammed up.

Still, small voices yet whisper in the storms,
"Immanuel . . . Immanuel . . . God is with us,"
While "scholars" shout and sputter . . .
    Impossible!
    He's just a good man.
    Indeed, a great man who shows us our potential.
But, the winds and the waters still obey his will,
And he yet speaks.

—Dr. Paul Wright

Prayer: Thank you, Immanuel, that you're still with me because you followed through with that awful mission which began in a Bethlehem shed.

⚓ Dec. 26 ⚓

Matthew 23

Proud Performance or Secret Service?

"How horrible it will be for you, scribes and Pharisees. . . . You give God one-tenth of your mint, dill, and cumin. But you have neglected justice, mercy, and faithfulness. These are the most important things in Moses' Teachings" (Matthew 23:23).

While on earth, any anger Jesus displayed was reserved primarily for certain religious leaders. Scathing rebukes were directed at these dignified men. Yet they seemed clean-living and devout. They prayed much, gave to the poor, and studied the Old Testament Scriptures meticulously, teaching them in the synagogues. So why was Jesus so hard on them?

Jesus knew something that was hidden to the public. He knew that when the Pharisees prayed long and loud on street corners and made their tithe-giving a circus act, they wanted praise from others. He knew that when they jockeyed for the most important seats at gatherings and enlarged the Scripture packets on their wrists and foreheads, they did it to become more conspicuous. These men would even carefully tithe their kitchen spices, yet would refuse to support their aged parents.

Jesus said that things like tithing were good, but should not be done at the expense of vital practices like judging fairly, showing mercy, and passing on a vibrant, humble faith to others.

Do we neglect the core elements of Christian living for the cheap thrill of momentary praise for our public religiousness? Let's not give in to the temptation of attention-grabbing performance when we should be performing in secret.

Prayer: Lord, when I begin thinking I'm hot stuff, remind me again who I really am. Give me a heart that serves you without a drum roll.

⚓ DEC. 27 ⚓

ECCLESIASTES 11:1–6

NO MAGIC FORMULAS

Just as you don't know how the breath of life enters the life of a child within its mother's womb, you also don't understand how God, who made everything, works (Ecclesiastes 11:5).

A well-known seminar became popular some years ago. Thousands of people flocked to it and came away with rave reviews. The first time or two I attended the seminar, I was also excited. Then unexpected nagging doubts plagued me. The leader seemed to have little step-by-step formulas to explain and solve almost every issue and problem a Christian faces. A little voice called Reality kept saying, "But life isn't quite this simple." God cannot be placed in a box, and real life for us mortals is usually refreshingly or perplexingly unpredictable.

Most of us would appreciate a life governed by the scientific method: follow these four steps and you'll get this result every time. However, in our daily living the results may flip-flop on us, or we blow the second step, or it takes five steps instead of four.

Peter had a nice, neat script for Jesus to follow. He said, "First, Jesus, you'll become a national hero. Second, we'll build you a tabernacle on the mountain. Third, you'll reign over a vast kingdom with us as your nobles."

The script didn't work. But out of the heartbreak of Jesus' crucifixion came an ending far more glorious than Peter could have scripted.

PRAYER: Father, help me not to try dictating scripts for you but to allow you to work uniquely in each situation.

⚓ Dec. 28 ⚓

Psalm 37:1–11

Fret Not over the Godless

Do not be preoccupied with evildoers. Do not envy those who do wicked things. They will quickly dry up like grass and wither away like green plants (Psalm 37:1).

A friend of mine works as head nurse at a hospital. She told me this story: A few months back, a middle-aged man was admitted to the emergency room with an acute heart attack. The man's wife and girlfriend met for the first time at the hospital. The man hovered between life and death for days. Finally, while still critically ill, he was sent to a convalescent center. Based on similar cases, doctors expect a patient in this condition to typically contract pneumonia and die within a few weeks. However, his wife took him home and nursed him back to health. As soon as the man was able to return to work, he left his wife and went back to live with his girlfriend.

This true story elicits from us an immediate call for justice. I ask, "God, when you knew what he would do, why did you let the man live? Why did he recover, while my mother who was faithful and kind all her life, died? Why?"

If your heart cries for answers, you're in good company. Jeremiah said, "O Lord, I want to talk to you about your justice. Why do wicked people succeed? Why do treacherous people have peace and quiet?" In our Scripture verse for today, God answers, "Your part is to delight in me. I'll deal with the godless in my own way and time. Trust me."

Prayer: Father, it's hard when evil seems to triumph. Enable me to be content with leaving the judgments to you.

⚓ Dec. 29 ⚓

1 Corinthians 1:17–24

God's Simple, Profound Manifesto

While I was with you, I decided to deal with only one subject —Jesus Christ, who was crucified (1 Corinthians 2:2).

A man was born in a stable, grew up in a poor carpenter's family, became an offbeat preacher—then at age thirty three was railroaded to death by a frenzied public. Not exactly the stuff of stately, intellectual manifestos. Yet the Christian gospel claims this humble man died for the sins of the world.

Why did God make the gospel so ordinary—so open to ridicule? It is as Paul says: God intentionally made the gospel seem simplistic to know-it-alls and proud intellectuals. God did this to shame the conceited and make it imperative that those who come to him will humble themselves.

Don't imagine you're the only Christian who has ever been tempted to feel embarrassed when you share this strange and simple message. However, in Romans 1:16 Paul said he was taking the offensive. He writes, "I'm not ashamed of the Good News. It is God's power to save everyone who believes." He refused to be ashamed because through the gospel God unleashes his power to completely transform human beings.

God does not command us to out-debate the atheistic philosophers of this world. He tells us instead to teach Christ crucified. It's pretty simple, isn't it?

Prayer: Lord, help me present the gospel with boldness, not embarrassment. Don't let me try to dress it up in fancy clothing.

⚓ Dec. 30 ⚓

1 Corinthians 1:25–2:2

God's Pecking Order

God chose what the world considers ordinary and what it despises—what it considers to be nothing—in order to destroy what it considers to be something (1 Corinthians 1:28–29).

Were you ever chosen last in physical education? The God of perfection—he selects those whose hearts are perfect toward him. But does he consign those who aren't outwardly outstanding to sit on the bench? No! God chooses those who aren't paraded as brilliant, good-looking, wealthy, or powerful. Sometimes God even seeks out the despised, the weak, and the disadvantaged to carry out his purposes. This way, when he accomplishes supernatural things through them, they won't claim it was due to their superiority.

This principle does not appear to mean that effective Christians can't be nice-looking, intelligent, well off, or influential. It's just a lot more difficult for these people to trust God in place of their personal assets. It's also easy for them to think their success is due to things like a magnetic personality or astute use of money.

God sometimes even allows a tragedy or ongoing problem into the lives of those he uses or blesses. In Paul's case, he refused to remove this problem. Again, its purpose was to keep the great apostle from beginning to think he was self-sufficient (2 Cor. 12).

You don't have to be humanly great for God to give you great assignments. In fact, it seems he'd prefer that you're not.

Prayer: Father, I'm glad you don't choose those who are great by the world's standards. I'm so grateful you chose me.

⚓ DEC. 31 ⚓

JOB 11:7–15
JUST THE BEGINNING

"If they want to brag, they should brag that they understand and know me. They should brag that I, the LORD, act out of love, righteousness, and justice on earth" (Jeremiah 9:24).

We have reached the end of our study, but it is really only the beginning. Our quest to know God and understand his mysteries will span eternity. Think of all the names of God and you will catch an inkling of the depth of his character: El Shaddai, Lord, Savior, Provider, Refuge, Emmanuel, Alpha, Omega, and on and on.

We are sensual creatures trying to understand and know an invisible God. We get to know him as we trace his paintbrush on a sunset, as we pore over his love letters in the Scriptures, as we enjoy moments of spiritual communion, or the gentle encouragement of a fellow pilgrim.

If God was always easy to understand, he would not be God. It is those who smugly think they've got God all figured out that are probably least familiar with him. What makes him unique are qualities like his infinity—his all-knowing, all-powerful presence at all times in all places. Somehow, we must continually try to know God better while remaining content with the realization that we can never understand him fully.

PRAYER: O God, walk with me on ordinary roads. I don't ask for the sensational—I only ask your companionship on short journeys and long. Let my routine life be transfigured by your presence.

Source Notes

JANUARY

7. C. S. Lewis, *Mere Christianity* (New York: Macmillan, 1943).
8. Ibid.
15. Alexandre Vinet in *Words Old and New*, edited by H. Bonar (Edinburgh: Banner of Truth, 1866), 345.
21. Jim Jones interview, National Public Radio, 1978.
23. Robert Ruark, *The Old Man and the Boy* (Greenwich, CT: Holt, Rinehart and Winston, 1953), 106, 109-110.
25. R. C. Sproul, *Essential Truths of the Christian Faith* (Wheaton: Tyndale, 1992).
30. A. W. Pink, *Attributes of God*, (Grand Rapids: Baker, n.d).

FEBRUARY

1. J. B. Phillips, *The New Testament in Modern English* (New York: Macmillan, 1957). Used by permission.
2. Oswald Chambers, *My Utmost for His Highest* (Uhrichsville, OH: Barbour, Copyright renewed 1963), July 28.
6. John Trent and Rick Hicks, *Seeking Solid Ground* (Colorado Springs: Focus on the Family, 1995), 136-137.
   Chambers, *My Utmost*, September 30.
8. Henry Ward Beecher in *Streams in the Desert*, edited by Mrs. Charles E. Cowman (Grand Rapids: Zondervan, 1925), 164.
   Terri Patterson, Uncopyrighted gospel tract, 1994.
10. Paul Rees, *The Warrior Saint* (n.p.: Schmul Publishing, 1987).Leroy Eims, *Be the Leader You Were Meant to Be* (Wheaton: Chariot Books, n.d.).
12. Chambers, *My Utmost*, July 30.
14. C. S. Lewis, *Mere Christianity* (New York: Macmillan, 1943).
18. A. B. Simpson, George Matheson, and J. R. Miller in *Streams in the Desert*, 200, 220, 240.
    Chambers, *My Utmost*, January 4.
20. Ruth Graham, *Legacy of a Pack Rat* (Nashville: Nelson, 1989), 157. Used by permission of Thomas Nelson Publishers.
22. C. S. Lewis, *Mere Christianity.*
    Oswald Chambers, *My Utmost*, July 24.
29. John Pollock, *Biography of D. L. Moody* (Grand Rapids: Zondervan, 1967).
    C. Anderson, *To the Golden Shore: The Life of Adoniram Judson* (Grand Rapids: Zondervan, 1967).
    Jane Wheeler, Unpublished letter to Wheaton College family, n.d.

MARCH

11. F. B. Meyer in *Streams in the Desert*, edited by Mrs. Charles E. Cowman (Grand Rapids: Zondervan, 1925), 74.
23. C. S. Lewis, *The Problem of Pain* (San Francisco: HarperCollins, 1940).
28. John Miller in *Streams in the Desert*, 29.
30. F. W. Robertson in *Streams in the Desert*, 240.

Source Notes

April

1. Stephen Renn, ed., *Vine's Amplified Expository Dictionary of New Testament Words* (Iowa Falls: World Publishing, 1991).
11. Thomas Carlyle in *Legacy of a Pack Rat* by Ruth Graham (Nashville: Nelson, 1989), 107.
20. Paul Brand and Philip Yancey, *Fearfully and Wonderfully Made* (Grand Rapids: Zondervan, 1980).
22. Richard Cecil in *The Thought of the Evangelical Leaders: Discussions of the Eclectic Society*, edited by John Pratt, (Edinburgh: Banner of Truth, n.d.).

May

1. Billy Graham, interviewed by John F. Kennedy, Jr., 1997.
2. Alistair Begg, *Made for His Pleasure* (Chicago: Moody Press, 1996).
   C. S. Lewis, *The Problem of Pain* (San Francisco: HarperCollins, 1940).
5. Frederick Buechner, *Listening to Your Life* (San Francisco: Harper, 1992), 166-167.
7. Adroniram Judson in *From Jerusalem to Irian Jaya* by Ruth Tucker (Grand Rapids: Zondervan, 1983).
10. Edmund Calamy in *Words Old and New*, edited by H. Bonar (Edinburgh: Banner of Truth, 1866).
12. Buechner, *Listening to Your Life*.
    Athanasius in *Words Old and New*, 17.
    Asahel Nettleton in *Words Old and New*, 325.
13. Sir Walter Raleigh in *Words Old and New*, 111.
14. Thomas Browne in *Words Old and New*.
15. John Evans in *Streams in the Desert*, edited by Mrs. Charles E. Cowman (Grand Rapids: Zondervan, 1925).
16. John Milton in *Words Old and New*, 178.
17. M. Drewery, *William Carey: A Biography* (Grand Rapids: Zondervan, 1979).
18. Philip Yancey, "Why Not Now?," *Christianity Today*, 5 February 1996, 112.
20. F. W. Faber in *Streams in the Desert*, 327.
    Oswald Chambers, *My Utmost for His Highest* (Uhrichsville, OH: Barbour, Copyright renewed 1963), April 25.
21. John Berridge in *Words Old and New*.
22. Evans in *Words Old and New*, 332.
    John Bunyan in *Words Old and New*, 213.
    Berridge in *Words Old and New*, 282.
    John Angell James in *Words Old and New*, 227.
    George Whitefield's Journals (Edinburgh: Banner of Truth, n.d.).
    W.H. Hewitson in *Words Old and New*, 349.
    Sermons of Robert M. M'Cheyne (Edinburgh: Banner of Truth, n.d.).
    Lady Powerscourt in *Words Old and New*, 354.
23. Basil the Great in *Words Old and New*.
    Amy Carmichael, *Thou Givest; They Gather* (Ft. Washington: Christian Literature Crusade, 1958).
24. E. Stenbock, *Miss Terri: The Story of Maude Cary, Pioneer GMU Missionary of Morocco* (Lincoln, NE: Good News Broadcasting, 1970).
26. Carmichael, *Thou Givest*, 46-47.

28. Charles Swindoll, *Come Before Winter . . . and Share My Hope* (Wheaton: Tyndale House, 1988).
29. Aristides in *The Ante-Nicene Fathers*, 1971, ch. 15.
Justin in *The Early Christians*, by E. Arnold (Rifton, NY: Plough Publishing House, 1975), 98.
30. M. Felix in *The Early Christians*, 89-90.
Tertullian in *The Early Christians*, Scapula 4. To the heathen, 1.3.
31. John MacArthur, *The Glory of Heaven* (Wheaton: Crossway Books, 1996), 11.

JUNE

3. Stephen Renn, ed., *Vine's Amplified Expository Dictionary of New Testament Words* (Iowa Falls: World Publishing, 1991).
4. Francois Fenelon in *Streams in the Desert*, edited by Mrs. Charles E. Cowman (Grand Rapids: Zondervan, 1925), 265.
9. Sir Walter Raleigh in *Words Old and New*, edited by H. Bonar (Edinburgh: Banner of Truth, 1866), 110.
11. G. Machen, *What is Faith?* (Edinburgh: Banner of Truth, 1925).
13. John Love in *Words Old and New*, 307.
18. *New English Bible: New Testament*, edited by delegates of Oxford University Press and syndics of Cambridge University Press, (Oxford University Press, 1961).
19. *The New Testament: A New Translation by James Moffatt* (San Francisco: Harper & Row, 1964).
A. W. Pink, *Comfort for Christians* (Grand Rapids: Baker, 1976).
23. Oswald Chambers, *My Utmost for His Highest* (Uhrichsville, OH: Barbour, Copyright renewed 1963), November 27.
Eugene Peterson, *Run with the Horses* (Downers Grove, IL: InterVarsity).
24. R. C. Sproul, *The Soul's Quest for God* (Wheaton: Tyndale, 1993).
25. Chambers, *My Utmost*, September 28.
26. Garry Friesen, *Decision-Making and the Will of God* (Portland, OR: Multnomah, 1980).
29. *Praying Hyde* (London: Pickering and Englis, n.d.).

JULY

10. Terry Whalin, "Nine Questions to Ask Before You Confront," *Discipleship Journal*, 71, 1992, 106-108.
12. Reuben Welch, *We Really Do Need Each Other* (Grand Rapids: Zondervan, 1982).
14. Oswald Chambers, *My Utmost for His Highest* (Uhrichsville, OH: Barbour, Copyright renewed 1963), September 30.
Ruth Graham, *Legacy of a Pack Rat* (Nashville: Nelson, 1989), 136.
16. Welch, *We Really Do Need Each Other.*
18. Corrie Ten Boom, *The Hiding Place* (Old Tappan, NJ: Revell, 1971).
19. Frederick Buechner, *Listening to Your Life* (San Francisco: Harper, 1992).
20. Daniel Taylor, *Letters to My Children* (Downers Grove, IL: InterVarsity, 1989).
24. John Fischer, *True Believers Don't Ask Why* (Minneapolis: Bethany House, 1989).
25. Welch, *We Really Do Need Each Other.*
27. T. Dixon, Jr. in *Legacy of a Pack Rat.*

31. F. Lehman, *The Love of God*, 1917, copyright renewed by Nazarene Publishing House, 1945.

AUGUST

2. F. B. Meyer in *Streams in the Desert*, edited by Mrs. Charles E. Cowman (Grand Rapids: Zondervan, 1925).
16. Charles Spurgeon in *Streams in the Desert,* 180.
17. *Twentieth Century New Testament* (Chicago: Moody Press, n.d.). *New Testament in Basic English* (London: Cambridge University Press with Evans Brothers, Ltd., n.d.). *New Testament: Berkeley Version in Modern English* (Grand Rapids: Londer, 1945).
21. Frederick Buechner, *Listening to Your Life* (San Francisco: Harper, 1992).
24. *Webster's Encyclopedic Unabridged Dictionary of the English Language* (New York: Random House, 1989).
26. *Twentieth Century New Testament* (Chicago: Moody Bible Institute).
27. Buechner, *A Room Called Remember: Uncollected Pieces* (San Francisco: Harper & Row, 1984), 140-141. John Fischer, *True Believers Don't Ask Why* (Minnesota: Bethany House, 1989).
30. Annie J. Flint in *Streams in the Desert.*

SEPTEMBER

1. Frederick Buechner, *The Clown in the Belfry* (San Francisco: Harper & Row, 1992), 41.
11. Max Lucado, *The Applause of Heaven* (Waco, TX: Word, 1990).
13. Alexander Whyte, *Bible Characters* (Grand Rapids: Zondervan, 1952).
14. Buechner, *Listening to Your Life* (San Francisco: Harper, 1992).
22. Joseph Caryl in *Words Old and New*, edited by H. Bonar (Edinburgh: Banner of Truth, 1866), 171.
24. *Diary of David Brainerd* (Edinburgh: Banner of Truth Trust).

OCTOBER

1. John Bale, *Words Old and New*, edited by H. Bonar (Edinburgh: Banner of Truth, 1866), 74.
2. Lord Tammarlane in *Streams in the Desert*, edited by Mrs. Charles E. Cowman (Grand Rapids: Zondervan, 1925), 21. Calvin Coolidge in *A Return to Virtue*, 161.
4. C. S. Lewis, *The Problem of Pain* (San Francisco: HarperCollins, 1940).
6. Frederick Buechner, *Whistling in the Dark: An ABC Theologized* (San Francisco: Harper & Row, 1988), 22-23.
7. Oswald Chambers, *My Utmost for His Highest* (Uhrichsville, OH: Barbour, Copyright renewed 1963), January 2.
8. Buechner, *Listening to Your Life* (San Francisco: Harper, 1992).
9. Bernard of Clairveax in *Words Old and New*, 42.
10 Chambers, *My Utmost,* August 30, July 28.
11. Buechner, *The Faces of Jesus* (San Francisco: Harper & Row, 1989), 136.
12 Lewis, *The Problem of Pain.* Francesco Petrarch in *Words Old and New*, 47.
13. Buechner, *Listening to Your Life.*
15. "Your Last Few Hours," *Our Daily Bread*, (Grand Rapids: RBC Ministries, 1980).

17. Dale Carnegie, *How to Win Friends and Influence People* (New York: Simon & Schuster, 1964).
John Wesley in *Words Old and New*, 272.
18. Chambers, *My Utmost*, April 22.
Buechner, *The Sacred Journey* (San Francisco: Harper & Row, 1982), 4.
19. *The Complete Works of John Owen* (Edinburgh: Banner of Truth).
Buechner, *Listening to Your Life*, 157.
20. Amy Carmichael, *Thou Givest; They Gather* (Ft. Washington: Christian Literature Crusade, 1958).
Blaise Pascal in *Words Old and New*, 204.
22. David Brainerd in *Words Old and New*, 287.
The Complete Works of John Owen.
23. Ralph Stockman in *A Return to Virtue*, 85.
26. John Calvin in *Made For His Pleasure* by A. Begg (Chicago: Moody Press, 1996).
Aristotle in *A Return to Virtue*, 106.
29. Walter Lippman in *A Return to Virtue*, 106.
G. K. Chesterton in *A Return to Virtue.*
Pocket Webster's School and Office Dictionary (New York: Simon & Schuster, 1990).

NOVEMBER

2. J. B. Phillips, *The New Testament in Modern English* (New York: Macmillan, 1957). Used by permission.
3. Charles Swindoll, *Come Before Winter . . . and Share My Hope* (Wheaton: Tyndale House, 1988), 231.
6. N. Miller, "Count Your Many Blessings," in *Life & Work Curriculum,* Young Adult Teacher Edition, Oct.-Dec. 1996, (Nashville: Sunday School Board).
8. F. B. Meyer in *Streams in the Desert*, edited by Cowman (Grand Rapids: Zondervan, 1925).
9. *Hudson Taylor's Spiritual Secret* (Chicago: Moody Press, 1970).
10. J. R. Miller in *Streams in the Desert.*
12. Frederick Buechner, *Listening to Your Life* (San Francisco: Harper, 1992), 220.
22. Joni Eareckson, *Joni* (Grand Rapids: Zondervan, 1976).
23. Buechner, *Wishful Thinking: A Theological ABC* (San Francisco: Harper & Row, 1973), 27-28.
25. Patricia Baxter, "Level at the Cross," unpublished poem. Used by permission.
27. Arthur Bacon in *Streams in the Desert*, 49.
28. Andrew Murray in *Streams in the Desert.*
30. Swindoll, *Come Before Winter*, 276, 279.

DECEMBER

1. Alexandre Vinet in *Words Old and New*, edited by H. Bonar (Edinburgh: Banner of Truth, 1866), 345.
2. Anne Tyler, *Saint Maybe* (New York: Ivy Books, 1991).
14. Paul Brand and Philip Yancey, *Fearfully and Wonderfully Made* (Grand Rapids: Zondervan, 1980).
25. Dr. Paul Wright, unpublished Christmas poem. Used by permission.

Index

INDEX